Lean Startup Marketing
WORKBOOK 1: PRODUCTIZATION

Step 1 of the 3-Step RAF Marketing Method for Actualizing and Marketing an Offering into a Profitable Business

Real-World Marketing, Step-by-Step, Idea to Launch and Beyond

Entropy Publications, LLC, San Francisco, CA

query@entropypublishing.com

Entropy Press® is a registered trademark of Entropy Publications, LLC.

Library of Congress Cataloging-in-Publication Data is available.

ISBN-13: 978-1-7325431-0-2 (Entropy Press)
ISBN-10: 1-7325431-0-0

1. Entrepreneurship. 2. Small Business Marketing. 3. Content Marketing.
4. MVP, Minimum Viable Product. 4. Digital Marketing. 6. Social Media Marketing.

Printed in the U.S.A

Cover design by TargetMediaDesign

Lean Startup Marketing
WORKBOOK 1 CONTENTS

Lean Startup MARKETING
Workbook 1: Get Ready—PRODUCTIZE

Step 1 of the 3-Step **RAF Marketing Method** for Turning Your Ideas into Offerings of Value, for Profit

-PRODUCTIZATION Preface-

I am privileged, and honored to be a native Californian, a part of the most innovated state in the U.S. Born and raised in L.A., after I finished college, I became an Art Director for the manic entertainment industry. I developed marketing campaigns for many of the major movie houses and networks, before tiring of the Hollywood scene and moving up to the San Francisco Bay area in 1995, at the start of the dot com boom.

My first experience marketing startups was for *Stac Electronics*, even before I left L.A. The engineers had developed a lossless disk compression system they called *Stacker*. Initially, their product was very successful. They even piqued *Microsoft's* interest, but after the *MS* engineers met with the *Stac* founders and reviewed their code as part of the due diligence process, *Microsoft* promptly produced their own data compression software, *DoubleSpace*. While *Stac* won their lawsuit for copyright infringement for $120 million a year later, they never found their footing again, and eventually sold their technology and remaining assets after the dot com bust.

My experience with *Stac* taught me that I'd rather help innovators, engineers and developers to market and launch their own companies, than help groping Hollywood moguls sell one more crappy movie or TV show.

After moving up to the Bay area, I began marketing startups, helping innovators launch new products, or get more traction with selling the products they'd produced, or to get seed-round financing for their ideas. My first client, *Softkey International*, developed educational software for children. It eventually became *The Learning Company*, which sold to *Mattel* in 1998 for $2.4 billion.

Ensconced in the entrepreneurial environment, I met a software engineer hoping to launch the multi-dimensional database system he'd created into a thriving startup. Like so many talented developers, he had no knowledge of marketing. He insisted his creation was uniquely brilliant, light years ahead of its time, and all he needed to do was tell people at the SIG (special interest group) meetings he attended in Silicon Valley what he was working on, and they'd line up to buy it. Marketing, he insisted, was on par with prostitution. His creation would surely sell itself.

It didn't. Three years after he'd quit his job to invent the technology, the software was complete. He'd been talking about it for well over a year when we met at a networking mixer. During the event, he gave me a detailed monologue about database technology, describing in technical terms what his software was. He was unable, even after I prompted multiple times, to tell me what it *did*, what solutions it provided, or why it might be of valuable to anyone but him.

Enamored with his passion and creative mind, I agreed to help him with some marketing strategies to sell his software. We spent the next day, and most of that evening talking about his invention—what he had created, what it *did*, what function or solution it provided, and *who* would likely want it.

Less than a year later, in 1997, he sold *MD²* for close to $1 million in a perpetual licensing agreement to *Sybase*, which is now part of *SAP*. We married, and moved to Boston for 2 years while my new husband integrated his software into the *Sybase* code base. I had our first child, while working with ad agencies marketing Fortune 500 accounts like *Toys R Us* and *Hewlett Packard*. But I missed working with startups, and the creative energy that I absorbed working with them.

We came back to California at the beginning of the new millennium, at the peek of the dot com bubble. It seemed everyone in the Bay was working on a startup, but few had a clue how to sell what they were inventing. My husband took a job at what he referred to as a "gold-plated" startup, gold-plated because they were dropping a lot of cash on "team building' trips to expensive corporate retreats. The founders had invented web-based software to track user experience. But in 2000, business websites just weren't that popular yet, so this new startup had technology, but no market to sell it to.

One of the founders, the CEO, hired me to create an identity package for his new internet company. I will never forget what he told me when I asked him to describe what his startup produced, what his technology *did*—what real world solutions it provided, and for *who*.

His response: "We don't need a product. Anything internet related is hot right now. We are selling *perception*, the *idea* that we have internet solutions."

A year later this startup was laying off their staff of 80+, including my husband. Without a product, or even a service, they had nothing to market. Perception may be marketable, generate buzz, but it can't generate an income with no product to sell. As the internet took off, and every business built a website, their software eventually found a place in generating data used for analytics. They eventually sold their technology to *IBM*.

The day my husband was laid off, he came home and said: "This startup (name withheld to protect identities), like so many I've worked for, used the 'Fire, Aim, Ready,' approach to building a company, which is why it is failing."

I laughed. "What's that?"

"They should be doing, 'Ready, Aim, Fire.' You know, actually develop a product first, *before* trying to sell it. They have technology, but no product. They have no one to sell their software to because they haven't stopped to consider what it actually *does*, in the real world, that would be of use to anyone."

His words ricocheted off the walls of my brain for years. Many startups I consulted for had the same issue. They'd hire me to brand their product and new company, or ask me to create campaigns, without any idea what they were selling, or who would find value in their offering. Most burned through the cash from investors within the first year. Many failed.

As the internet has become an integral part of doing business, new marketing approaches became popular. Instead of integrating these new strategies with traditional marketing methods, many entrepreneurs ignored the foundation of marketing, deemed it irrelevant, and threw away the best practices known for eons to generate response and conversion (click, buy, subscribe).

Today, many software engineers like to think of themselves as marketing pros. Growth hackers—software developers who think they can produce response-oriented marketing by A/B testing campaigns, or using keyword tricks to reach #1 in search engine ranking (SEO), are often the only people producing marketing for the company. If there is a marketing department at all, these people will tell you it's all about 'Reach.' All they need to do is get a lot of Likes and Shares, or get people to follow their company on social media to generate sales.

This is a fallacy. While achieving #1 in Google ranking, and split testing campaigns may help *improve* response on your marketing efforts, using traditional marketing best practices will produce greater conversion than can be achieved by split testing campaigns with low initial response. Today's marketers have thrown out the baby with the bath water. Abandoning the 'Ready, Aim, Fire' marketing method is *the reason* 90% of all startups fail the first year.

Disheartened by all the startup failures both my husband and I witnessed while working with so many over the last two decades, about 7 years ago I wrote a blog, *Marketing 101*, highlighting the foundation of effective marketing, as well as three timeless best practices that must be performed *in order*—'Ready, Aim, Fire'—to get the greatest response on any marketing effort. This blog eventually became the **Lean Startup Marketing** (**LSM**) course taught at UC Berkeley, Stanford, and other accredited universities in L.A. and the Bay area.

Over the last 6 years, LSM has helped hundreds of students launch and market a startup with the RAF ('Ready, Aim, Fire') Marketing method.

1. Get **Ready**, and **Productize** your offering.
2. Take **Aim**, and **Brand** your offering.
3. **Fire**, and **Launch** your marketing efforts.

This three-step process gives innovators practical, doable steps to build a *sustainable* business. It also provides startups struggling to get traction with their marketing efforts, a clear and direct process to achieve much greater response on their marketing efforts, at launch and beyond.

LSM is *not* marketing theory. Each of the three workbooks, filled with slides, challenges and projects, are **step-by-step guides** you'll refer to again and again, to assure you are on the proper path to building a thriving business. The **Lean Startup Entrepreneurial** (**LSE**) **series** provides specific, low-budget, actionable steps for marketing your offerings, to sell directly, or launch your first offering as a profitable startup.

Lean Startup workbooks are designed to teach you the process of turning an idea or product in development into an offering of value, and then marketing it for profit. Each workbook also guides learners through the process of creating and producing marketing for your new venture that gets the greatest response. Learn by engaging in the process, and you'll be able to actualize most *any* idea you have now, or any that may come, by simply following the steps of the RAF Marketing Method, *in order* (kind of like working a math equation... ;).

Welcome to LSM Workbook 1: PRODUCTIZATION

To actualize any idea into a reality you must begin at the beginning. You can not build a building without architectural plans. You can not create a cupcake without a recipe or list of required ingredients. And you can not start a business without some sort of plan.

LSM gives you the framework for marketing and launching a startup, but before you market any offering you must begin by understanding what you plan to sell.

LSM Workbook 1: PRODUCTIZATION, is the process of getting *intimate* with your idea, or developed product. Neglect to productize your offering, and at best, your marketing efforts will get little traction. At worse, ignoring Productization leads to startup failure.

Productization is unquestionably the most neglected step in the product and startup development process, but this *first step* is imperative to implement *before* creating marketing for your offering. You can't possibly brand and advertise your product or service if you are not intimate with what you plan to sell and who you plan to sell it to. Implementing the steps of Productization, *in order*, allows you to produce tightly targeted marketing campaigns that motivate viewers to click, try, or buy your offering.

LSM Workbook 1: PRODUCTIZATION provides the following steps to get your offering Ready (RAF Marketing method) to market:

- MBA to marketing novice, learn all the marketing you'll ever need to know to become proficient at marketing...anything.

- Create Productization lists filled with targeted content to use in your branding, marketing and advertising campaigns throughout the life-cycle of your business.

- Identify specific Target Markets and Targeted Users who will find a solution or value in your product or service—customers that are most likely buy your new offering.

- Learn how to utilize your Productization lists to create tightly targeted marketing that gets the greatest response *and* conversion.
- Construct an Elevator Pitch to succinctly chat up your new venture.
- Perform Competitive Analysis, and find differentiators that make your offering special, unique, valuable.
- Project Horizontal and Vertical products and markets for current and future offerings.
- Choose an effective Profit Model to make money on your offering at launch, as well as two years and five years down the line.

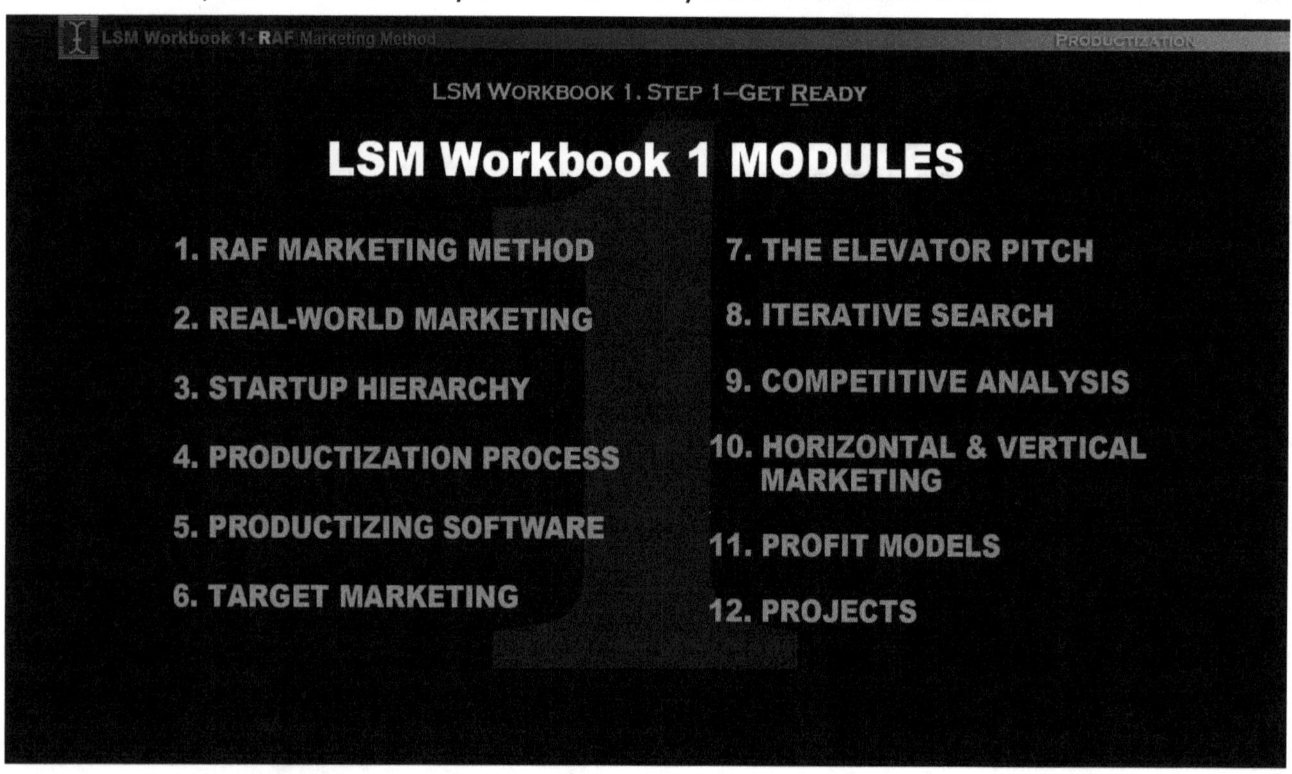

LSM Workbook 1 guides you *step-by-step* through the process of developing your idea into a software application, product, or service that adds value, or solves a problem for specific groups of people (Target Marketing). This workbook provides an in-depth examination of the Productization process to turning an idea into an offering of value, for profit. If you already have a salable product or service, and have yet to productize your offering, do it now! Better late than never. Executing Productization lists, pitches and profit models will enable you create, or direct those you hire to produce targeted, response-oriented marketing for your new venture.

Projects for LSM Workbook 1

There are **three multifaceted projects in LSM Workbook 1**. Completing each will give you targeted *content*—keywords and phrases related to your offering, that's directed at your likely audience—to use in the branding and advertising campaigns you'll learn to create in LSB Workbook 2. Completing each project will also make you aware of your competition, help you identify what makes your offering unique, project future products and markets to sell to, as well as create pitches to promote your offering in-person and online.

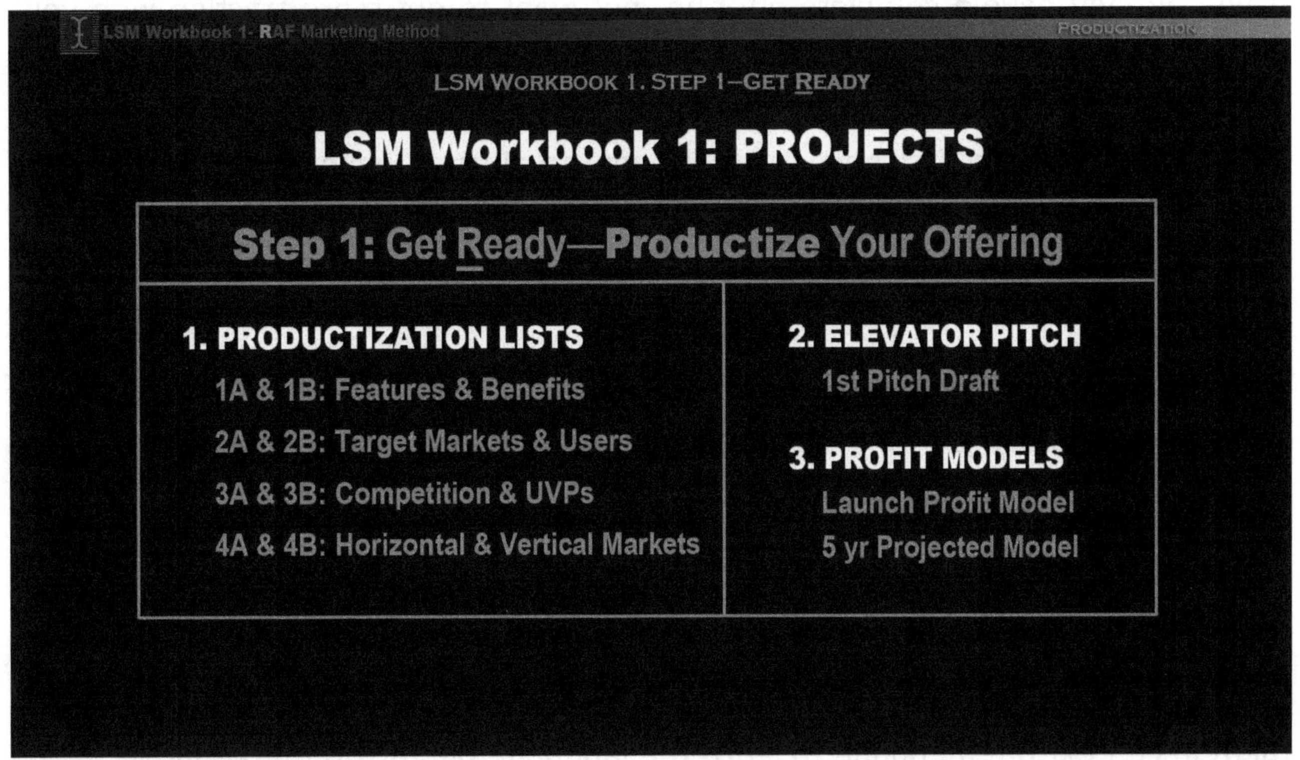

There are twelve projects throughout the entire LSE series. As each is completed, *in order*, you will have the marketing material required for the pre-launch and launch of your new venture by the last module of LSL Workbook 3.

The knowledge you'll gain doing each project, in the order each is given, will give you a greater understanding of your offering, the company you are developing, and the steps you must take to market them effectively. Even if you choose to hire designers or ad agencies, you'll be better equipped to direct those you contract, to economically produce tightly targeted campaigns that get the greatest response.

You can read each of these workbooks twenty times, memorize them in fact, and not learn as much as you will from doing the work. To *really* understand how something works—you must *work the process*.

Challenges

Challenges are different from projects. They'll appear throughout Workbook 1, with a few scattered in Workbooks 2 and 3, usually at the end of important content. Completed Challenges will *not* be used to market your product or startup, but are provided to help you get familiar with the process of marketing...anything.

If you already have a complete offering, but want to get more traction with your marketing efforts, the Challenges will help you broaden your understanding of the intricacies of how marketing works.

As with the projects, I strongly suggest you do all the Challenges! Beyond using each project to create and then produce your marketing campaigns, both the projects and challenges in the LSE series have been designed to accelerate your learning of the Lean Startup Marketing process.

The Private Language of Any Industry

Most every industry, from baked goods to software, has their own private language. Learning the language of business marketing is essential for startup success. Throughout LSM Workshop 1, as well as the entire LSE series, you will see words in **bold**. You'll also find acronyms—abbreviated initials of broader concepts—used every day in the entrepreneurial industry. It is imperative these terms and acronyms get inside your head. Pay extra attention to the words and phrases in bold, and the acronyms that follow them. Even if you don't always remember their meaning, over the course of the entire LSE series, you'll see them in context often enough to learn the language of startup marketing.

Access to LSM Workbook 1 Slides

You will find all the slides in LSM Workbook 1 at this URL address:

- https://startupmarketingonline.com/lsm-workbook-1-slides/
- Password: LSM-Productization

-

-

STOP! Do CHALLENGE #1 before moving on.

◆◆◆

CHALLENGE #1: Generating Product Ideas

If you already have an idea you'd like to produce, a product in development, or a fully actualized offering you are in the process of marketing, skip this Challenge.

It is highly recommended that you have an idea to actualize, to realize the full potential of this course. The idea is less important than working the process, so don't dwell on creating a brilliant offering, or even one that you will produce right now (if ever).

Imagine creating something that's fun to do, or solving a recurring problem. Now, come up with a basic (even vague) idea of something you'd enjoy doing, or a fix for your recurring issue.

STEP 1. THINK of [at least] five (5) PROBLEMS you frequently encounter, and write them into a document titled: "MY FREQUENT PROBLEMS." Number each problem as shown.
Examples:

1. Trash bags that don't stay fixed to the rim of the can.
2. Spending an hour or more looking for a movie you'll actually *like* on your streaming video services.
3. Internet access that keeps crashing while you're watching the *Netflix* movie it just took you an hour to find.
4. Your kids are not doing their chores, or well in school, or...?
5. You have no one with whom to share how you really feel, and you can't afford therapy.
6. You don't have the time or energy to be a full-time parent and build a full-time career, but you want kids and need money.
7. You get tired by 3:00p.m. and want a wake-you-up, but slow burning energy snack.
8. You can't get a good job without work experience. And you can't get work experience without a job.
9. You know it's unhealthy for your dog to be locked inside all day, but there's no way to let him run and play during your workday.

STEP 2. Use a corresponding number to LIST [at least] five (5) SOLUTIONS to your list of problems.
Examples:

1a. Trash bags made with a 3" thick rubber-band around the top rim.
2a. A recommendation system that figures out individual preferences.
5a. Online therapy with qualified pro counselors available when you need to talk.
7a. My organic, low-fat, gluten-free, great-tasting cupcakes and scones.
8a. A web platform to match students or recent grads with corporate internships.
9a. A P2P service of local, professional pet care advocates, with pick-up

and drop-off, to personal doggy assistants.

STEP 3. Pick ONE of your SOLUTIONS. If you don't already have an idea, or product in development to sell, use the solution to the problem you've discovered in this challenge as *the* idea you'll actualize and market for profit, to follow the steps presented throughout the LSE series. (Check out the next Challenge for an alternate startup idea generation technique.)

◆◆◆

Real World Startup Marketing

So, you think you have a great idea for a new software app, product or service. Perhaps you've started a startup with what you *thought* was a great idea, but are getting little to no traction on your marketing efforts. Or, maybe you don't have any ideas *yet*, but want to become your own CEO and run your own show, doing something you love.

What's an idea worth?

Nothing. Unless you actualize it. And beyond just building the product, service, or software application, you have to *market* your offering, *for the entire life-cycle of your business*—pre-launch, launch, and beyond.

Talented innovators are creating awesome apps, from social platforms, to lifestyle organizers, to peer-to-peer online services. Others are developing goods and products from cupcakes, to fashion, to nutritional supplements. Entrepreneurs are busy in their garages, dining rooms, and offices, designing solutions that will enable us to be more efficient, productive, and have more fun! Most are hoping to create thriving companies. And the fact is, most will never become sustainable businesses without effective marketing.

Now, more than ever, with globalization and automation, it is urgent we learn to create our own jobs, and possibly start companies that will employ others. The Lean Startup workbook series teach you how to turn your ideas into products and services you can sell directly (*Amazon, Google Play, Etsy*), to start a "microbusiness," or create a startup of many offerings to come, from the ground up—idea to launch. The LSE series will also help existing startups realize greater response with their marketing efforts.

The Lean Startup Marketing series has been taught live, in its entirety, at Stanford University, and UC Berkeley, since 2012. LSM has empowered entrepreneurs, mompreneurs, retirees, developers, designers, and business professionals to turn their ideas into quality offerings of *value*, and grow sustainable startups, for a nominal monetary investment.

Get ready for the journey of your professional life, when you commit to directing your own career, creating and *selling* something you are passionate about. With LSE, it won't cost you much money to start your business, but it's going to be hugely time consuming, and at times absurdly frustrating. It'll surely be scary scary scary at times, leaving you questioning if you are on the right path. Often you won't be, and you'll have to recalibrate and try again and again. More often than not, it'll feel like you're getting nowhere. And, of course, there will always be friends and family who tell you your idea won't ever go anywhere, and to give it up and focus on your *real* job, try to be the best employee you can be.

You will encounter many challenges starting your own business, but you'll look forward to coming to work every day. And wouldn't you rather be spending the greater portion of most every day of your life doing something you *like* to do, instead of working for someone else?

The best bit—you don't have to quit your day job if you aren't rich, or don't have a benefactor to float you financially while you develop and market your startup. Just stop blowing away your evenings and weekends binge-watching *Netflix* (or however you choose to waste time). Invest those hours into actualizing your idea into a product or service someone actually *wants*, then learn how to sell it to them with the RAF Marketing Method. Follow each and every step, IN ORDER, of the step-by-step process introduced in each workbook. Completing all three LSE workbooks will enable you to launch a product or service of value directly, or build a startup, with the first of many offerings to come, and then market your new venture, for profit.

◆◆◆◆◆◆

MODULE 1: RAF MARKETING METHOD

Startups Fail by Starting BackAsswards

Over 400,000 startups launch annually in the U.S., according to Gallup statistics, 2016. Over 90% fail within the first year.

Most innovators launch a startup backwards. They spend a year or more creating a product or service, then put up a website and slam the internet with less than effective digital marketing campaigns because it doesn't cost anything to publish online. These entrepreneurs don't get much traction with their pre-launch and rollout marketing efforts, so they keep tweaking their original offering when it doesn't sell, adding more and more features, services and tech. They invest additional time and money into marketing, but still don't get more than a few customers, who likely don't last long.

As previously mentioned, we'll call this the "Fire, Aim, Ready," method of starting up, which invariably leads to startup failure.

The "**Ready, Aim, Fire**" or the **RAF Marketing Method** delivers a 3-step *process* that gives you practical, *doable* steps to build a solid foundation on which to create a sustainable company. Implement each step *in order*, to market your idea or developed offering into a *valuable* product or service, *and* get greater response on your marketing efforts, at launch, and beyond.

The RAF Marketing Method is delivered in three rigorous workbooks:

1. **Lean Startup MARKETING (LSM) Workbook 1. Step 1: Get Ready**, and **PRODUCTIZE** your idea into an offering of value, *before* producing it.

2. **Lean Startup BRANDING (LSB) Workbook 2. Step 2: Take Aim**, and **BRAND** your offering in development with identities and marketing campaigns, that tout the solutions and/or unique benefits the features of your offering provide.

3. **Lean Startup LAUNCH (LSL) Workbook 3. Step 3: Fire**, and **LAUNCH** your tightly targeted branding and advertising campaigns at your potential target audience.

You do NOT need a fully functional offering to effectively implement the RAF Marketing Method presented in this first workbook. You do *not* need to produce your idea, yet. In fact, it is recommended that you don't!

Weird as this sounds, Workbook 1 of the LSE series does not require your idea be produced at all. The Productization process presented in Workbook 1 is designed to help you develop and produce an offering with the right "product/market fit." Initializing Productization will align your product development with target markets and users most likely to benefit from the offering you hope to create and sell.

Don't waste time (and money) implementing an offering that you've yet to confirm anyone wants. Producing a minimum viable product (MVP) to sell, only happens once you've gone through the first step in the lean startup marketing process: Productization. Selling products, services, or a message (as with nonprofit organizations), you first must productize your offering to determine if your idea or product in development is worth developing.

If you already have a complete offering, and are in the first year, or the seed-round financing of your startup, implementing the Productization process will yield tightly targeted content to use in your campaigns that will increase the response to all your marketing efforts.

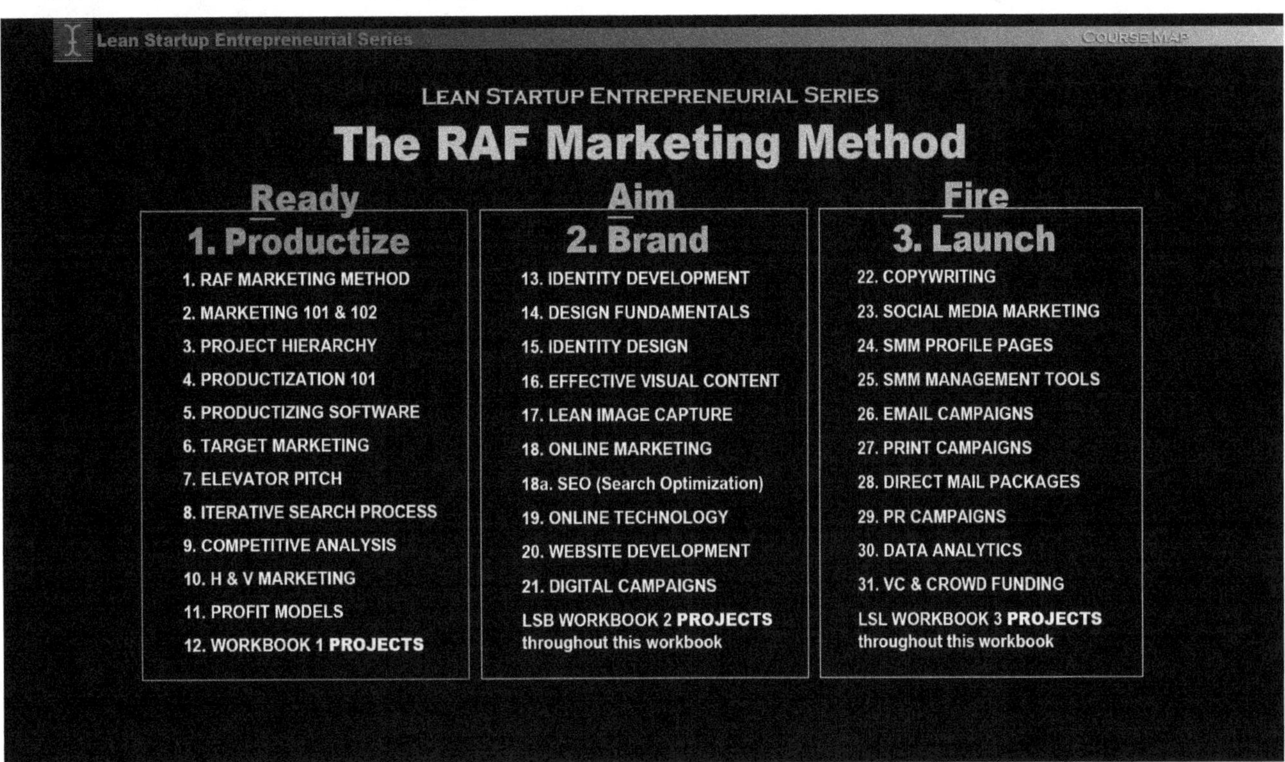

Performing the steps of the RAF Marketing Method *in order* will compel you to *think differently.* You'll learn the foundation *and* applications of real-world marketing, like you never have before, even if you're a marketing professional with an MBA.

Becoming your own boss isn't rocket science, and it doesn't have to cost a lot of money, at least initially. But running your own business, even a small one, is a *big commitment* to a lot of work if you hope to achieve any level of success. The LSE series will give you the direction and tools to become your own greatest resource, and empower you to realize the boundless possibilities you'll find when you actualize your creative mind.

Avoid Startup Crash and Burn

Don't become one of the 90% that fail when they endeavor down the startup road! Now, you too can create a startup success story. When you embark on the startup journey with the RAF Marketing Method, step-by-step, *in order*, you will set up a solid foundation to build a sustainable business by avoiding the three primary reasons most startups fail:

1. No one PRODUCTIZES the offering. An innovator goes through a lot of time and (sometimes) expense putting together an offering from an idea they had, or heard, without ever considering *how* or *why* anyone else will find value in its creation. Once the idea is manufactured, no one, even the marketing department, identifies how the offering's features actually benefit anyone. They don't have a clue who the target audience is, for their product or service. They design a logo, put up a website, and publish a bunch of advertising online, without identifying a *need* or even desire for their offering. They don't bother to look for competitors already producing the same or similar offerings. And they don't project how the product or service will make money now or in the future.

2. The startup LAUNCHES without infrastructure to support brand or fulfillment. Once Productization is complete, branding must be created and *standardized,* so it appears the same across different media—from online advertising to print campaigns—to build brand awareness. Most startups launch without creating and distributing brand standards to all stakeholders, so marketing efforts fail to build brand awareness.

Launching with no infrastructure to support fulfillment means the startup fails to fulfill orders of their offering, or their website platform cannot scale, and crashes with an increase in users or site activity.

Startups must deliver on promises *out of the gate*, and be able to fulfill all orders, and have the infrastructure to scale seamlessly, and fast. Delivering on commitments builds trust. And trust garners believers—repeat customers. And satisfied customers talk about what they like, both in-person and online. The more positive talk an offering receives, the more likely that product or service will 'go viral,' or garner a wide, generally global audience. The #1 way we sell today, and yesterday, is through recommendations for products, or a service, or a message, from family and friends.

3. Startup does not invest in research and development. The launch of their first offering goes well. Their sales out of the gate are great! The problems arise when the startup rides on this initial wave of success too long. They have no plans, and no one in the company is working on new offerings or features (2.0, 2.1, etc.).

Today, potential competitors are going to know about any *successful* offering, *fast.* And there will be those who will copy, and *surpass* the original startup's success. This fact makes it imperative that the development of new products and/or services be *ongoing*. With each new product, or even upgrade, there will be additional horizontal and vertical target markets and users to sell to. New offerings should be released every nine to twelve months, minimum! Welcome to the internet age.

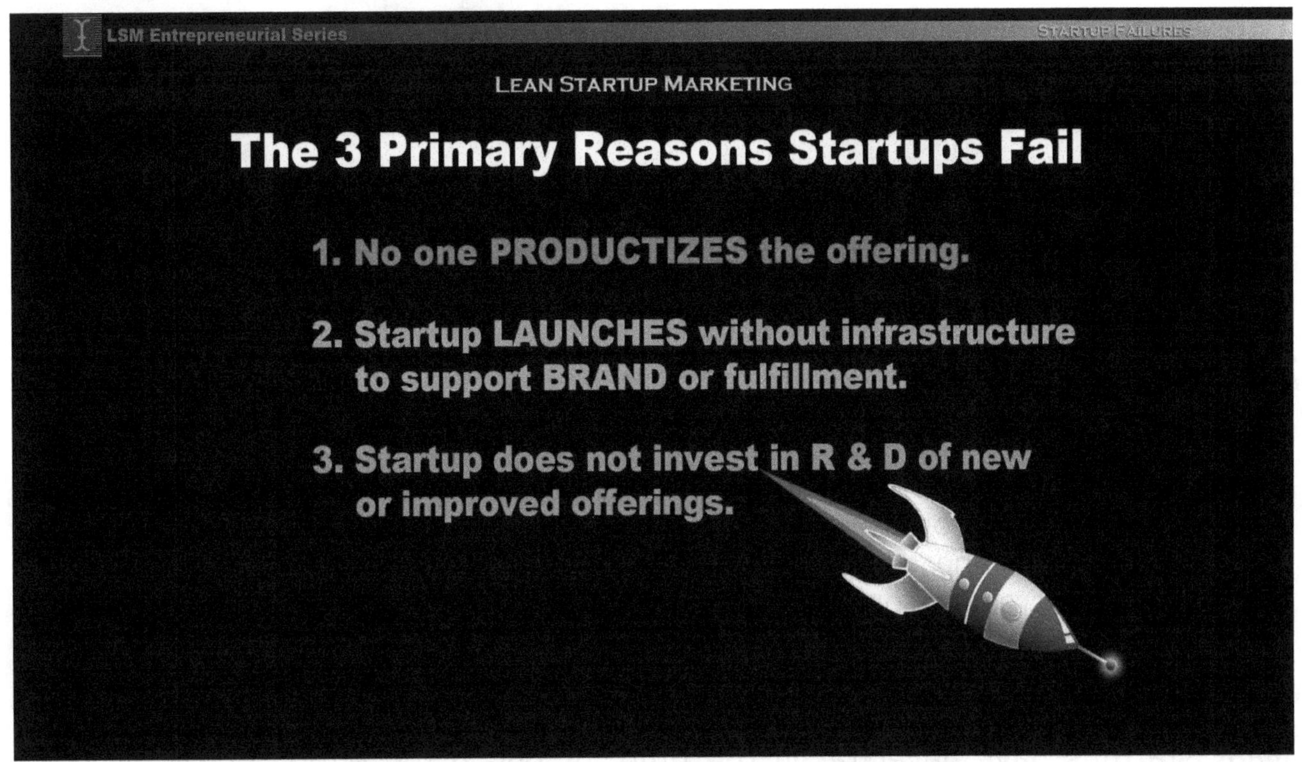

Avoid these common startup failures with the gorilla (not *guerrilla*, as marketing should never be stealth) RAF Marketing Method, delivered step-by-step, in three workbooks, *each building on the previous steps*. Follow the steps *in order* to guide you through the process of turning an idea, or even a completed product, into an offering of value, something someone, besides you, *wants*. Each workbook will drill down and detail the steps you must take to market a product or service to sell directly (on *Amazon*, *Etsy*, *eBay, GooglePlay*), or your first offering of many to come by launching a startup.

Each workbook in the LSE series assumes you have the knowledge and means to *produce* the offering you envision. LSM Workbook 1: PRODUCTIZATION does *not* require that your idea already be actualized. **Productizing your idea should happen simultaneously with developing it.** If you are planning to create a startup during this course, by LSB Workbook 2: BRANDING, your product should at least be in the works when marketing your pre-launch campaigns. By LSL Workbook 3—LAUNCH, you must have a complete and *quality-tested* offering to sell.

Remember, to effectively actualize an idea for profit, and to vastly increase your odds of startup success, you must implement the RAF Marketing Method *in order*:

LSM Workbook 1. Step 1—Get Ready, and **PRODUCTIZE**.

LSB Workbook 2. Step 2—Take Aim, and **BRAND**.

LSL Workbook 3. Step 3—Fire, and **LAUNCH** marketing campaigns.

Target Marketing starts wide, and drills down to individuals (targeting *users*), which is exactly how the LSE series unfolds. Next, we delve deep into each of the three workbooks, and examine the steps that must be implemented to create a valuable offering, and market it for profit.

LSM Workbook 1. Step 1: Get Ready

Productize Your Idea into an Offering of Value

The Productization process is a must for startup success, but also to *grow* any business into a lasting company of value. Turning an idea, or even a developed offering into a product someone actually wants, requires defining your potential offering's *characteristics,* clearly, concisely, and specifically.

Productization is an essential component of the lean startup marketing process. Many startups have never taken the time, or put in the effort, or simply don't know how to productize their offering/s. Productization comes *before* branding because the process produces correlated content directly inline with what you are planning to market and sell. You will utilize this content to create your company's brand. Identifying the features, benefits and solutions of your product, as well as the target markets and users likely to find value in your offering, gives you a framework for branding it.

If your startup has launched without an *intimate* understanding of what your offering IS, DOES, and WHO will find value in using it, it's likely your marketing efforts won't receive the conversion, such as purchases of your product or sign-ups for your service, that are needed to sustain and grow any business.

Whether you are hoping to market an idea, or a product in development, or more effectively brand and market an existing offering, the Productization process will help you set up your business for sustained success. It provides an infrastructure that defines the best, and most unique characteristics you must actualize, to create a *valuable* offering desired by a large group (or many groups) of people.

We *begin* the journey of marketing any business idea by implementing the Productization process.

To productize your potential offering, begin by identifying what its features and benefits are, and what solutions your projected product provides for specific target markets, as well as likely individual customers.

Next, you must find out if anyone else has already produced your idea. If you find competition for your projected offering, don't give up on your business idea! Come up with differentiators—new features and benefits for your projected offering that are unique, and *better*, than your competitors.

Potential new targets, such as horizontal and vertical markets, must be identified in the initial Productization phase, to ensure you have a continual stream of potential customers.

Constructing an elevator pitch will give you the *words* to chat up your offering quickly and concisely. Stealth mode is bad marketing. Create *buzz,* even before your offering is produced, for startup success at launch, and beyond.

And finally, how will your startup make money? Determining an initial profit model for launch, as well as a couple of years after rollout, and then 5 years down the line, will keep all stakeholders on the path to creating an offering of value to sell, for profit.

Whether we've already developed our idea into a product or service, or it's still just an idea in our head, Productization gives us insight into what we *think* we have. Initializing this ongoing process enables us to understand the people most likely to find a purpose for, or value in, our projected offering, even if it is simply to be entertained and have more fun!

Productization also gives us direction in developing and producing an offering of monetary value that is able to compete with similar offerings already available. Additionally, adhering to this process, *in order,* assures us we have an ongoing stream of target markets and users. And the best bit, Productization gives us marketing *content*—lists of keywords and key phrases—the features, benefits and solutions our projected offering provides. We'll use the words in these lists in the branding process to create marketing and advertising campaigns that build brand awareness of our offering and company, and ultimately to garner sales for our product or service.

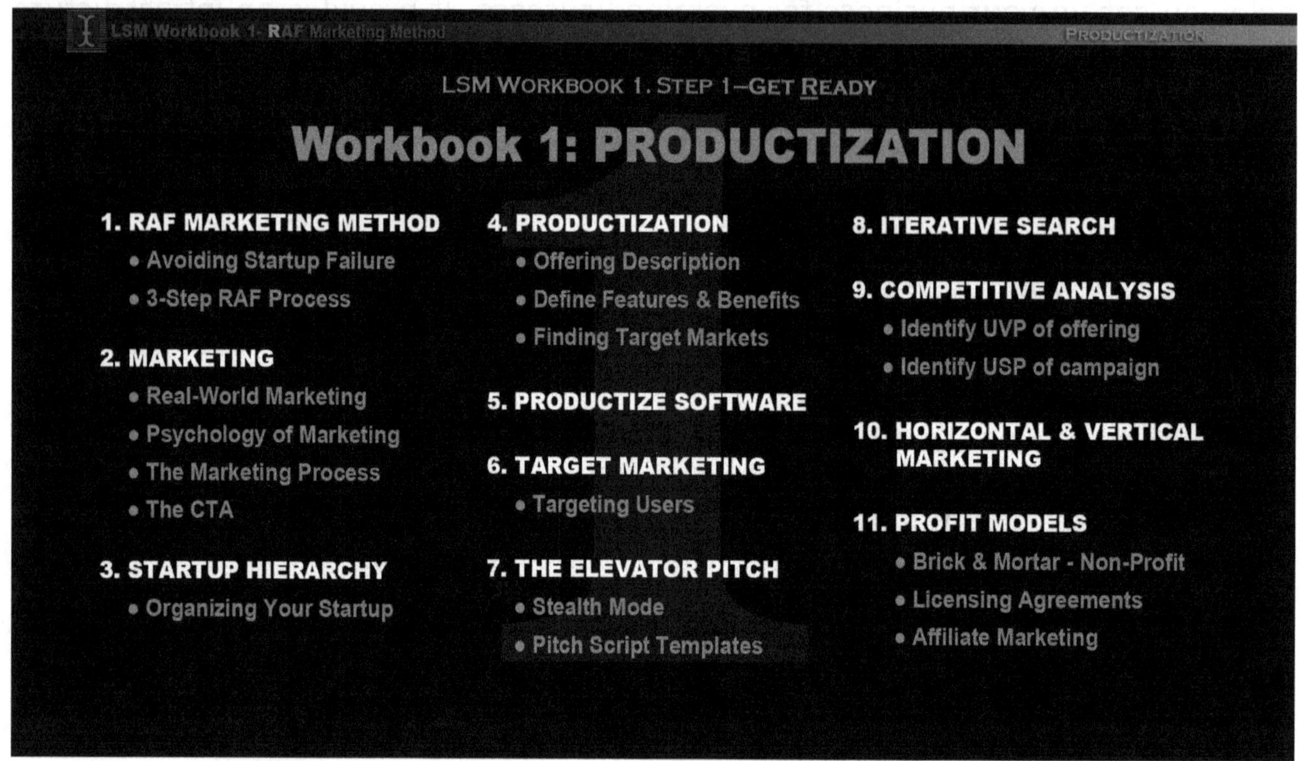

By getting ready and engaging in the Productization process, you may discover your projected offering is lacking in both features and benefits, or provides no real world solutions for anyone. Or maybe your offering has great value, but some competitor has developed your idea already. With each discovery, you may have to iterate your original idea, or even existing product, to make it more marketable.

The Productization process is a marketing *tool* to help us truly understand—get *intimate*—with our projected offering, and identify target markets and users, competitors and differentiators, that allows us to create a unique offering of value that specific groups of people are likely to buy.

LSB Workbook 2. Step 2: Take Aim

Brand Your Offering to Target Markets and Users

When you brand your offering (or product in development) to your target markets, you are effectively putting a 'face' on your idea, so it becomes something tangible, instead of just a concept or passing notion. The initial branding process does not require your offering be produced. You can create brand identities and pre-launch advertising and marketing campaigns that generate excitement about your upcoming offering *simultaneously* with producing it.

Whether branding a product, service, and/or a new company, even a nonprofit organization, the branding process begins with a name. Naming a startup is like naming a newborn, which your new venture virtually is—your new baby.

We give children language to communicate. We give our new venture a 'voice' with taglines—an essential component of the corporate identity, to communicate who we are and what we have to offer.

In LSB Workbook 2, we'll marry graphic design and marketing, explore the partnership inherent to these two disciplines, and learn to create advertising that gets greater response. We'll closely examine the design process, color theory, and typography, as well as digital and print reproduction of many types of marketing tools and campaigns produced in the branding process.

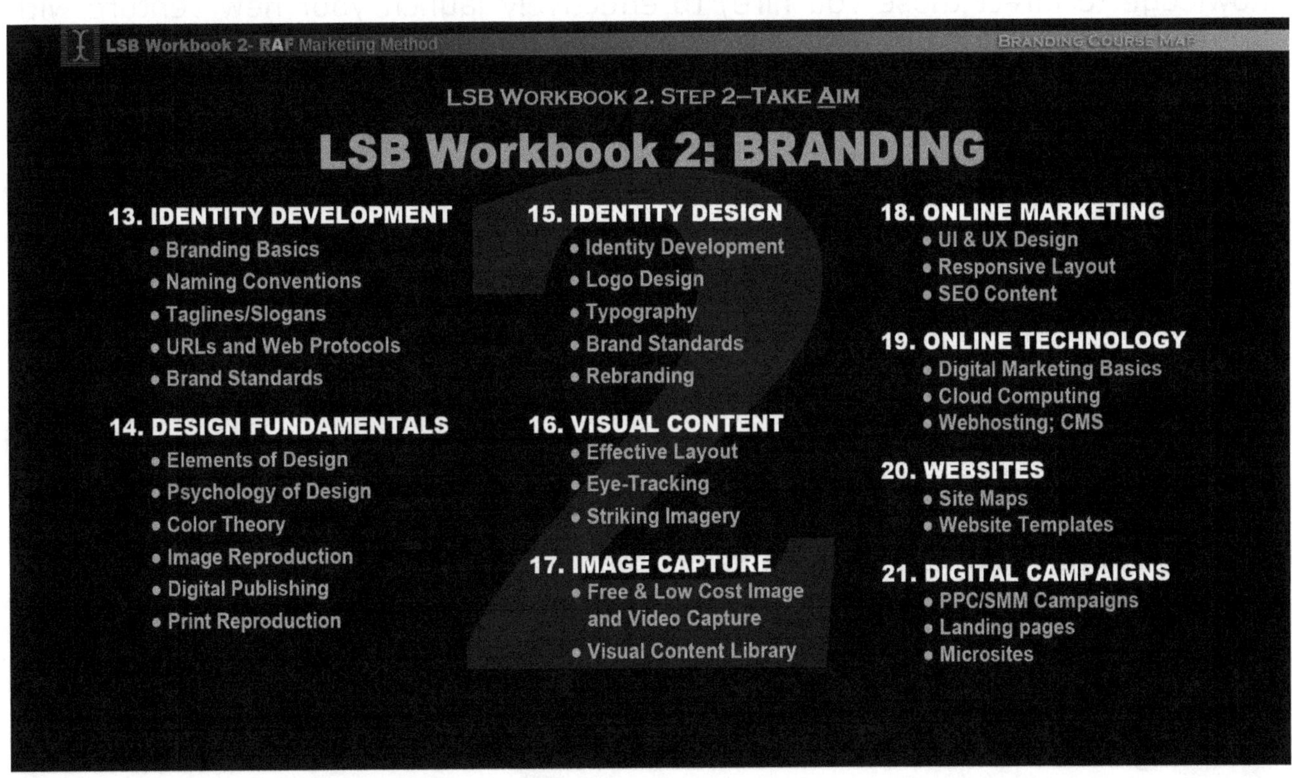

Product and corporate I.D.s, also known as logos, must be as dynamic on a *Twitter* feed as on the side of a building. You must create a complete identity for your startup, and also for *each offering* released. Brand Standards must be established to assure your identities look consistently fabulous across all media to build your brand awareness.

Branding is an ongoing process for any business to grow and thrive. Advertising and marketing tools and campaigns must be continually developed for launch and throughout the life-cycle of your business. LSB Workbook 2 covers online technology basics, from **user interface** (**UI**) design—what you see on your device screens, to **user experience** (**UX**) strategies that keep users engaged with your digital marketing, to **responsive** design that looks great on your laptop, as well as your mobile devices. Then we parlay this knowledge into building stunning websites and online marketing campaigns that command attention, at little to no cost.

You'll begin a professional image library of pictures and video clips to use in your marketing efforts. And you'll learn tips and tricks of SEO copywriting to creating attention-grabbing headlines, email campaigns, and micro-posts that improve your search engine ranking (SEO), and that get response (click, download trial, sign-up) to your marketing efforts.

LSB Workbook 2: Branding will give you the step-by-step process (and the knowledge to direct those you hire) to effectively launch your new venture with marketing efforts that get response. We'll walk through the steps of the branding process, to produce professional identities, websites and other digital and print marketing and advertising that achieve optimal conversion rates (buy, try, or subscribe) with each campaign.

LSL Workbook 3. Step 3: Fire...Launch

Launch marketing campaigns with consistent branding across channels and media.

Utilizing the tightly targeted branded marketing tools and campaigns that you created in Take Aim, you now FIRE—Launch those campaigns at your target markets and targeted users. After publishing your pre-launch campaigns, you should iterate your offering, and/or marketing efforts, to integrate initial feedback. At this final stage in the lean startup marketing process, to effectively launch your offering and/or startup, you must have a complete, and *quality-tested* offering to sell (meaning you know it works, can scale with users or orders, it won't crash, or break) with your launch campaigns, and all your marketing efforts that follow.

LSL Workbook 3: Launch examines **Social Media Marketing** (**SMM**), and how to use digital marketing effectively, to extend your company's reach directly to the people who'll likely benefit from what you're offering. You'll learn how to build social networks for your company's offerings through profile pages on platforms where your target audiences likely hang out.

We'll drill deep into email marketing. Email campaigns often generate more conversion than any other digital media, *if* the intended recipients are likely interested in what we have to offer them, and the email avoids SPAM filters. Your email provider will detect marketing efforts over personal correspondents and never deliver your campaign to your intended recipient if they suspect it is a promotion. We'll resolve both these issues, as well as explore various types of email campaigns, from drip promotions released over time, to direct-sales eblasts.

While many entrepreneurs mistakenly believe marketing begins and ends on the internet, print marketing actually has higher ROI (return on investment) than digital campaigns. Direct mail (snail mail) often has great conversion—viewers of your marketing efforts either buying, trying or subscribing to your offering—that are equal to or higher than email. And surprisingly, print doesn't cost near as much as you think, especially digital printing.

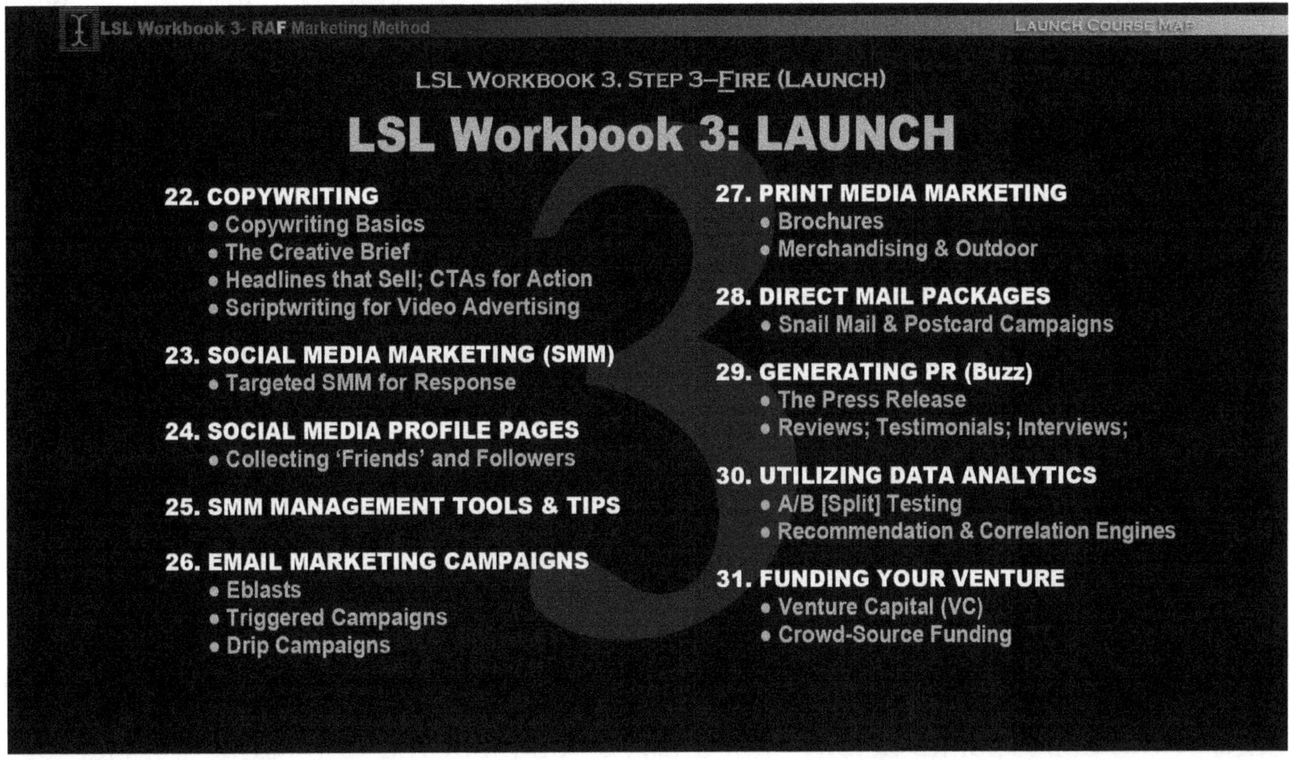

Live audio/visual (A/V) presentations or online webinars help generate buzz. We'll explore effective techniques for creating live and online presentations, as well as learn how to generate Press Releases to reporters of your favorite digital or print magazines within your company's industry.

Your initial pre-launch campaigns, and every other campaign you launch during the life-cycle of your business, garners data—how many opened your emails, or didn't, or saw your digital and/or print campaigns, who ordered your product, or started to order but stopped in the process...etc. The more campaigns, the more data. Marketing is becoming increasingly data driven. The *Privacy Train* has already left the station, with so many sources capturing information about each of us daily. LSL Workbook 3 examines the myriad of data mining and analytic tools available today, such as *Google Analytics,* to the digital data being gathered on most every site you market on, from *Facebook* to *Twitter* to *LinkedIn*.

Are you tired of living poor while investing your life and sweat equity into creating your startup? Want someone to believe in your product or service as much as you do, and support their faith with cash? Of course, it's easier to get funding if you've launched your startup already, and your offering is not only selling but getting great reviews and repeat customers. But if you are still in the pre-launch phase of your business, you can still get funding by effectively presenting what you've got to offer. This final phase of the RAF Marketing Method, we'll explore ways to solicit funding, from venture capital (VC) firms that make an investment in you, your team and company, to crowd-source funding by individuals who believe the product or service you are creating will likely have great value.

The Complete RAF Journey

Combining all three LSE Workbooks gives you the complete step-by-step process of actualizing your idea into an offering of value, for profit. Whether you are selling an offering directly, like a video game, a novel, or fashion line, on *Google Play, Amazon,* or *Etsy* (respectively), or producing and marketing the first offering of many to come from your startup, following the steps presented throughout this course *in order*—Ready, Aim, Fire—will give you the knowledge to generate the marketing tools, branding and advertising campaigns to launch a startup by the last module of the Lean Startup Marketing series.

You will need the following marketing tools and campaigns to market an idea, or offering in development, into a product or service of *value*, then effectively brand and eventually sell your offering and company. Each Workbook will drill down and examine the required marketing efforts for pre-launch, launch, and beyond to create, build and grow a startup into a thriving business over time. We'll examine each of the bullet points below, *intimately*, throughout the RAF Marketing Method, so no worries if you don't understand them all from this broad introduction.

Pre-Launch Tools and Campaigns

- **8 Productization lists**
- **Elevator Pitch (Drafts)**
- **Profit Models**
- **Corporate Name and Identity**

- **Product Names and Identities**
- **Product and Corporate Standards Guide** (or video)
- Purchased **URLs**
- A **webhost—**from *Wordpress* or *Wix*, to *Amazon Web Service (AWS)* for self-hosted digital marketing.
- **Digital Marketing** Campaigns: "Logo reveals" and "Coming soon" campaigns. UX games, contests, savings incentives, pre-orders, sign-up [newsletter/blog] interactive campaigns.
- **Print Marketing** Campaigns: [for Brick and Mortar] "Coming soon," *plus* coupon or incentive direct mail (snail-mail) campaign. (% off, or discount coupon of a local restaurant or store opening.)

Launch Campaigns

- **Website**/s
- **Landing pages**
- **PPC advertising campaign** (that double as SMM campaigns)
- **SMM** (Social Media Marketing) **Profile Pages** (on Facebook; LinkedIn...etc.)
- **Email** (and direct [print] mail) campaigns
- **Fully integrated, interactive, multi-channel marketing campaigns** including digital, print, PR, SMM, display (where applicable—trade show booths, in-store Brick and Mortar).
- Both digital and print marketing efforts should focus on touting the features and benefits of your offering (or campaign messaging), that fulfills a desire or solves a problem of a specific group of people. All marketing efforts must have an implied or direct CTA, that tells the viewer what action to take, even if it's simply remembering your brand (as with implied CTAs).

Marketing for the Life-Cycle of Your Business

- **All of the launch campaigns, plus**:
- **Data collection** and applied **analytics**
- **Website and Profile Page edits and updates**
- **Press releases for product and company updates**
- **Live Meetups, Talks/Presentations**
- Online **Webinars, How-To videos** (utilizing your offerings)
- **Positive press,** such as recent hires, corporate earnings, or company's philanthropic contributions or events.
- BE CREATIVE, and deliver unique advertising experiences and interactive marketing campaigns, focused on the *benefits* your offering provides for *specific groups of people* for the greatest response to all your marketing efforts for the life-cycle of your business.

Tom's Wisdom

I've brought Tom Edison into the LSE journey because Tom was an entrepreneur who actualized his ideas into products for profit.

Legend has it, that after over 5,000 attempts at producing a long-lasting light bulb, Edison finally created one that didn't explode. Only then did he understand what it took to achieve even transient success, since the incandescent light bulb is soon to become a footnote in history with the development of LED, and other clean-energy light sources.

"**Genius is 1% inspiration and 99% perspiration**," Tom said, and he will be remembered for [at least] this bit of wisdom.

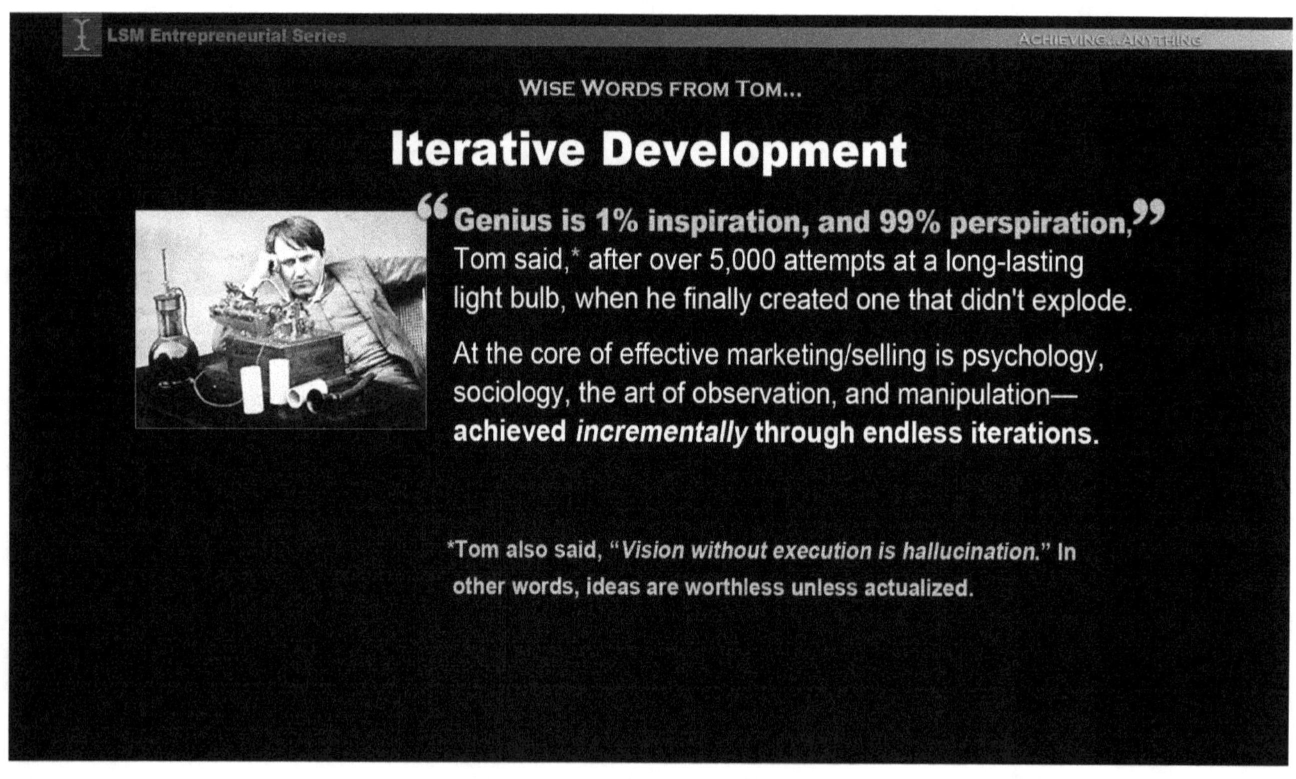

Very few startups launch with the original idea. As you move through the Productization process, you'll discover competitors doing close to or the same things you've envisioned (or that you're currently in the process of developing). Other roadblocks will pop up along your startup journey. Whether you find that not enough people will benefit from your particular offering, or you find you can not produce your initial idea economically to allow for acceptable profit margins, it is likely you'll have to change—*iterate*—your original idea to make it more marketable.

In all probability, you, or your product development team, will have to iterate most every offering you (or they) conceive for your company. Producing "the next big thing," for any industry is generally achieved when product development works in coordination with marketing personnel (including graphic designers) to produce offerings of value, that will likely benefit a large number of people.

Effective **marketing is selling** a product, service, message or idea, as with nonprofit organizations. Sales are achieved by producing products and/or services with features that *benefit* someone besides just you. Identifying the most likely features and benefits that will fulfill a desire of particular groups of people is achieved incrementally through multiple iterations.

So, do the work. *Don't quit*, even when you hear the voice of fear.

ITERATE.

The #1 Way to Launch a Successful Business

The RAF Marketing Method is one of the most efficient and effective ways to launch a new product and/or startup. Following the steps of the process presented in the LSE series, *in order,* will also increase the response and conversion rates of every marketing effort you launch. However, even if you follow this process step-by-step: Get Ready and productize your idea, then Take Aim and brand your offering with tightly targeted advertising and marketing campaigns, then Fire and launch them across all media...

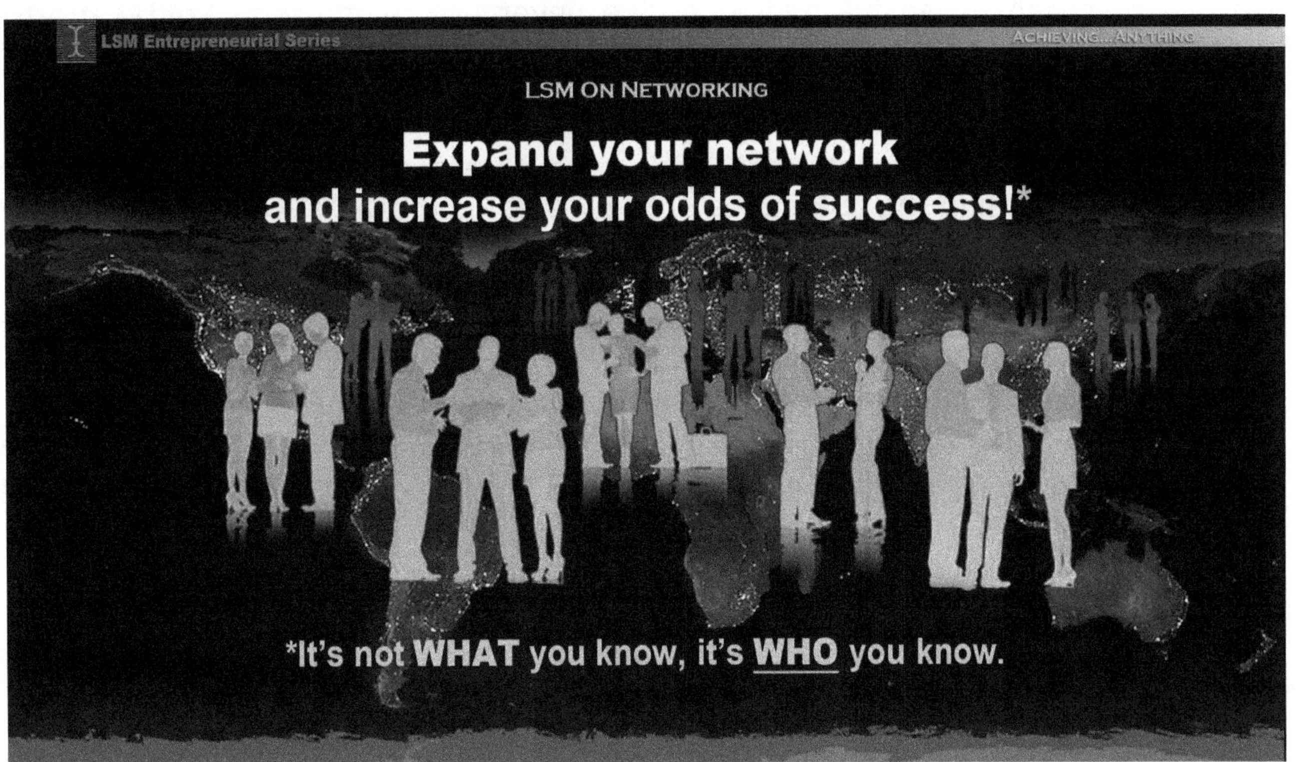

The *best way* to get traction for you new venture is through the people you meet along the way.

NETWORK. NETWORK. NETWORK.

I can not stress this enough. It applies to every level of business, whether you're looking for a job, or creating a startup, or hiring for your company. **NETWORK**.

After all, it's not *what* you know, but *who* you know that will help pave your path to success.

This is Lean Startup MARKETING

To create a startup, your marketing efforts must promote the benefits or solutions the features your offering provides. To create a *sustainable* business, your marketing must continually solve a problem or fulfill a desire of an expanding group of people.

While the foundation and purpose of marketing remains the same as it's always been, today's marketing methods are different than ever before, with the advent of the internet. We can now *market* a product or service before it's ever built—create buzz, excitement, even before launching the offering. At product launch, we can reach an expansive audience, like never before, through **social media marketing** (**SMM**), and more. And we can do all this with the RAF Marketing Method, at little to no cost.

Invest the time to actualize your ideas, and create a job you love. Walk the process you'll learn in the LSE series *step-by-step*, and dramatically increase your odds of startup success.

Again, the LSE series assumes you have the knowledge and means to *produce* the offering you envision. But taking an idea, and turning it into a product or service that actually makes money, requires an intimate knowledge of marketing. Whether you have your MBA, or are new to the marketing game, all the marketing you need to know to launch and grow a successful business is in the next module. Marketing Fundamentals is next.

MODULE 1: RAF MARKETING METHOD REVIEW

• The three primary reasons why startups fail:

  1. No one productized the projected (or complete) offering.

2. **Startup launched without infrastructure to support brand or fulfillment.**
3. **Little to no Research and Development (R&D) for new products or services.**

- The RAF Marketing Method is an acronym for "Ready, Aim, Fire," to help you remember to perform **PRODUCTIZATION**, **BRANDING**, AND **LAUNCH**, *in order*, to effectively actualize an idea into an offering of value, for profit.

- **Get Ready** means you must **PRODUCTIZE** your idea—identify its features, and the **solutions** or **benefits** your offering provides for a *specific group of people*.

- **Take Aim** means **BRAND** your potential venture—put a 'face' on your upcoming business with product and corporate identities, and a body of branding and advertising campaigns to market and sell your offering/s.

- **Fire** means **LAUNCH** your marketing campaigns to your *tightly targeted* audience, as targeted marketing gets the greatest response.

- We often must **iterate** our original idea into a different product or service than originally conceived to effective market and sell our offering.

- **NETWORKING** is the #1 way to get traction for your new venture. NETWORK. NETWORK. NETWORK! It's really not *what* you know, but *who* you know that will help pave your path to startup success.

-

-

STOP! Do CHALLENGE #2 before moving on.

CHALLENGE #2: Generating PRODUCT Ideas

If you already have an idea you'd like to produce, a product in development, or a fully actualized offering you are in the process of marketing, skip this Challenge.

Unlike finding solutions to problems, as in Challenge #1, in this exercise you will look to create a product or service by what you enjoy doing. While I'd like a trash bag that stays on the can, I wouldn't find much joy in developing this particular product, as I have no interest in plastics, rubber bands, or trash.

To endure the missteps and do-overs required in launching *any* business takes real tenacity, that will be challenged again and again with each disappointment. You'll *want* to give up, but *don't quit!* Build a business around something you enjoy doing, a task you [generally] like to perform (whether you're being paid or not). A job that engages, excites, will help you weather this onslaught of hardships, as you'll be iterating on what you already enjoy doing.

1. **List three of your top interests.** *Be as specific as possible!* What do you *love to do* (or even *like* to do)? Are you a gamer? An athlete? Like to bake? Shop? Read? Enjoy traveling? Gardening? Crazy in-love with your dog, or cat, or parrot?

2. **Make a list of the things you like to do.** Don't worry about how profitable they may be. Just list what you what you enjoy doing. Note, you won't *always* enjoy even tasks you generally like. I'm a writer, and often find the writing process frustrating, but overall I love to write. I even enjoy the editing process, rearranging and deleting words to communicate more clearly, and concisely.

3. **Come up with ONE IDEA for a product or service that is in-line with one** [or more] **of your interests, and/or pleasures**.
   - *You're the developer of an MMOG game that's better than* 'Call of Duty.'
   - *You love reading and want to recommend books you love, to as many as possible, with your own book review blog.*
   - *You've grown crops of eatables in your back yard, and come up with tons of recipes, along with fertilizing techniques for abundant yields.*
   - *You bake the best scones on Earth, and you want the world to taste 'em.*
   - *You're a science fiction fan, and want to share your thoughts on reads, movies, shows and other finds on an* All Things SciFi *vlog.*

Use this ONE IDEA to actualize and market with the RAF Marketing Method, and create an offering of value, for profit, with a job you'll enjoy doing daily.

◆◆◆

◆◆◆◆◆

MODULE 2: MARKETING 101 & 102

Marketing 101

Marketing is a *tool* to sell products, services and messages. As the CEO of your idea, or even developed offering, your #1 job is to *sell it*—market it—to potential partners, customers, employees, and investors.

Out of the gate, let's shatter a myth. Digital marketing, print advertising, merchandising, in-store display, marketing on the internet, or marketing on Mars, we are *always* marketing to *people*. And what motivates our behavior to take an action, such as buy or try a product, or subscribe to a service, hasn't changed since we became human.

Turning an idea into something other people will value, and then getting those people to purchase our offering, or into our message as with non-profits, requires an intimate understanding of the foundation, purpose and execution of the marketing process.

No doubt, you'll find much of the Marketing Module ahead disturbing. It'll go against what you've been taught is morally correct. However, *real* marketing, in the real world today, and maybe since marketing began, isn't about morality. It is about generating sales. The LSE series is designed to get you to *think differently*, about marketing, but also about *people*, because we are always selling to people, not markets. You must *see us*, as we *really* are, not the faces we wear, or the fabrications we all tell ourselves and each other, if you hope to become effective at marketing. The LSE series provide real-world marketing, for the greatest possible response and conversion rates (buy; try; subscribe) on all your marketing efforts.

-

-

-Marketing Fundamentals-

Marketing, as defined by *Google's* dictionary is, "the action or business of promoting and selling products or services, including market research and advertising," whatever *that* means. What *action*, being taken by *who*, exactly? This definition is a bit vague, as are most definitions of marketing, because the actual *practice* of marketing is more an art than a science, even with today's big data analytics. And the *art* of marketing takes many forms.

To date, the marketing industry has had no universal definition on what Marketing actually *is*, until now...

Marketing is manipulating people to do what you direct them to do.

I've gotten a lot of push-back from this definition. My students get disturbed by the word "manipulate," as a moral issue. While, it's true, I could have used the word "motivate," that would be the rhetoric they sold you in business school, and a lie. Most of us would not willing choose to overpay for an *iPhone*, that has less power and fewer features than their competitors, if *Apple* wasn't manipulating you to believe their **user interface** (**UI**)—what you see on your device screen—is somehow special, or that using *Apple* products in public gives you the *perception* (akin to belief) of being 'creative and cool.'

And, right about now, if you're an *Apple* fan, you're mentally defending the company and your purchase choices, believing beyond *any doubt* that *Apple* produces the best electronic devices out there. In doing so, you are simply confirming that they are marketing to you effectively.

I, too, used to be an *Apple* devotee. When the *Macintosh* first came out (Jan. 24, 1984), it was blow you away better than any other personal computer out there. I fell in love, and stayed in love for years, until the cost of upgrading the *Mac's* memory to run programs like *PageMaker* and *Photoshop,* nearly cost me my business. I finally sought alternatives, when *Apple* lost their exclusive license agreement with *Adobe*, and *Photoshop* and these applications became available on other personal computers (PC) in the late-1990s. I found PCs, even laptops that had come out years earlier with quadruple the memory, at half the price of a

Mac, with easy to navigate visual **UI**s, right down to the little trash can for deleting files. I had believed *Apple's* relentless marketing, promoting their UI as the *only* interface that was simple to use. The *Toshiba* laptop I purchased turned out to be more powerful, with more memory, with a higher screen resolution, and the UI was just as easy to master as my *Mac*. And it was half the price of the competing *Apple* laptop.

We are *all* manipulated by effective marketing.

We *all* market messaging and our *brand* virtually daily to be *perceived* in the way we want to appear to others. Dress to impress at work, or on a date? You drive a *BMW* or *Prius*? Does *Ikea* or *Pottery Barn* furnish your apartment or home? What faces do you wear in public, at work, regardless of how you are really feeling?

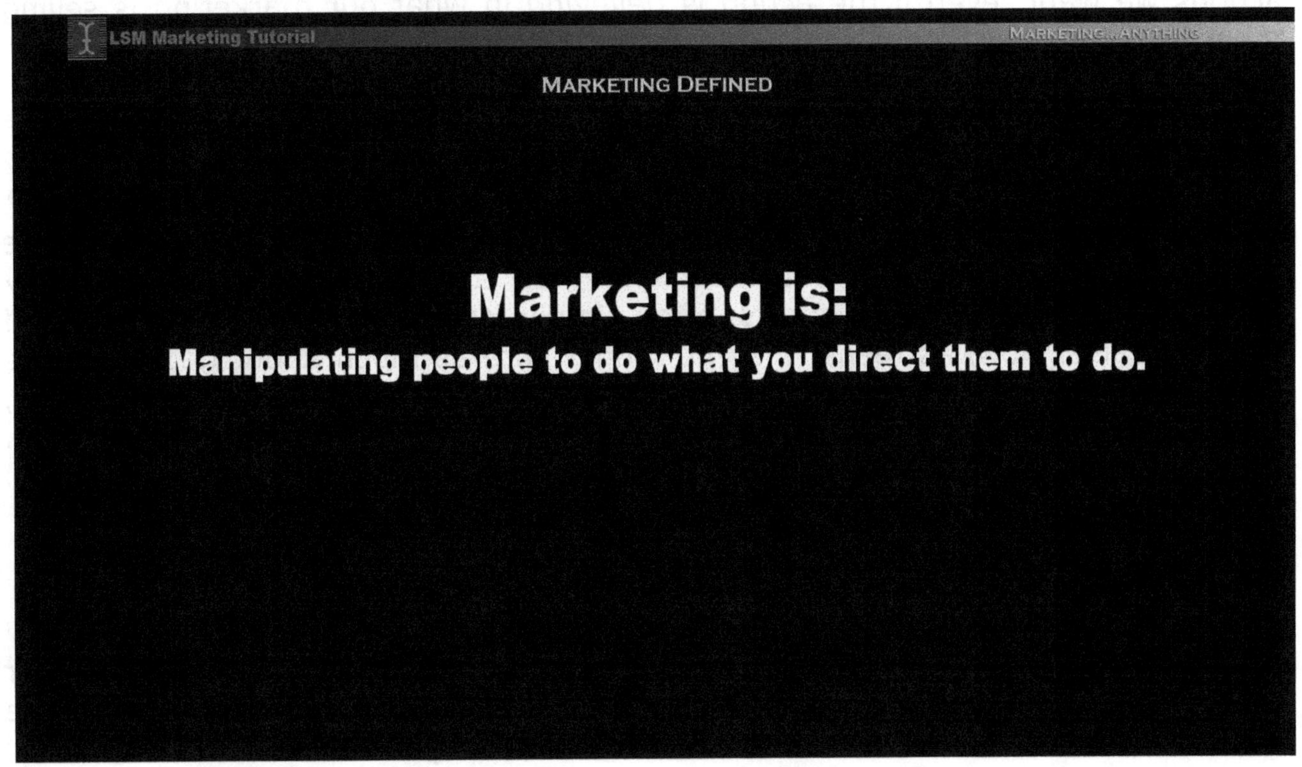

According to *Google*, "manipulate" means: "to handle or control (a tool, mechanism, etc.), typically in a skillful manner."

OK. Let's go with *Google's* definition. Strip away the moralistic rhetoric and social consensus, and "manipulate" is just a verb, a very specific *action*, not theory at all. What makes manipulation a moral issue depends on who you are trying to manipulate, and for what purpose.

I manipulate my kids daily to do what I think is best for them, like get A's in their classes to get into a good college to compete in the global, automated job market they'll enter. I've preached—*marketed*—this messaging to my kids since they were in middle school. I try to *sell* them on dealing with their real feelings, instead of hiding in bravado. Eat right. Sleep 8 hours a night. Get off their fu**ing cellphones. If I were ad campaigns, our home would be stuffed to the brim with 17 years of memes, tweets, blog posts, brochures, fliers, post-its, videos, and emails to my kids trying to get them—*manipulate* them—*sell* them on doing as I say, or as I'm directing them to do, from learning to speak, to potty training, to applying for college.

So ultimately, **MARKETING is SELLING**.

Every marketing effort should be designed to get someone to take the action or actions we want, even if the *action* is *believing* in what our marketing is selling them, such as education is a valuable asset to attain.

Marketing, as a theory, is really quite simple. But between theory and reality is the Grand Canyon. How do we actually get people to *act* as we direct? Manipulating people simply means getting them to do what they wouldn't normally do on their own. Marketing does this by using a motivator—an *incentive* —to respond as directed. As babies, and then toddles, my children naturally responded to my marketing efforts, often simply for the reward, the *motivator* of getting praise. Now, as teens, they no longer care as much about getting kudos from their mother. They'd much rather share *YouTube* videos with their friends, than study. So I have to up my marketing efforts, change according to their new demographics, to make any impact. I'm working on that as I type this... ; }. (Marketing is an *iterative* process.)

Marketing is manipulating people to take the action we direct.

In business marketing, "manipulating" people means *selling* them on our products, services and messages. But how do we do get people to buy what we want them to, or to believe that our offering or message has value for them?

Marketing has many proven methods and practices that work (generally over many campaigns) to manipulate our potential target audiences to become paying customers, and/or true believers in our messaging, offerings and company. Throughout this module, as well as the entire LSE series, we'll examine the elements of real-world marketing, and how to apply them to achieve the greatest possible conversion rates on all your marketing efforts.

The Conversion Funnel

A classic marketing model called a **Conversion Funnel** uses an inverted triangle to graphically shows how getting a sale generally works. A sale can mean many things, from selling **massive-multiplayer online games** (**MMOG**) through *iTunes*, or books through *Amazon*, to getting newsletter sign-ups, to convincing someone to hire you. Whether selling a product, service, or message, the Conversion Funnel is the de facto gold standard of marketing theory. This model is only *theory*, as it tells us what we must do to market our offerings effectively, but neglects to tell us how to do that.

As theories go, the Conversion Funnel is a good starting point—a foundation to build an understanding of the marketing process. There are generally five phases in the conversion process to get people to take the desired action of buying your offering or into your message.

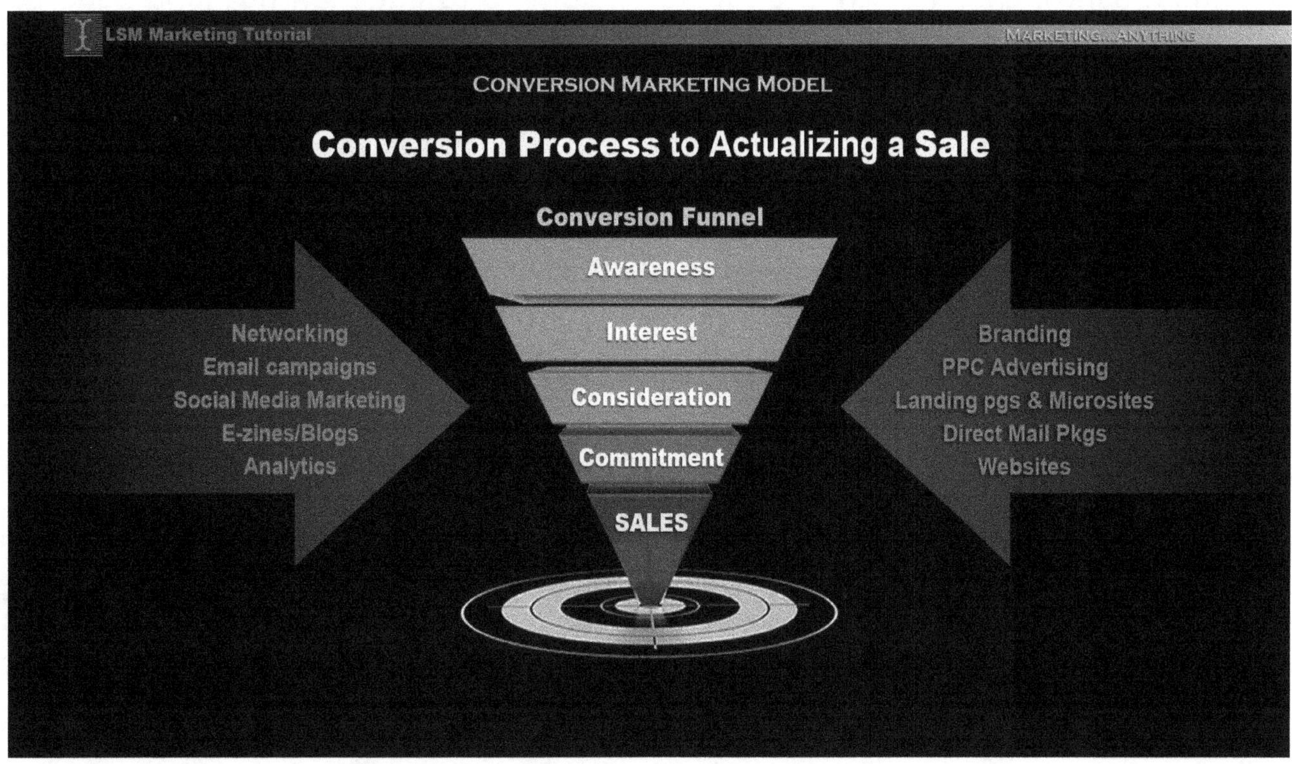

Phase 1: You must make someone AWARE you have a product or service. You must grab their attention with striking marketing to get them to notice your offerings, message, and/or company.

Phase 2: You have to spark their INTEREST, to see if your offering is something they may want. Is what you are selling offering a solution to an immediate need they have? Does your product or service fulfill a desire of theirs, like a low calorie dessert, or having more fun, or even helping the homeless or feed starving children, as with nonprofit message?

Phase 3: Potential buyers interested in what you are selling CONSIDER if they *really* want your offering. We all weigh factors of perceived need, wanton desire, cost, but there are hidden motivators that have us considering whether to buy a particular product or service, or download that app onto our mobile phone. I may crave the Mocha Frappuccino from *Starbuck's* this morning, but it's fattening, and bad for me. And I'd spend over $5, which I can't afford to waste on unhealthy snacks. So, I won't take the action and stop at the *Starbuck's* on my way to work today, as the commercial I saw on the morning news tried to get me to do.

What would get me to stop at *Starbuck's* and buy an offering of theirs today? It depends on what motivates *me* to take any specific action. *Starbuck's* could offer me rewards points to redeem some of their healthier products, such as their breakfast sandwiches (which is a lot better for me to eat than downing sugared caffeine for breakfast). In doing so, it's likely they have manipulated me with one of my **primers**—eating healthy is important to me. The **trigger** to get me to act, is the reward points that gives me discounts, or freebies with other purchases.

Your job, when marketing your offering, is to find out what those conscious *and* unconscious motivators of your target audience are, and what primers and triggers to use in manipulating them to do as your marketing directs.

Phase 4: If you've marketed effectively, your potential target audience will decide they actually *do* want (or feel they need) your product or service, and make a COMMITMENT to buying it (or subscribing, or signing up, or clicking on your ad, or whatever your campaign directed them to do).

In the above *Starbuck's* example, upon seeing the ad while checking my email this morning, they made me *aware* of an offering I found *interesting*—getting a discount on their breakfast sandwich. This would have **triggered** me to make the COMMITMENT and stop at *Starbuck's* on my way to work, their marketing campaign effectively taking me through the conversion process. Likely, I'd have made the COMMITMENT to purchase only minutes after seeing the ad, and consciously or unconsciously made the decision to stop at *Starbuck's* before I left my house.

Phase 5: This final phase of the Conversion Funnel is the actual SALE of your offering, where your target audience takes the action of purchasing your product, or buys into your message. But between *commitment* and SALES is the Grand Canyon. On my way to *Starbuck's* many things could have changed my *commitment* to stop there on my way to work. I could have had an accident, or been running late and couldn't afford the time it would take to stop there. I could have gone there and the line was too long, too slow...etc.

While the Conversion Funnel seems obvious, how we actually make a sale happen, in the real world, especially with expensive offerings, is quite a bit harder than the funnel theory provides.

Put Theory into Practice

So, let's put some of this theory into action, and practice what we must do to actualize these conversion steps, *in order*, and get a sale.

Before we introduce our product or service to anyone, *we* must be aware of what our offering *does*, and *who* will find value in it. In other words, we must productize our offering so that it fulfills a desire for a specific group of people, which we call our likely customers, or **target audience**.

Phase 1: This very first phase of actually selling your offering is often the most neglected. It is advantageous to make potential customers AWARE of your product or service *while you are developing it*, and before you produce any campaigns. Your first marketing effort should be an initial **elevator pitch**—a brief description of what you are planning to create. This pitch helps you clearly and concisely chat up your product or service wherever you are, often long before the offering is produced. At networking events, at home, to colleagues, family and friends—talking about your potential offering in broad strokes to whoever will listen, is the beginning of building awareness of what you are hoping to eventually sell. We'll closely examine creating your elevator pitch later in this workbook, and why *stealth mode* is bad marketing, but for now, let's focus on how to build awareness of your potential offering.

Beyond pitching at networking events and family gatherings, we build awareness of our product or service with multi-channel marketing efforts, tightly targeted to our potential target audience, which we established during the Productization process. Websites, print and digital advertising, video marketing, social media marketing (SMM) campaigns, webinars, presentations, trade shows...etc., are all marketing tools we use to build awareness and garner interest.

Our marketing efforts must command attention. We do this in a variety of ways which we'll explore throughout the LSE series, but a proven way of attracting attention is by using striking images or engaging videos. Color, movement, flashes of light, or high-contrast imagery will usually get noticed over just text content.

Phase 2 & 3: Headlines (second only to imagery) attract attention, but also, headlines are generally how we spark the INTEREST of our target audience. Promoting the *best thing*, or the **unique value proposition** (**UVP**) of our offering—the solution or desire our product or service fulfills—will attract the INTEREST of our potential customers.

Continually reminding people with email campaigns, **pay-per-click** (**PPC**) digital ads on social media platforms (*Facebook* or *YouTube)*, profile page updates, as well as PR and positive press, will keep our offering on their minds, and help them to CONSIDER our product or service more often.

Humans have 'goldfish' memories. We may see an advert for something that sparks our interest, and the next minute see another advert, or something else that diverts our attention, and we forget all about what we saw that captured our initial interest. Continually advertising our offering is an *ongoing necessity,* if we hope to sell it, and eventually build a thriving business. Marketing tools and campaigns must be produced and published constantly, to build brand awareness, to get our potential target audience to buy our offering, to keep the customers we have, as well and to convert new customers, or even just *remember* our product or company.

Phase 4: Getting people to make a COMMITMENT to buy our offering, or believe in our message, is the hardest part of marketing. People talk a lot of crap, say they just "love it," but then don't want to spend the money to get it, or worse, forget about our offering entirely. So, how do we get people to actually make a COMMITMENT to purchase our product or service, or to act upon our messaging?

This question is at the foundation of all marketing, but one you first must ask yourself: What motivates *you* to commit to buy something?

We all purchase necessities like food, clothing, shelter. But *what* food, fashion, and living space do we buy, and what motivates our choices?

Income, race, religion, age, location, are obvious factors in our decision making. Most college students likely can't afford a mansion in Beverly Hills. It's more likely they'll rent a flat near campus. If you're marketing a great new app for finding affordable rentals, it would be wise to target your advertising and marketing efforts at college students. Known as Target Marketing, which we'll closely examine later in this workbook, it is easier to get a sale if we market to the people who will likely find value in what we're selling.

Tightly targeted marketing gets the greatest response.

During the Productization process, you'll discover how to identify your likely target markets and users. Throughout the LSE series, we'll delve deep into creating and producing tightly targeted campaigns, to achieve greater response on all your marketing efforts.

Phase 5: Assuming we already have our target's *attention*, and *interest,* and even *commitment* that they want our offering—we're just trying to close the SALE—we can use a variety of known marketing tools to do this.

Consistently releasing striking marketing efforts that offer solutions, or satisfy a desire of our target audience, is a must throughout all the conversion phases. Touting testimonials and great reviews in our marketing efforts, lets your target audience know that others love your offering, which will often help close a SALE.

Another great way to turn *commitment* into a purchase is the personal touch. Sending an actual salesperson to close a SALE is expensive and often unnecessary. Instead, try putting a chat interface on a your website or sales page, to give potential customers the opportunity to engage in an online text chat with a live person to assist them with questions or concerns. These customer service representatives can help funnel your committed customer to follow through with the purchase.

The greatest motivator to get people to follow through on their *commitment* to purchase your product or services are **incentives**—sales, special offers at the counter in brick and mortar venues, or discounts sent directly to their mobile. Perks, like free stuff, or memberships, will often convert *consideration* to *commitment* to *conversion*, and close the SALE.

The Conversion Funnel is marketing theory that can be put into practice, utilizing some of the methods described above. We will examine many more throughout this workbook, as well as the entire LSE series. To complete the conversion process and get an actual SALE, may take a minute, like buying a coffee at your local cafe, or years, as when purchasing a *Ferrari*. But it's important to remember that the purpose of marketing, in person, in print, or online, is **manipulating people to do what our campaigns direct them to do**.

-

-

STOP! Do CHALLENGE #3 before moving on.

◆◆◆

CHALLENGE #3: Engage in Self-Awareness

The **Conversion Funnel** illustrates how a sale is made, from the top down—AWARENESS to SALE. **CHALLENGE #3**, you will *reverse this process*, and begin with the SALE, for a greater understanding on the **primers** and **triggers** that motivated *you* to make a purchase. Be sure to write down your answers. The process of writing them down will help you think about them clearly. The writing process will also help you remember what motivated your behavior.

Think of an expensive purchase you've recently made. Did you buy a car? Auto insurance? A top of the line cellphone or laptop? A pricey piece of clothing or jewelry? Tickets to a show, or conference?

1. **Think back to what motivated your COMMITMENT to purchase** (or subscribe to) the offering? What was the final push? List *the* **triggers** that got you to give the company cash or your credit card and seal the sale.

2. **What got you to even CONSIDER the purchase** you made over similar offerings by competing companies? List the **unique value proposition** (**UVP**), or the *best bit* you heard from a friend, or perhaps saw in a marketing campaign, that got you to purchase the expensive offering from that particular company.

3. **What piqued your INTEREST about the offering?** What **primers** got your attention? What benefits, real and/or perceived (*Apple*= 'cool, and easy to use') sparked your interest in the marketing campaign you saw, or the viral messaging that you heard from a friend? List some *specific* **primers** that captured your INTEREST enough to even consider purchasing the offering.

4. **How did you first become AWARE of the expensive offering you eventually purchased?** Did your mom, or sibling, or friend tell you about it (viral marketing)? Did you see a print ad the first time you became AWARE of the expensive offering you recently bought? Or perhaps your pricey purchase came up in search results when you were searching *Google* for something similar. List the first, and subsequent times you were made AWARE of your recent purchase *before* buying it.

   Reversing the Conversion Funnel shows you how to manipulate and motivate [at least] one target customer—*you*—to make an expensive purchase. And there are a ton of people on the planet a lot like you, regardless of how unique you think you are. There are people that are the same race, the same age, the same sex, religion, income level, often from the same location, and will likely act on the same or similar **primers** and **triggers** as you will in their purchasing behavior.

   Marketing uses demographics, geographics, psychographics, and other data to identify and categorize people into groupings. We then use these categories to focus our marketing efforts on reaching the target markets and target users (customers) most likely to find value, i.e. *benefits* in the features of our offerings.

5. **Project an ideal target user** (*specific* customer) **for <u>your</u> potential**

offering. Now, perform CHALLENGE #3 for this ideal customer's journey from SALE to AWARENESS. This process will help you find new ways to reach existing customers, and even identify potential new target users.

The Conversion Funnel is marketing theory, but you can put it into practice by implementing advertising campaigns and marketing efforts that are laser-focused to address each stage in the marketing and branding process.

◆◆◆

Marketing Means Selling

As stated, Marketing is a *tool*, to sell products, services and message. The purpose of marketing is to manipulate people to do as our campaigns direct. And, as previously pointed out, this can mean many things, from marketing to my kids to do the *right* things, to marketing software applications, to marketing a message like global warming.

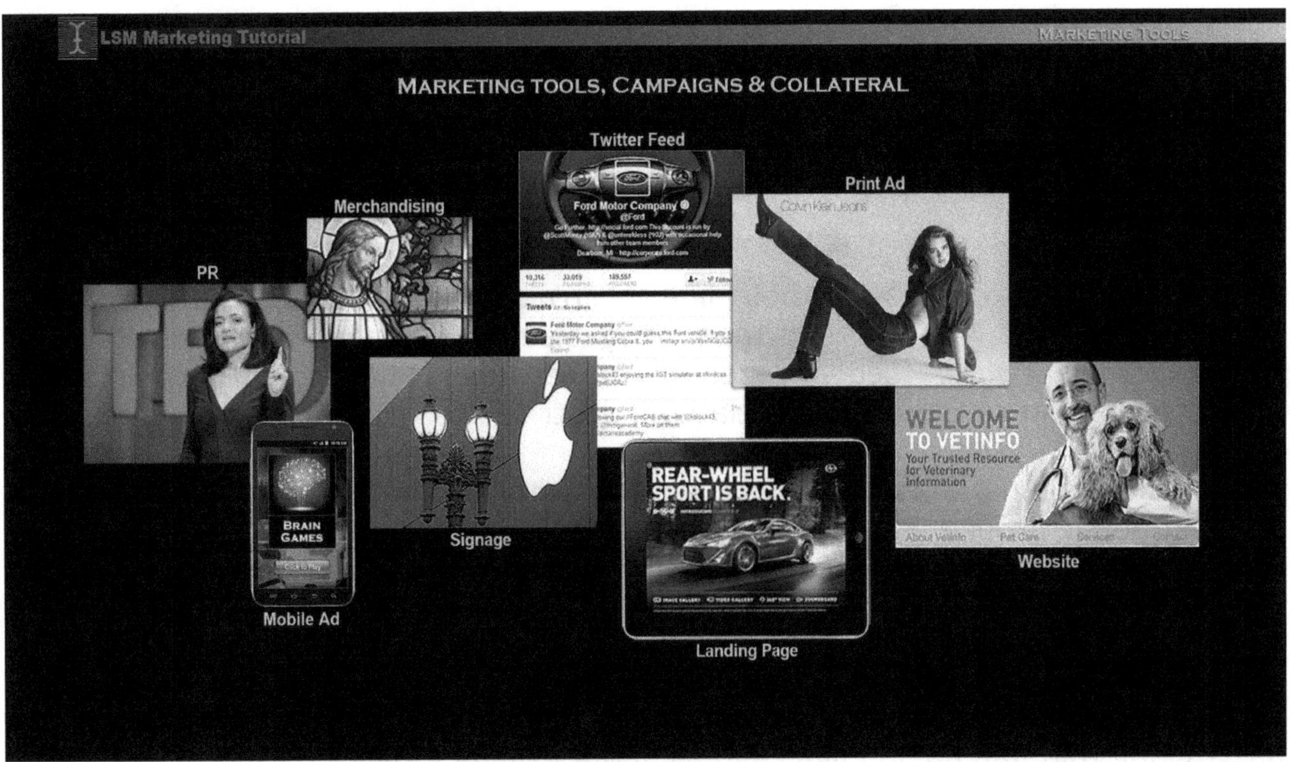

Selling a message, such as a political perspective, or a belief system, requires many forms of marketing. Utilizing **live networking** by building communities though local venues and events, and **social media marketing** (**SMM**) of digital ad campaigns across most every platform on the internet, religious organizations spend trillions (collectively) on marketing annually to convince us to believe, and/or keep the faith.

Nonprofit organization generally sell a belief in their message, though they often sell merchandise or tickets to events to raise funds. Philanthropic groups like the Gates Foundation, a $38 billion organization funded by Bill and Melinda Gates, give grants for projects in health, education, and social welfare. While the Gates Foundation has many websites that encourage nonprofit groups to apply for funding, the foundation doesn't market for money, since Bill Gates, founder of Microsoft, has plenty. But what about non-profits always looking for funding? Similar to marketing a product, most non-profits must create campaigns constantly, not only to build AWARENESS of their cause, but also to spark INTEREST, and eventually get a COMMITMENT to support their agenda with donations throughout the life cycle of their organization.

Beyond just a website, or business cards, all companies, from micro-businesses to major corporations, must continually produce marketing tools—digital and print branding and advertising campaigns, presentations, merchandise, trade shows, live networking...etc., to grow.

Apple utilizes brick and mortar locations at many retail outlets around the world to market their electronic devices. They use a full array of marketing tools, such as signage, eg. the *Apple* logo on their storefronts, merchandising—the layout of their products, and the advertising displayed in their stores—to soliciting people to come in and buy.

Ford Motors not only sells their line of trucks with loud TV and *YouTube* commercials filled with muscled men, they also build their brand awareness by updating their *Twitter* feed a dozen or more times *daily*, to help their target markets—men in construction or related industries—to remember their vehicles.

Calvin Klein jeans became widely known with a print ad campaign, where actress/model Brooke Shields posed, full body, in skin-tight *CK* jeans, and an open blouse. This *Calvin Klein* ad was making a subtle promise to women, that they too could look like Brooke if we wore *CK* jeans. And women bought *CK* jeans in droves, buying into the *perception* that they looked as good in them as they did on Ms. Shields, regardless that most didn't look anything like her. *Calvin Klein's* marketing offered what many women of the time desired, and perhaps still do—to look thin and be 'in,' like sexy, coveted Brooke Shields.

Marketing is selling. Branding, advertising campaigns, and live networking are *tools* we use to sell. And after the Productization process presented here in LSM Workbook 1, you'll learn how to create effective marketing tools and campaigns (LSB Workbook 2) to build brand awareness, spark interest, and ultimately convert CONSIDERATION to COMMITMENT, and eventually *sell* your offering.

◊◊◊

MODULE 2: MARKETING 101 REVIEW

- There is no difference between **digital** and **traditional marketing**. We are selling to *people*, regardless of the marketing tool. Our human psyche has changed very little since we became homo-sapiens, so we use **psychology** to market to people.

- **MARKETING is SELLING.** They are one and the same. The purpose of marketing is to **manipulate people to buy** our products, services and/or a belief in our message.

- A **Conversion Funnel** is a visual marketing model that illustrates how a SALE is [generally] made.

- *Effective* marketing tools build brand AWARENESS, spark INTEREST in our offering and company, get people to CONSIDER our offering over competitors, COMMIT to purchasing, or believing our message, and eventually **trigger** people to take an *action*—buy, try, or subscribe.

- **Target marketing** is the process of finding groups of potential customers and individual users who will likely find a solution or value in the real or perceived features of our offering.

- **Incentives**, such as sales, gifts, and special offers, are an effective marketing tool to convert CONSIDERATION into a COMMITMENT to purchase.

-
-

STOP! Do CHALLENGE #4 before moving on.

CHALLENGE #4: Engage in Learning About People

Most of us live inside our own heads, thinking about *whatever*, but rarely watching others closely. Time to step outside your own head, and *think differently*. To become proficient at marketing, you must watch what people do to understand what attracts our attention, and motivates us to act.

1. **For ONE WEEK, seven full days, observe and journal about the people you see** (at school, at home, at *Starbucks*). Watch what we actually do, (not what we *say* we will) and write down what you observe, into your laptop, onto your phone, or actual pieces of paper.

    - **Keep each observations under 100 words** (preferably less). Observe and journal only scenes to which you play no part. You must be an *impartial observer* of what you choose to describe.

    - **Create seven documents** (or a separate piece of paper for each day), with [at least] five observations per day of any individual's behavior, or of two or more people interacting. Observations can be of family dynamics at the dinner table, or someone at a cafe, but you must not have any interaction within the scenes you observe and document.

    - OBSERVE CAREFULLY, and write down *only* what your see and hear. Do NOT add or embellish anything you see when documenting your observations. Do NOT judge, or give your opinion on what you see. Simply transcribe each event as they unfold.

Choose to document scenes of interest. Do NOT describe someone passing you on the sidewalk staring at their cellphone like everyone else you pass by. NOTICE the subtleties, if they exist. What are they doing on their phone (if you can see)? Three out of the five cellphone screens that I could see at Back-to-School night at my kids high school, the people—mostly women, mid 30s to late 50s, White and Asian, upper-income—were checking their email, or *Facebook* feed, or playing some inane online game.

Pay close attention to your subject's mannerisms, how they talk—expressive, with a lot of hand gestures? Low key, quietly leaning in to whomever they are speaking? You may see an extreme expression like a frown, or a broad smile or outright laughter, but try NOT to interpret an express as "they looked bored," or "happy," or any other judgment call. Do NOT give any interpretation of what you see. Write *only* what you observe and hear, watching any individual, couple, or group of people.

2. **Log Demographic, Geographic, Psychological and Behavioral data:**
    - Title each entry with the DATE, TIME and LOCATION of each observation.
    - Start your observation with gender, age (approx.), race, and other obvious demographic data, like someone wearing a religious symbol, we can assume they follow that particular religion.

- Note mannerisms and behavior. Does your subject look away when someone looks at them? Do they boldly stare back? Solicit conversation with someone close by, or are so absorbed in their cellphone they hold up the line at your cafe?
- Note purchases at shops in the mall, or at the grocery store when you're waiting in the checkout line. What is being purchased, in what sizes (small or large), in what quantity, by whom?

Example: I'm in Nordstrom's, watching a 20-something, slender Black woman in a tan blouse tucked into a straight, knee-length navy blue skirt, try on nine pairs of shoes. She finally purchases a pair that looks identical to the pair of the black pumps she wore into the store.

We'll explore how to apply the information you gather about what people *really* do, beyond what we say, throughout the entire LSE series.

◆◆◆

-

-

-MARKETING 102-

Effective Marketing Always Sells the Same Thing

Marketing is selling, manipulating people to buy into our messages, and our products or services. And even though we are all selling different offerings, from politics to pottery, off or online, effective marketing—advertising that motivates people to *act* as our marketing directs—is always selling the same thing:

Effective marketing sells features and benefits of an offering, that fulfills a desire (or perceived need) **of a specific group of people.**

Whether marketing a sale on your offering, or sign-ups for your company newsletter, *effective* marketing sells the *benefits* that the features of your product, service or message provides. Your offering must satisfy a [perceived] need, offer a solution, or quenches a desire for a particular group of people (your target markets and users).

Throughout these workbooks, we'll drill down on identifying and effectively communicating with your target audiences, but first we must examine what motivates response (click, like, share—even *talk* about an offering or company), and conversion (buy, try, sign-up, subscribe).

How We Get People to Do What We Want

What motivates people to act? This is a very important question, because marketing is about getting people to do what we direct them to do, or to *act*.

At the foundation of marketing is the practice of **Psychology**. To be effective at marketing—motivating people to buy our offering, or believe in our message—we must monitor, categorize, and seek to understand human behavior.

Psychology is more an art, than a science. Humans are complex beings, dynamic: our [perceived] needs and desires constantly changing with age, and life circumstances. We lie to ourselves—tell ourselves we need things we don't, or make promises we never keep, like dieting, exercise, control spending, less time on our electronic devices, *YouTube*...etc. We lie to each other, because we believe it ourselves, or we want to appear smarter, kinder, wiser. We ALL fib, exaggerate, fabricate, remember wrong, because memory has been proven to be faulty. Humans are fickle, which is what makes figuring out what motivates us particularly difficult when we often don't know ourselves.

We are just beginning to identify a few basic behavior patterns common to most of us through big data collection and analytics. However, assessing and categorizing behavior does *not* automatically give us the reason *why* someone chose to take an action.

Remember, humans are dynamic, complicated, and motivating us to take any action is hard. But regardless of our age, education, income level, or lifestyle, there is one motivator that is undeniably effective at getting people to do what we want them to.

What consistently motivates most people to act?

Self-interest.

This is not an indictment of humanity. This is *who we are*, an unalterable part of our nature. And marketing *must* deal with this fact. What this means, in applicable terms, is we must offer people something they want, or they *think* they need, in order to get them to buy our offering or into our message. Whatever we sell must provide some value, or the *perception* that obtaining it will gratify us. To achieve the greatest possible response rates on all your marketing efforts, be sure to address how your offering will solve a problem, or fulfill a desire, i.e. *benefit* your potential customers with every campaign. We'll examine techniques utilizing the psychology of self-interest, to create branding and marketing campaigns that get the greatest response in LSB Workbook 2. For now, let's continue to explore the foundation of real-world marketing in detail.

Objective Manipulation employs our psychology to funnel viewers towards an objective, usually to purchase, sign-up, subscribe, or believe in our message. Utilizing storytelling—creating a narrative to sell our offering (as in, you'll look sexy in tight jeans regardless that you don't have the body-type of a model)—also known as *'selling perception,'* is a common form of Objective Manipulation used in marketing today.

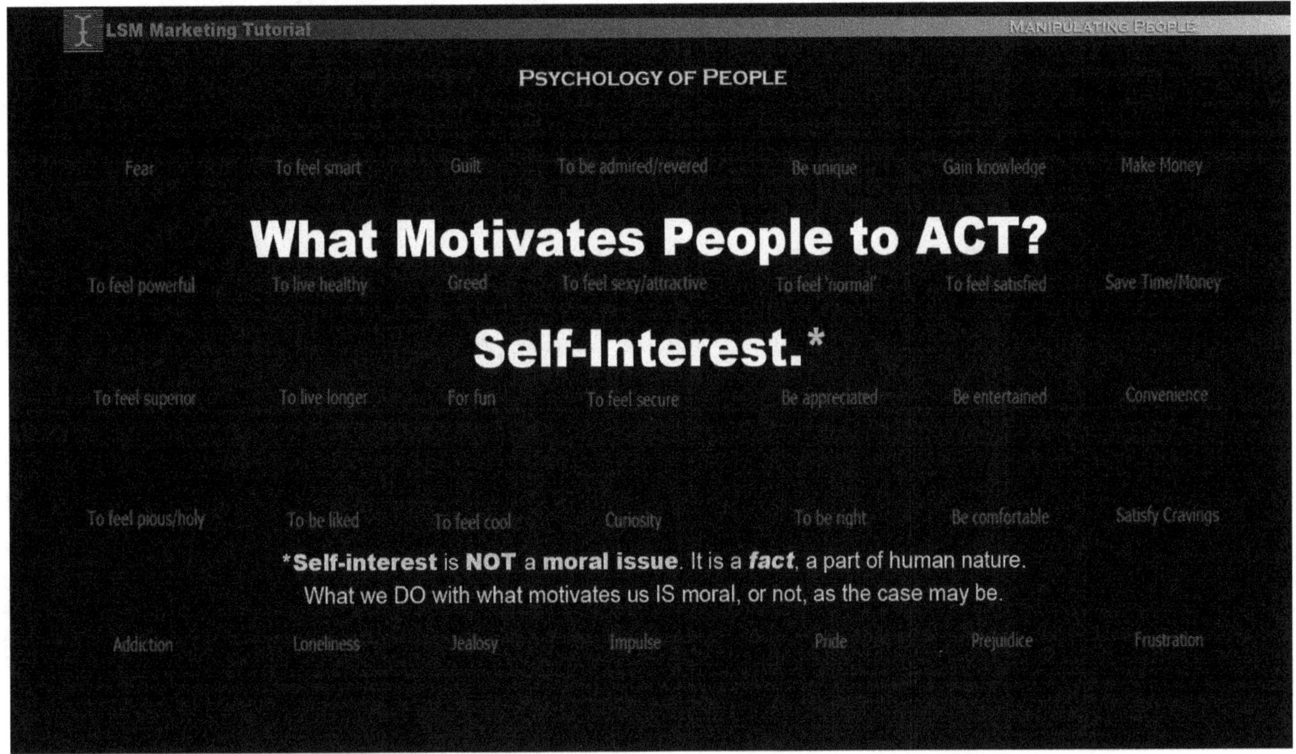

In the psychology of humanity, and most every other living being on this planet, there is no such thing as altruism. Even 'saints,' like Mother Teresa, who spent her life feeding the poor, caring for the sick, did so out of self-interest, *not* altruism. Altruism is a religious construct to motivate good deeds, to get people out of our own heads, even for a moment, to consider others. In fact, most religions promote altruistic behavior with rewards in life such as Karma—do good and good will come to you—and promises of Heaven—an afterlife of bliss—when we do right by each other.

No doubt, many of you reading this are bridling right now. "*Of course* altruism is real! It's what we strive for, our highest attainment—to give *selflessly*—because we are fundamentally caring, loving beings."

Not so much. Humans are fundamentally self-serving.

This is not a judgment call, but a *fact* of human nature. What *can* be judged is *what we do* with this fact of our nature.

Case in point: A classic scenario cited as a metaphor for true altruism is a parent running into a burning house to save their children, regardless that it's suicide to do so.

Would I run into a burning house to save my kids? You bet! Why? Not altruism.

Most any reasonably sane person would not run into an inferno *knowing* it would kill them if their intention was to save someone else. So, there must be other reasons why a parent would enter a burning house without regard to their own safety to recuse their children.

As a mom of, now, two teens, I'd impulsively run into that burning house without ever stopping to consider that it may be deadly. Saving my kids, or even trying to, would be the only way I could continue to live with myself, if, by some bizarre twist of fate, I lived and they died in the fire. The loss of the most intense love I've ever known would be so profound, I'd spend every day of the rest of my life tormented by the *chance* that I could have saved my children, and blaming myself for not attempting to do so. Additionally, as a mother, I am satisfying my biological wiring by caring for my offspring. My body produces 'reward' chemistry, 'happiness' hormones—Dopamine, Serotonin, Oxytocin—which helps motivate me to attempt [the *action of*] rescuing my kids. So, unless I was looking to commit suicide, is running into that burning house to save my kids altruism or self-interest?

What would *you* run into a burning building to save? And *why*?

To be effective at marketing, it is essential that you broaden your perspective to *think differently*, and get off the *politically correct* train. Our very human condition that we all *act* in our own self-interest is at the core of our psychology. In the real world of marketing, we characterize behavior, then develop campaigns with primers and triggers that motivate people to *act*. To produce *effective* marketing that manipulates your target audience to take the *action* your campaigns direct, you must *first* consider their psychology.

Still absolutely believe you've witnessed, or even performed [on occasion] acts of altruism?

Missionaries from many religions around the world spread their beliefs with every starving child they feed. Of course, the impoverished don't need the religious indoctrination they are served with each mouthful, but these missionaries are fulfilling their function as representatives of their belief system. And their brains reward their efforts with 'happiness' hormones that make them feel good, accomplished, proud. *Oh, so good*, that they are able to tackle the next day, and the next, of abject poverty.

The kind of illness and injustice these missionaries experience most days would cripple me. I'd get so depressed, I'd become non-functional, watching people struggle for basic survival under fascist dictators and lunatic militias. Regardless of my belief system, I can not contribute to aiding the poor in the manner missionaries do, because it would not make me feel good in any way. I'd be profoundly sad every day, knowing religion will never save these children. People, beyond religious sects trying to win followers, are going to have to do that.

Self-interest, *without exception,* **is <u>the</u> motivator that gets people to ACT.**

To get anyone to buy your product, service or message, you must understand human psychology. *Study people!* Observe what we *really do*, not just what we *say* we will. '*Techie posers*' are [generally] men, who wear wire-rimmed glasses, dress in Levi's, T-shirts, athletic shoes, and often hoodies—today's personification of a Silicon Valley tech worker, modeled after what Steve Jobs (founder of *Apple*) wore, and how Mark Zuckerberg (founder of *Facebook*) dresses. But this particular grouping of *posers* don't know how to code, nor is their job in tech, except on the lowest levels. *Techie posers* are a specific target audience, especially for video gaming.

We produce conversion-driven marketing, by tightly targeting *groups of people with similar characteristics* that will most likely to be interested in our offering. To be effective at marketing, you must seek to understand what your target users *think* they need, or desire, and *why.* Then offer them features, benefits and solutions your product, service or message provides that are in their real, or perceived, and often unconscious **self-interest**.

Marketing to Self-interest

Bernie Madoff, an American fraudster and a former stockbroker, marketed effectively to a lot greedy people. He fulfilled their desire to get rich without effort when he convinced them to invest in his pyramid scheme. Investors eventually lost $64 billion in capital, some committing suicide after losing everything they had, before Bernie's Ponzi scheme went bankrupt with Madoff's arrest.

On the other end of the spectrum, *Toyota* acted in self-interest when they invented the *Prius*, a hybrid, economical compact car. The target markets for fuel efficiency and electric powered vehicles was growing fast over rising gas prices, and amid new concerns over global warming (this issue first highlighted in the media in the late 1990s). And *Tesla* is motivated by self-interest as well, expanding their existing target markets to include middle-income users by releasing a consumer version of their all electric vehicle with a reasonable price-point. Less cost for consumers. Less pollution in the air. *Tesla* makes more money. Everyone wins!

Humans are self-interested beings. What we do with this fact, how we *act* is what matters, not that we *are* self-interested.

Toyota and *Tesla* produce the cars they do to make money. And while serving themselves, they are moving closer to serving the greater good, by producing cars that maximize fuel consumption, and have low emissions.

Martin Andrew Green is an Australian professor at the University of New South Wales. He's dedicated his career to developing solar cells. Mr. Green's self-interest is scratching a mental itch. He's curious about light energy, and in learning how to manipulate it, his brain rewards him with the same 'happiness' hormones missionaries get for doing what makes them feel good. The reward center of Mr Green's brain makes him feel powerful, smart, valuable, serving his emotional needs whenever he's 'scratching' his mental itch, i.e. working on what interests him. He is also contributing to the greater good of humanity, and nature, by developing alternative 'clean' energy.

Self-interest in not a curse. It is simply a state of being... *human*, in our case, but seemingly, it dictates the behavior of everything else that lives on Earth. *Survival of the fittest* is how species thrive over millennium. Not survival of the kindest, whatever 'kind' means. Martin Green is not kind, but self-interested, scratching his mental itch. Missionaries are not kind, in spreading their belief system. Educating the impoverished to manage their own needs, stand up against tyranny and create a just society would serve the greater good far better than preaching religious doctrine while supplying aid.

There is no need to fear the fact that human behavior is driven by self-interest. Regardless of the religious assertion that altruism is not only real, but mandatory for society to function, self-interest is *imperative* for our continued survival.

To get people to take the action your advertising and marketing campaigns direct, make sure to address how your offering serves your target customers' interests. The list below are areas of self-interest that we utilize in our marketing efforts to manipulate our target audience to think, or *feel* a certain way, that's likely to motivate them to buy our offering, or believe our message.

—To be liked.
—To fit in.
—To feel cool (as in hip, or trendy).
—To be appreciated.
—To be right.
—To feel proud.

—To feel important.
—To make money.
—To save money.
—To save time.
—For convenience.
—To feel secure.
—To feel attractive.
—To be comfortable.
—To appear original.
—To appear smart/er.
—To win.
—To feel happy.
—To have fun.
—To gain knowledge.
—To be healthy.
—To appear humble.
—To gratify curiosity (scratch a mental itch).
—Out of fear; greed; guilt...etc.

-

-

STOP! Do CHALLENGE #5 before moving on.

◆◆◆

CHALLENGE #5: Build Your Awareness of Self-Interest

To understand how people feel and think, *why* we do what we do—our psychology—first you must figure out, and continually monitor what motivates *you*. To do so, we'll look at the Conversion Funnel through a different lens, on the *emotional*, or psychological levels. You'll describe from the top down—AWARENESS through SALE—what motivated *your* behavior. Answer the following questions (in writing!):

1. What was your last <u>unnecessary</u> purchase?

- How did you become AWARE of the item? Did a trusted friend turn you on to it? Did you see an ad or commercial for the offering?
- What sparked your INTEREST in the product or service? What role did the reputation of the brand play in your interest? Women purchasing a *Prada* purse have very different *psychology* than those buying a handbag from *Target*.
- What got you to CONSIDER this offering over that of its competitors? *Be specific!* If you purchased an *iPhone* over a *Samsung* mobile phone, there is an *emotional* reason for your choice. Describe your feelings about the offering *and* brand—the image the company

symbolizes for you—that lead you to your decision to purchase. Did it make you feel smarter (a book, or a course), attractive (make-up, or clothing), powerful (a sports car or *Harley Davidson* motorcycle), creative (anything *Apple*)?

- Why did you buy it over its competitors' offerings? What about the brand or offering stood out for you? (*Apple* devices have visual **user interfaces** (**UI**) that are easy to navigate, which is a functional reason why you may have purchased your *iPhone*, but emotionally, buying *Apple* products makes *Apple* devotees *feel* younger, more savvy, and more creative than non-*Apple* users. If you are an *Apple* fan, *why*? Don't tell yourself it's their easy-to-use UI, as most of today's devices are equally user-friendly.)

Go through this process in **CHALLENGE #5** with every purchase you made, large or small. Start making mental notes of purchases that you see, at the supermarket or mall. Pay attention to purchases your friends and family chat up. Make mental notes about who bought what when, and why, assuming you know, or ask. Over time you'll see patterns emerge. A truth about humanity is we all share the same basic emotional drivers that guide our behavior. Walking the process of **CHALLENGE #5**—asking yourself *why* with every purchase, both in the functional and *emotional* realms—will show you primers that manipulate, and triggers that motivate each of us to act.

◆◆◆

Marketing is an Ongoing, Iterative Process

Getting people to do what we want is a process. It takes time, and requires multiple marketing touch-points, from networking, to print, to digital social media marketing (SMM) advertising and branding campaigns. It's likely you'll get discouraged when you begin the launch process, and don't get much traction with your roll-out campaigns, but this is typical.

Marketing is an iterative process. We collect data with every marketing effort, and apply what we learn through analytics, and common sense, to improve our response rates on the next campaign. We do this again and again to build brand awareness, and eventually sales. In LSB Workbook 2: BRANDING, we'll take you step-by-step in creating advertising and marketing campaigns that get the greatest response. Effective branding—getting people to remember your offerings and company in a positive light—is built on the marketing process, upon the foundation of *psychology*, which identifies realities of human behavior that motivate us to *act*.

We are *all* self-interested, and likely won't consider buying a product or service, or even a message, if we don't get something we want, or perceive that we need. Making a purchase, filling out a form for a newsletter, business report, or free 'gift,' is done with the *belief* that we will receive an offering of value for our action. If this belief is concretized, and the offering we receive does possess value, and has a real benefit that serves us, even if it's only entertainment, then it's likely that business just won themselves a customer.

Remember, the second place startups fail, is they launch without infrastructure to support brand or fulfillment. When you're starting up, out of the gate, *your offering must perform as your advertising and marketing campaigns promise*. Living up to your word builds trust. Do *not* make promises you can not fulfill. Make sure your offering is as ready to launch as your marketing efforts. Practicing the RAF Marketing Method will keep you on track, performing the proper tasks, in the *proper order*, to get the greatest return on your time, energy, and likely money that you've invested into marketing your new venture.

Understanding and monitoring human psychology will give you insight to more effectively manipulate your target audience, by providing them with what they desire, or *think* they need. To manipulate people to buy our product, service or into our message, or even remember our offerings or company brand, we first must understand the psychological difference between WANT and [perceived] NEED.

WANT vs. NEED

WANT is a desire, and desire is dynamic, changing all the time. At the base levels of our psyche, we all function on WANT—fulfilling a desire, even if that desire is simply a solution to a problem. You don't even need to eat, if you don't care about living. Absurd as this sounds, as of 2017, suicide is the 10th leading cause of death in the U.S. And clearly, many of us aren't paying attention to longevity with our substance abuses, our sedentary lifestyle, sitting and staring at a computer screen all day long, poor food choices and eating habits. Our *need to live* is trumped by *desire* quite a bit in the human psyche.

Marketing must seek to understand what people *really do*, and *why*, if we hope to manipulate them to do what *we want*.

We *all* hide behavior from others that we don't like in ourselves. Instead of demonstrating 'poor' behavior, some of us sneak fattening snacks when no one is watching. Many join a gym and never attend. Most of us harbor negative feelings we believe to be facts about other races, that, to appear *politically correct*, or socially acceptable, we don't vocalize. Guilt is a powerful manipulator, and used often in marketing to motivate an *action*.

To be effective at marketing, we must look beyond surface behavior—the facades we all wear—and drill down to what *really* is motivating someone to take any given action. Why does an obese person continue to overeat, especially with massive health problems? Why do many buy a book and never read it, or clothing and never wear it? Why do some exercise consistently, and others won't get off the couch, even though all of us know exercise is good for our health?

Humans take an action because we *desire* a certain outcome, even if that outcome is a feeling, as in feeling smarter because we bought a popular book. Stephen Hawking's, *A Brief History of Time*, tops out the list of the most unread books purchased, according to *Amazon* statistics, which refers to the reader who buys but doesn't read the book as the *Hawking's Effect*.

NEED is merely a projection of WANT, or desire. Since none of us actually NEED anything, marketing must seek to understand the psychology of WANT, i.e. **desire** to effectively market...*anything*.

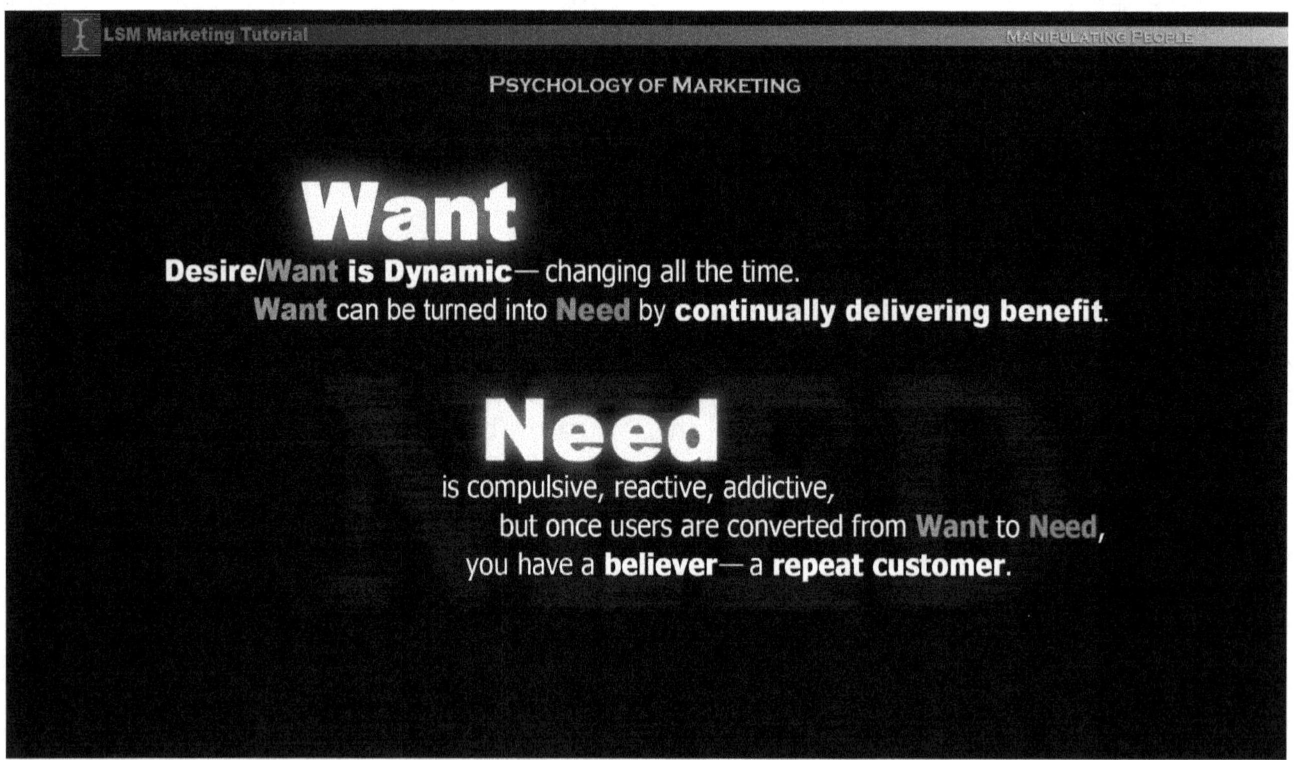

Getting my kids to work hard academically is likely my longest running marketing campaign. I can't sell them on '*hard work is its own reward*.' It isn't for them. So, I first must consider what they desire. I market to them with typical parental refrains, primers like, *you need a good education to get, or to* create, *a job you like, that makes good money, so you can live comfortably and provide for your kids*. Teens today, mine included, fear making it on their own with globalization and technology shrinking the job market. Fear is another great manipulator, used frequently in marketing to motivate an action.

Continually campaigning to our kids, or marketing our products, services and company, the process of creating marketing that converts—getting people to buy our offerings or believe our message—remains the same.

Effective marketing sells features and benefits of our offering, that fulfill WANT/desire of a specific group of people.

Desire is fickle, and we often believe we NEED what we merely WANT. Smart marketing understands this as a fact of human nature. And exploits it. People who want to continue living need to eat. But what we choose to eat can have an inverse effect on our continued existence. Think of "impulse" offerings—the trashy snacks and candy—packed on racks at the checkout line in the supermarket. After shopping for foods we've put in our baskets, we are hungering for something immediately. We NEED a treat, *now*. Consuming sugar and carbohydrates stimulates our brain's pleasure centers. Our bodies release the 'happiness' hormones consuming these types of foods supply, making us believe we NEED them. Marketing understands the human condition of hunger, and, combined with our desire for immediate gratification, tries to manipulate us to give in to our craving for a sweet or salty snack, which motivates us to take the action to buy crap we don't need.

Marketing any company into a global brand requires turning WANT/desire, into *perceived* NEED. **Turning WANT to perceived NEED is achieved by continually delivering benefits**, or the *perception* of benefits that your offering delivers. To build a loyal customer base, what Silicon Valley calls "brand advocates," marketing efforts must work to convince target users that they NEED our offering, or anything, even merchandising (like T-shirts with our logo emblazoned across it) related to our brand.

Steve Jobs, of *Apple Computer*, effectively turned WANT into NEED by continually delivering visual **user interfaces** (**UI**) that were easy to learn and easy to use. Some people now believe they NEED *Apple* products. *Apple* started up by marketing easy to operate personal computers (PC), like nothing before them. The real value their initially marketing promised, their first offerings, in fact, delivered. Having their line of PCs pay off their marketing built trust in *Apple* users, eventually branding them into a respected name in technology devices.

Brand advocates of *Apple* now have faith the company will continue to deliver great products, whether or not this continues to be true. *Apple* buyers are now *Apple believers*. *Apple* has effectively converted desire—WANT—into NEED.

Perceived NEED is compulsive, reactive, *addictive*. And once we convert someone from wanting something to thinking they *need* it, we've created a believer—a repeat customer. A **brand advocate**. Like any believers, these converts have faith our offerings will continue to fulfill their desires, whether or not this turns out to be true. As previously discussed, *Apple's* competitors now produces similar, and/or higher quality products for far less money, but *Apple* has lost few of their devotees by maintaining their unique brand image.

Startups, emerging companies, *new* ventures, fold when they fail to live up to their roll-out advertising—their *promise* of delivering quality offerings of value *before* becoming an established brand. Once your business or company has attracted a global audience, your brand recognizable across continents, it is easier to maintain market share, regardless of the quality, or even utility of your future offerings. However, no matter how big you are, continually delivering overpriced crap, whether product or bad service, will eventually destroy your business. (Think now defunct: *Pets.com; Beepi; Yahoo; Babe Clothing; GameStop, eToys*, etc.)

Remember, **we are all self-interested beings**. We must consistently get what we WANT, or believe we NEED, from your company to support your brand. For the greatest conversion with all of your marketing efforts, first consider what your current, and potential customers desire, or *perceived* that they need. We'll define how to do this next, with the Productization process, to avoid the *first* of the three primary reasons startups fail. To build trust in your offering and brand, and avoid the *second* most common reason that startups fail, be sure to deliver the benefits your roll-out marketing promises about your new offering/s, to build loyalty, i.e. faith, and win brand advocates.

-

-

-The CTA-

Motivate Response with a CTA

Never forget that **marketing is selling**. They are one and the same. With every campaign you generate, you must have an **objective** that will eventually lead to a sale. Before creating *any* marketing effort, even viral, in-person pitching, you must first consider what you hope that campaign will achieve.

If you are just starting up, it is likely your initial pre-launch campaigns will be for branding—letting your target markets know you are *'coming out,'* and what you'll have to offer them when you launch. Pre-launch campaign objectives often including getting viewers to click on "Visit Our Website," or "Download Free Trial," of your service or software. The objective of a pre-launch video campaign is to get people to click on the *Play* icon and watch your video. **NEVER create**

marketing without an objective in mind, even if it's just to build your brand awareness, followed by additional campaigns that will eventually lead to sales.

Getting response on most marketing efforts is particularly difficult because WANT/desire is fickle, and people often don't know what they want until it is presented to them. Branding and advertising campaigns are *tools* to make our target audience aware of our offerings or message, then, following the phases of the Conversion Funnel, ultimately getting them to do what as our marketing efforts direct—to try, buy, subscribe, believe in, or simply remember our company.

Effective marketing *directs people to do what we want*. We manipulate people to do what we want, by giving them something they consciously or unconsciously desire, or *think* they require. But after we have their attention, even their consideration that what we have to offer will serve them, how do we motivate them to take the actions our campaigns direct?

To get people to do what we want, we must tell them what we want them to do.

We must tell our target audiences what we want them to act on, what we want them to *do*—whether we want them to buy our product, or sign up for our newsletter, or learn more about our program, or receive our free gift, or download a trial of our software, or believe the message we are promoting.

We motivate people to take an action with a marketing tool called a **CTA**—a **Call-to-Action**. Each CTA directs the viewer to do what we tell them.

A CTA is mandatory in ALL marketing efforts.

From websites, to landing pages, to ads, to pitches, to print campaigns, you must have a CTA on every piece of marketing you produce, to get anyone to buy your product or service, or into your message. Even if the CTA is for branding, to get people to remember your company name and/or some feeling for what you do, a CTA is required on all marketing material, even viral messaging, as when a friend says, "You've gotta check this out."

Digital ad campaigns, to print brochures, to billboards you pass on the highway, *the* differentiator between fine art and marketing, is that **all marketing efforts have a CTA**. Remember, **marketing is selling**, and to motivate people to buy our offerings, or into our message, we must *sell* them with our marketing to take an *action*. Each campaign must direct the viewer to *do something*, take *some* action, even a passive action like remembering our brand.

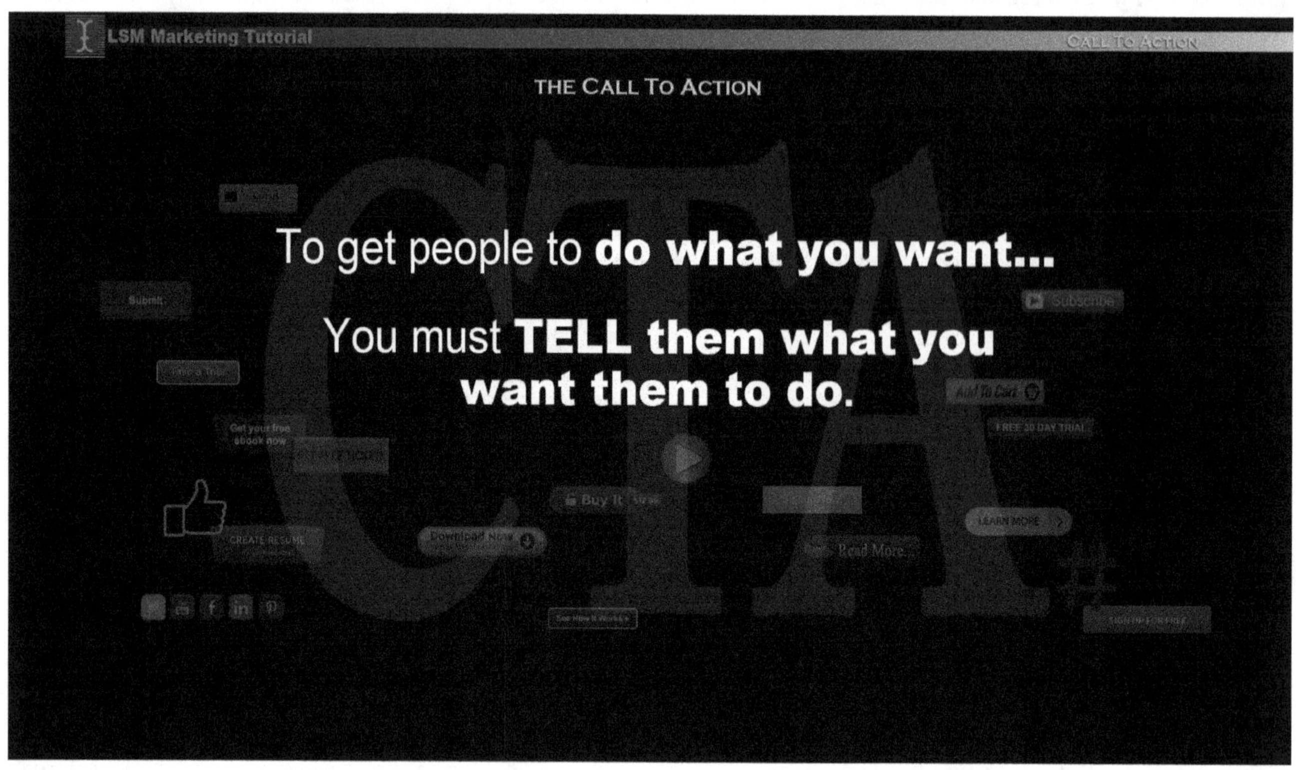

Regardless of how beautiful the marketing campaign you are creating is, you are *not* creating art. The *only* reason we create marketing is to *sell* a product, service or message. So, don't forget—a CTA is required on all marketing efforts because **to get people to do what we want, we must tell them what we want them to do**.

The Direct CTA

There are two (2) basic types of CTAs: **DIRECT** and **IMPLIED**.

A **Direct CTA** tells the viewer what to do directly, as in "Buy Now! Click here." We usually see direct CTAs on large or colorful graphic buttons, to command our attention and motivate us to click or call.

The purchase box on most *Amazon* checkout pages usually has many Direct CTAs. The first line in the purchase box is often an Implied CTA, *suggesting* you'll receive a savings of some sort, whether a discounted price, or free shipping. Most everything else on *Amazon's* purchase box is a Direct CTA. *Buy now. One click. Send. Deliver. Give. Add. Enter. Share.* These words are all *verbs*—action words—directing us to do something specific.

Websites often have Direct CTAs on their home page, with verbs commanding us to "Add to Cart; Download Trial" and/or "Read More." Navigation links, like those that appear on top of a website homepage are often Direct CTAs with verbs like "Explore; Discover; Contact Us."

Landing pages—a single web page that appears in response to clicking on its associated digital campaign—are often used for lead generation (finding new customers). They typically have Direct CTAs: "Register; Start Free; View Demo," but no matter what the CTA says that is clicked on, the link takes the viewer to a fill-in form to capture information, usually a name and email, of the potential new lead.

Share, Retweet, Like, Upvote/Downvote icons on many social media platforms are considered Direct CTAs, because they are directing the viewer to take the action each verb directs.

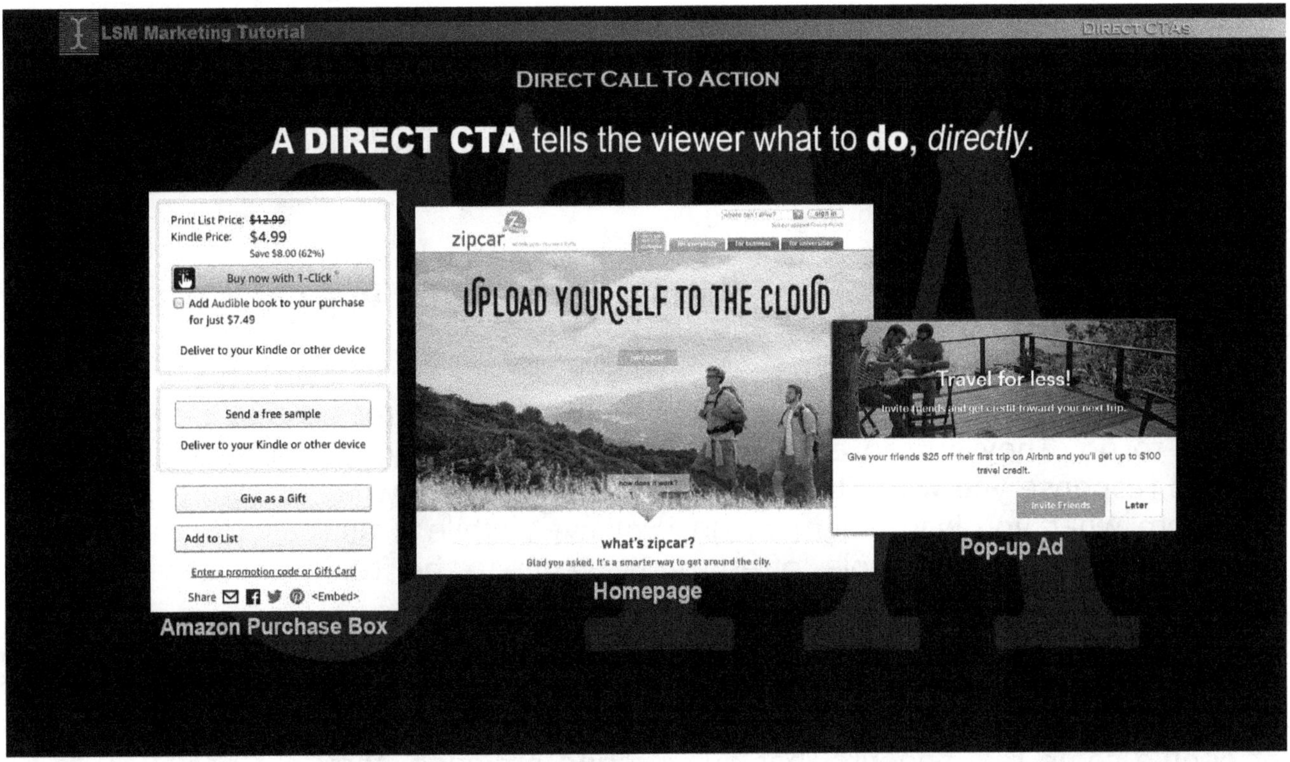

It is important to note, **use only ONE <u>primary</u> CTA per campaign**. Even with multiple CTAs as on *Amazon's* checkout box, the biggest, brightest button by far is "One-Click Purchase." All the other smaller Direct CTAs are trying to **upsell** the viewer—add more to their purchase—but buying the item we came for is *the* action *Amazon* wants us to take.

The reason to use only one primary or dominant CTA per campaign hearkens back to our 'goldfish' memories. Send two or more questions in an email, and you'll likely get a response to only the first, or the last question. Over 20 years of emailing multiple questions to family, friends and colleagues, and getting back a response to only one, I've learned if I have more than one question for the same person, to *send a separate email for each question* I want answered, making it ten times more likely *all* my questions will get a response.

The same works for CTAs. If your campaign is calling for an action on the part of the viewer, don't confuse them with too many requests. In other words, do NOT have multiple CTAs of the same visual command on any given ad, or even in an email campaign. Do not ask the viewer to 'download a trial' of your software, *and* to purchase it with separate buttons of the same size and brightness. One or the other, but *not* both. You are implicitly suggesting they buy your application if they like it, with your CTA asking them to *try* it.

Landing pages often have several Direct CTAs, even navigation links, as on a website. However, to create effective Landing pages that get response, use **only one primary CTA** to get the viewer to take the *most important action* you are trying to achieve. If the objective of your campaign is to get leads, and you want to get viewers to fill out a form, entice them with an incentive such as "Get Your Free Trial," or "Start Learning Today," which should appear as the largest, brightest button on the Landing page.

For the greatest response on all your marketing efforts, **use only ONE primary CTA per campaign!**

Direct CTAs make it crystal clear what our campaign messaging is asking the viewer to do. They are an excellent tool to employ in your marketing efforts to get the response you want, because to get people to do what you want, you must tell them what you want them to do. However, while a direct CTAs tells people exactly what to do, people often don't want to be told, or cease to hear advertisers yelling at them to ACT NOW.

Remember the Conversion Funnel? Conversion happens at different rates. Even if we've targeted our potential markets correctly, and can offer that particular group of people some real benefits that our offering provides, they are not likely to fill out our form, or download a trial of our software, without knowing anything about our offering or brand. While clicking for a discount on an ice cream may be more likely than clicking on a purchase button for a Ferrari, *neither* is likely if we don't know, or can not perceive the quality of the ice cream, or have never heard of the car company, Ferrari.

Since **a CTA is mandatory on all marketing efforts** (even in-person pitching, which we'll review in the Elevator Pitch module of this Workbook), we often need a more subtle approach than the Direct CTA.

Implied CTA

Implied CTAs are often the more effective marketing approach to get our target audience interested in what we have to offer. An Implied CTA is a *suggestion* to act, usually by touting the *best benefits*, or the **unique value proposition** (**UVP**) your offering provides.

Implied CTAs are generally used for branding. Simply remembering the name of a product, service, or company, is an *action*. The word "remember" is a verb. When we use Implied CTAs in our marketing efforts, we are asking our audience to remember our offering or company with positive associations, effectively building our brand.

It's often hard to tell that an ad campaign, Landing page, or website has any CTAs at all, as there are no buttons that give a direct command. In these cases, it's likely you are seeing an Implied CTA without even knowing it. If there *really* are no CTAs on the ad, no direct command or even *suggestion* to take an action by the viewer, it's likely the marketing effort will garner little to no response.

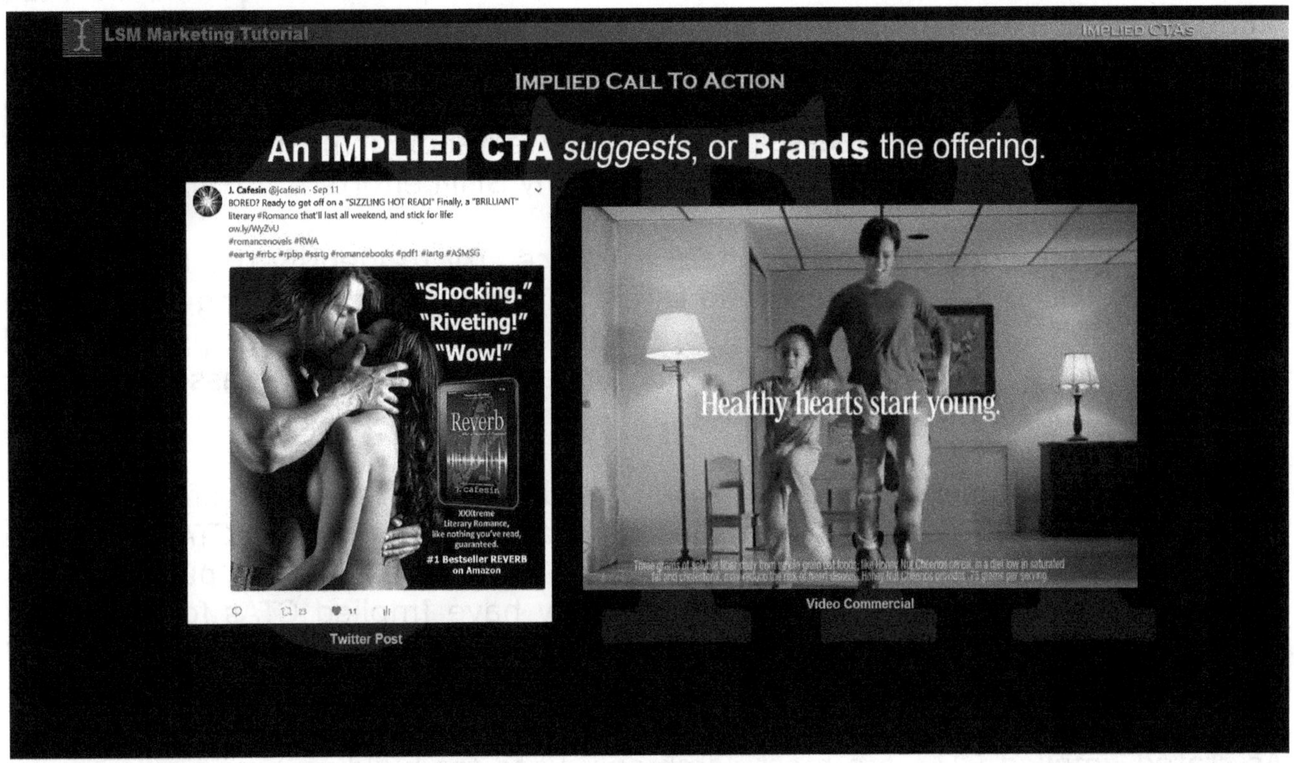

I utilize **social media marketing** (**SMM**), and post ad campaigns to my timelines and feeds on *Facebook, LinkedIn*, and *Twitter*, to market my books. Not many will buy my books if I simply post, "Buy Now," or, "Click to Purchase,"

regardless of how tightly I target my campaigns to specific types of readers.

People need convincing to buy books, not because they are expensive, but because reading is time consuming, and we all want to know that our time will be well spent. Instead of using a Direct CTA, I post Implied CTAs, such as good reviews, to show viewers that others think my novel is a great read. I use enticing images in my SMM campaigns that represent the story inside by books, to draw viewer's attention. I use these Implied CTAs to spark interest, and *suggest* to the viewer that reading my books will be a positive use of their time. And while I'll include a text link to the book's *Amazon* purchase page, nowhere on my post will it say, "Buy Now."

I use several **hashtags (#)** associated with what I'm promoting in the text area of my posts, as well as in most of my digital marketing efforts. Hashtags are Implied CTAs because they're not directing you to "Download Trial," or, "Buy Now." Hashtags simply categorize subject matter to help people find similar interests.

We use hashtags in our online marketing, so our campaigns will show up in search results when someone queries a specific topic. If I use the hashtag #Entrepreneurship in my SMM posts, I'm effectively addressing people interested in innovation and/or startups. If they search *LinkedIn*, *Facebook*, or *Twitter* with the word "Entrepreneurship" my post will likely appear somewhere in the timeline associated with "Entrepreneurship," effectively extending my reach beyond the market I'm targeting to garner more views of my SMM efforts.

Implied CTA are subtle, and often hard to notice. Try to identify the Implied CTA in an ad or online post, if you see no Direct CTA button commanding you to take a direct action. Implied CTAs are *suggestions* meant to tickle our psyche, build brand awareness, and often get us to unconsciously click on the associated text link in the campaign.

Beyond digital marketing, Implied CTAs are used in most forms of marketing. Print magazines often have advertising campaigns with Implied CTAs, because the viewer usually can not take a direct action while reading the publication in their doctor's waiting area. Billboards generally have Implied CTAs for the same reason—the viewer can not take immediate action. Same goes for TV commercials.

As stated, implied CTAs are most commonly used for building brand awareness. *Cheerios* #BeHeartHealthy campaign doesn't show anyone eating their product. No announcer says, "Buy now." The commercial shows quick cuts of various moms dancing with their tween kids in their kitchens. They are branding their cereal as nutritional, fun, even heartwarming, a *suggestion* for healthy living.

Cheerios is effectively building their brand as a lifestyle choice most of us strive for, making it more likely we'll buy it next time we're at the store.

Using Implied CTAs will help to build awareness of your offerings and company during pre-launch, launch and beyond, and effectively establish your brand. Maintaining a *positive* brand image is essential. Using hashtags, and the @ symbol to address a particular person or organization in your SMM campaigns can also extend your reach, i.e. get more views with each post. (We'll closely examine the *actual* ROI of most digital campaigns, including SMM, in LSL Workshop3—Launch.)

Direct or Implied CTAs are required on every piece of marketing you produce. Marketing efforts without CTAs are akin to fine art, only pretty graphics to please the graphic designer, *not* the targeted markets to which we are trying to sell. Don't forget, *every* piece of marketing you create, whether SMM, digital or print advertising, or even viral pitching, *must begin* with an **objective**. The CTA is the tool we use to get viewers to fulfill our campaign objective.

Whether an Implied or Direct CTA, remember to develop your campaign messaging around its **call-to-action**, its **CTA**. If your campaign objective is to get people to download a trial of your software, or buy your offering, than a Direct CTA is likely applicable. If the objective of any giving campaign is to get viewers to remember your brand, than an Implied CTA is the obvious choice. But without exception, when you are creating marketing material, a CTA is mandatory on every campaign you produce, because *to get people to do what you want, you must tell them what you want them to do*. The CTA tells, or *suggests* your target audience, take an action in respond to your marketing efforts.

MODULE 2: MARKETING 102 REVIEW

- **Effective marketing sells features and benefits fulfilling WANT, or perceived NEED.**

- **Tightly targeting** our marketing efforts to a specific audience likely to find value in our offering, will garner the greatest response.

- Converting WANT to NEED requires consistently delivering benefits to win and grow customer loyalty, and garner **brand advocates**.

- Get people to do what your campaigns direct, by giving them direction on what action to take with every marketing effort.

- Before creating *any* marketing effort, you must establish an **objective** for each and every campaign—to try; buy; sign-up; subscribe; or simply *remember* your brand.
- We direct people to respond to our marketing efforts with a specific action by including a **CTA**, a **call to action**, in every campaign.
- We can choose a **DIRECT** or **IMPLIED CTA**, but a **CTA** must be integrated into every marketing effort we produce.
- MBA or marketing novice, apply these **marketing fundamentals** to every campaign you produce for the greatest response on your marketing investments.

-
-

STOP! Do CHALLENGE #6 before moving on.

CHALLENGE #6: Create CTAs that Motivate Action

To understand how an effective **CTA** works, first, examine your own psychology, and what motivates *you* to take the action of even noticing an ad or other marketing effort.

1. **Create a list of 7 – 10 active BRAND blogs** that have a large number of quality posts. Some good ones to get you started (add a **.com** after each company name to access their URL):
    - *Target*: corporate.target/A-Bullseye-View
    - *Amazon Business* (business blog): amazonbusinessblog
    - *Whole Foods*: wholefoodsmarket/healthy-eating
    - *LinkedIn*: blog.linkedin
    - *Etsy Journal*: blog.etsy
    - *Hubspot Marketing:* blog.hubspot/marketing
    - *GatesNotes*: gatesnotes (Bill Gates blog)
    - *Nordstrom*: blogs.nordstrom/fashion

    There are tons to choose from. Simply google the BRAND you want, and add "blog," i.e. "TARGET blog."

2. **Peruse the first page of each site, and note articles, or advertising that grabs your attention.** Take a screen grab, or document the headline, content, CTA, and describe the imagery of at least seven posts or ads that stood out for you.

3. **Add a brief description of WHY the post or ad attracted your attention.** Did you click on the link to read the full article, or the CTA button on an advertisement? Did you sign-up for a newsletter, or to get a discount coupon, or free gift? What was the **IMPLIED** or **DIRECT CTA** that motivated you to take an action, if you did? If the post or ad got your attention, but you did NOT click, why?

   Understanding what CTAs motivate you to act, will help you get intimate with at least one type of target user—*you*.

4. **Now, project an ideal target user for your offering**—the product or service you're hoping to sell. List at least three IMPLIED, and three DIRECT CTAs that you think would motivate your ideal target user to purchase, sign-up, or click on a link in your ad. The CTA can be in the form of a headline, picture, content, button...etc.

Projecting a target user's journey to conversion—doing what your CTA directs—will help you get intimate with your projected customers, making it more likely you'll convert them with your advertising and marketing efforts.

◆◆◆

Engage in Marketing Your Startup

Right about now you may be thinking, "Hey, the LSE series promised to teach me how to market MY IDEA into a business, but all it's talked about so far is Marketing!"

Before you can sell *anything*, you must first understand how to market it. Even viral, in-person pitching must be based on marketing best practices, to get anyone excited about what you are selling. Software developers often pitch technology, which few understand, and most don't care about. Potential users are only interested in how they will *benefit* from using the application.

Stripping away theory, and political correctness, this Marketing module was designed to help you to *think differently* about the marketing process—how to apply **psychology**, and an **objective** to every marketing effort, to create effective campaigns, online, in print, or on Mars.

Now that we are all on the same page as to purpose and function of marketing, from here forward, and throughout the rest of the LSE series, we'll put real-world marketing methods and best practices in motion. Many steps will be introduced in the LSE series to direct you in producing and marketing a product or service or message, and even a company from the ground up.

Follow the integrated series of steps of RAF Marketing Method step-by-step as they are sequentially introduced in each module, to produce a guide for actualizing and marketing most any idea into an offering of value, for profit. If you are wise, like our inventor friend, Ben Franklin, you'll **Get Ready**, and begin by getting organized!

◆◆◆◆◆

MODULE 3: STARTUP HIERARCHY

To Create an Organization, You Must Organize

"Every minute spent organizing, an hour is earned," Benjamin Franklin said.

How many hours have you wasted looking for stuff? How many times have you purchased the same item, only to find the one you originally purchased weeks, or years later? How often do you perform the same job task required to complete a project because you could not find the necessary documentation, images, videos...etc., you are sure you have...*somewhere*?

To start a startup, or even market one effectively, requires literally hundreds of components, you will use again and again in producing marketing for your new venture. You'll begin by creating dynamic Productization lists, that will give you the words that describe your offering—the benefits and solutions your product, service, or message delivers. You'll continually identify target audiences that will find the greatest value in what you are developing, or have already produced. You'll keep a running tally of your competitors. You'll design corporate identities, social media marketing campaigns, print advertising...etc., and you'll need the same logos, taglines, images, videos, even words to chat up what you have to your target markets and users.

Time is money, as the business colloquialism goes. And it's true! But beyond wasting time looking for stuff you know you have done already, it is imperative to use the same elements—**brand standards**—to build brand awareness of your offering and company with every marketing effort.

Whether creating your own campaigns, or hiring marketing professionals, it is essential every stakeholder involved in marketing your startup has access to the components and elements required to create tightly targeted campaigns. And how can you access or supply these if you can't find them?

It is imperative to set up an initial **STARTUP HIERARCHY**—folders that will house the sets of documents, links, images, audio and video clips you'll find, collect, and generate for your new venture. This will keep everything in one location, and accessible to all pertinent stakeholders, to prevent wasting time searching for docs, images and files that are randomly placed on your (or your graphic designer's) computer.

Begin to actualize your idea, or market your existing offering, with an organized startup hierarchy. If you already have an existing startup, and have yet to set up your company's hierarchy, well, better late than never! Do it at this juncture. Like, *now!*

Much like a sitemap, you must set up an effective structure to stay organized as you productize your offering and scale your marketing efforts, with *'a place for everything, to put everything in its place.'*

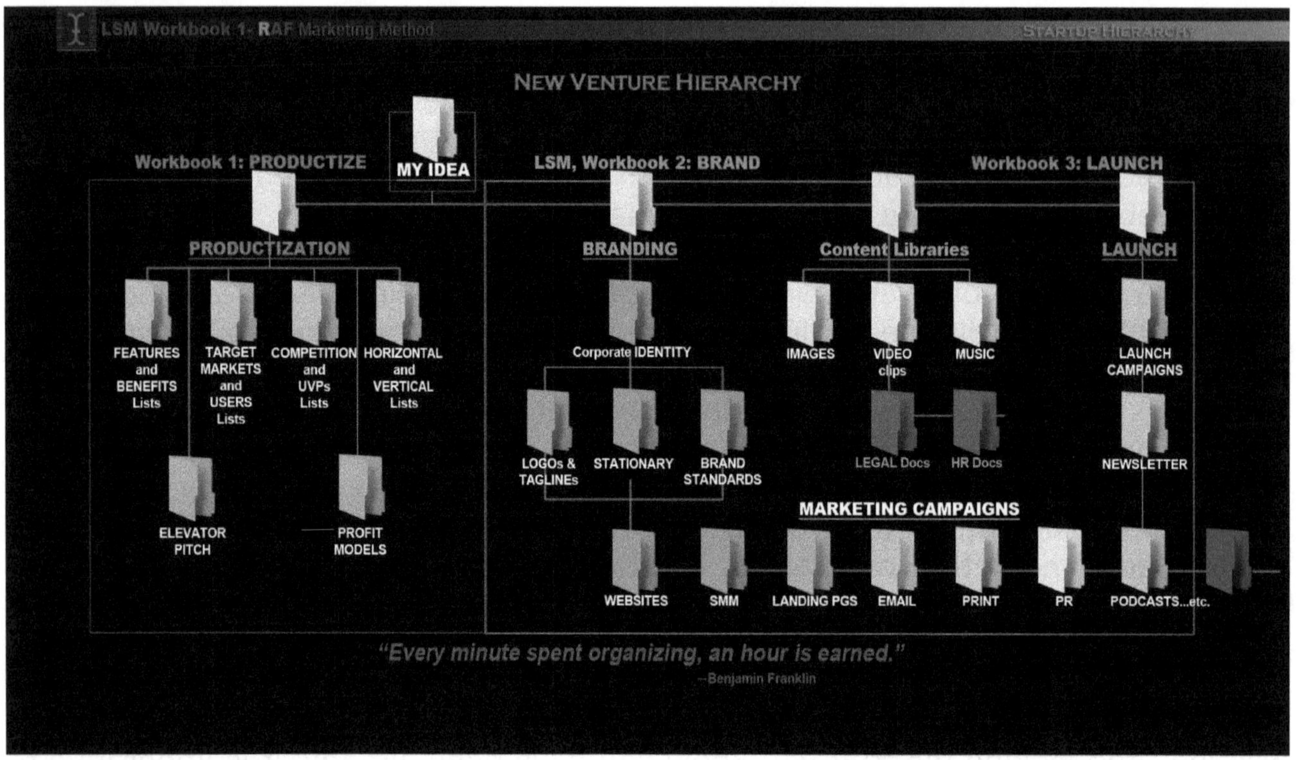

Step 1: First, create a new folder titled, MY IDEA, or give your idea a working title. If you have an existing company, use your company name as the title of this first folder.

You will put your original product description (which we'll review next) into a .doc file, then put it in this folder. You'll also keep this brief description on a post-it note, stuck on your monitor, while you are working on your offering and startup.

Step 2: Create another folder inside your IDEA folder, titled, **Productization**. Open this folder, and create four more folders:

- **Features & Benefits**
- **Target Markets & Target Users**
- **Competition & Differentiators**
- **Horizontal & Vertical Markets**

Create your actual lists in a Word program, or whatever text program you like to use. Do *not* create these lists on *Google Docs*. Productization lists should reside on your hard drive. Not *Google's* cloud.

We'll begin the Productization process next, but you must have a place to put the documents you will create. Building this hierarchy gives you a place to store and access them. These lists will not only help you define your idea for yourself, and others, but they'll be used throughout the life cycle of your business, as direction and content for your marketing and advertising down the line. You will fill these lists with bullet points of words—**keywords** and key phrases—specific to your offering. You, or those your hire, will use the content you create down the line for your websites, landing pages, in your email campaigns, in most all of your marketing efforts.

LSM Workbook 1 examines the Productization process. It is imperative that you begin with productizing your offering *first*, to get intimate with what you are planning to sell, or are currently selling. Productization lists should be dynamic, added to all the time, every time an additional feature is implemented, or a new benefit or solution uncovered. And the Productization process begins anew with every new offering developed.

Step 3: Go back to your main Productization folder, and in it, create another folder titled **Elevator Pitch**. You will fill this folder during the Productization process as well, with multiple drafts of a 5 - 15 second concise and exciting speech about your offering. Your elevator pitch should be dynamic, changing all the time as your offering develops, and always touting the *best thing* about your product or service, even if it's just entertainment. Your pitch should also change to address the person to whom you are talking. Pitching to VC (venture capital) to invest in your new venture, is very different than exciting someone you meet at a local pub about your offering.

Step 4: Finally, create another folder under Productization, titled **Profit Models**. You will fill this folder with documents of various profit models, from traditional direct selling through value added resellers (VAR), to potential licensing agreements of your software offerings. You'll create a profit model for your offering at launch, as well as a year, and five down the line during the last phase of the Productization process.

Establishing a profit model for launch, and beyond, will keep all stakeholders in your new venture on the path to actualizing an offering of value, for money. (Yes, even non-profits want money. Business *exists* to make money. If we were all rich, or it didn't cost money to live, we'd likely be doing something different with most of our waking hours than working so hard to make money.)

Startup Hierarchy Beyond Productization

LSB Workbook 2 takes you step-by-step through the entire **Branding** process, from identity design through the development of strategic marketing campaigns. Once you begin the branding process, you will add additional folders to your startup hierarchy. All branding tools and components, as well as each marketing campaign, will get their own folder. You will fill them with copy documents, images, videos, and even audio files to utilize when marketing your business. You will create content libraries, that centrally house your visual and audio content, so you, and all stakeholders helping you produce campaigns, will have easy access with *a place for everything*—the proper files in the proper folders, correctly marked with clear, descriptive titles.

Every file you create should be put in their appropriate folder, so you *never* have to waste time trying to find specific documents or images, and you have a location to point others to when working with teams, or outside vendors.

Make sure to use naming conventions that you, and others will understand—that will help every stakeholder in your new venture identify every image, file and folder you create, quickly and easily. Save yourself and your hires an enormous amount of time and energy by simply naming your folders, files, images, videos, and docs with titles that accurately describe their content.

Setting up an organized project hierarchy for your new venture will serve both you and those you hire to create a startup, from the ground up, that runs as efficiently as possible. Save time, with *everything in its place*, and you'll be saving money as well! Throughout the LSE series, and the life-cycle of your business, you'll add folders to your startup hierarchy, and fill them with files of business contacts, email addresses, marketing strategies and logistics, for launch and beyond.

The startup hierarchy presented here is just one example you can use when setting up your company's hierarchy. Each of us has our own particular style of organization, so don't limit yourself to following the paradigm presented here. However, a word of caution when developing your own, unique hierarchy. My daughter's organizational paradigm is to throw everything on her bedroom floor to "see it all." This type of organization serves no one, not even her. She is constantly looking for stuff, freaking out when she can't find it, and wasting not only her time, but mine as well, when I help her search for what she needs all too often.

When you are developing a business, you need to consider all those you will be working with, to realize your new venture. While you can productize your idea, or even developed an offering on your own, you will never be able to launch a sustainable company alone. To grow any business into a brand, you need qualified people to help you along the way.

The folders required for your startup hierarchy in this initial **Getting Ready** phase of the RAF Marketing Method, are four (4) **Productization** folders, a folder for your **Elevator Pitch**, and another for your **Profit Models** to house the documents you will create in LSM Workbook 1.

MODULE 3: PROJECT HIERARCHY REVIEW

- Building a business from an idea into a company requires a foundation of **organization**. Begin your new venture with an organized **STARTUP HIERARCHY** of files and folders, all within the main folder for your offering. Doing so will save you a lot time, and therefore, money.
- An organized **STARTUP HIERARCHY** gives all stakeholders access to text documents and **content libraries**, insuring clear communication to everyone working on your new venture.
- Do NOT write or store your startup documents or images on *Google's* cloud. *Google* (and hackers) can access your information. Don't let them!
- Store your main **STARTUP FOLDER**, with all related sub-folders and files, on *your* networked servers (like on your personal PC), and *backup all folders and files* often! As you scale, and need more connectivity to communicate, rent virtually space on *Amazon Web Services* (AWS), or other secure cloud service provider.
- Assign **administrators** to select folders and files to preserve company security while assuring all stakeholder have access to the documents and imagery they need to do their job.

Productization Initiates Profits

Productization is the process of marketing an idea into an offering of value—something that serves a purpose, or has a function that will benefit a specific group of people. Even if you have a complete product, service or message, it is imperative that you are *intimate* with what you are selling—you understand, *and* can articulate the best, most unique characteristics and qualities of your offering.

The Productization process in not rocket science, but there are many components that need to be implemented, *in order*, to effectively productize a product, service or message into an offering of value, for profit. We'll examine each of these with an overview of the process of Productization first, to give you a framework in which to productize your offering, or *any* potential offering into a marketable business.

Once you have a thorough understanding of Productization basics, LSM Workbook 1 will take you step-by-step through the process of productizing your offering.

Productization 101 is next. Productizing software, your potential product, service or message, or *any* idea or fully developed offering, follows.

◆◆◆◆◆

MODULE 4: PRODUCTIZATION PROCESS

Your Great Idea

So, you think you have a great idea for an app, product or service to sell directly (microbusiness) through *Amazon* or *Etsy* or *Google Play*. Or maybe you're already creating your first offering of many to come, with the hope of starting a sustainable startup. Fantastic! Time to **Get Ready** and begin the marketing process.

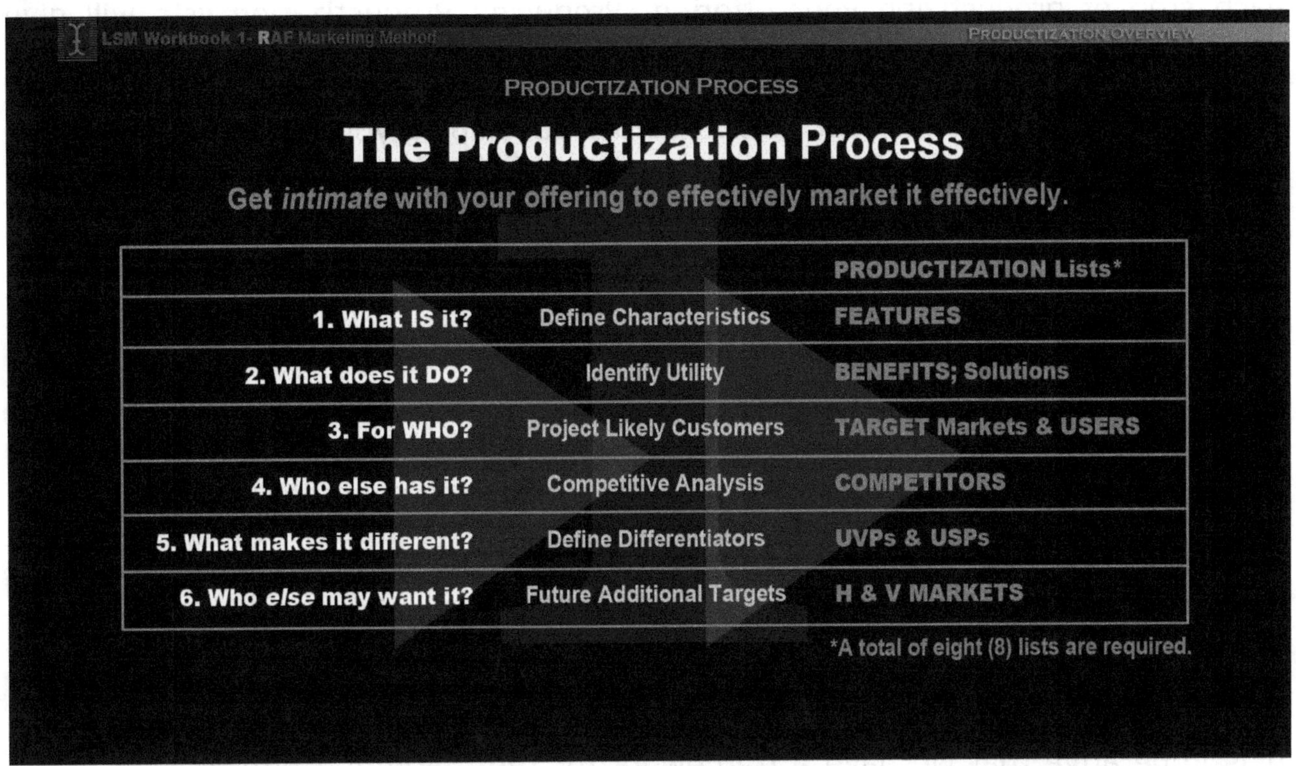

As previously stated, it is highly recommended that you have an idea, or offering in development to market, to realize the full potential of the LSE series. Remember, the idea is less important than *working the process*, so don't dwell on creating a brilliant offering, or even one that you will produce right now. The LSE series is about marketing a product idea into a sustainable business, and you need a potential offering to do this. You do *not* need to produce the idea, yet. In fact, at this first stage in the Lean Startup Marketing process, it is recommended that you don't invest the time, energy, and often money into producing an idea that may have little to no benefit for anyone, besides you. The Productization process helps us identify *if* and *where* our original product idea has product/market fit or fits, in the marketplace of sellable offerings among similar or competing products.

If you still have no clue what you'd like to create, go back to **CHALLENGE #1:**

Generating Startup Ideas, and **CHALLENGE #2: Generating Product Ideas**. Follow the step-by-step process, to come up with an idea to actualize during this series. Learn by engaging in the Lean Startup Marketing process, and you'll be able to actualize most *any* idea [you have now, or that may come], by simply following the steps of the RAF Marketing Method *in order,* (kind of like a math equation... ;).

If your offering is already produced, and you're not getting the traction or sales you'd like with your marketing, it's likely time to go back and **Get Ready**—work each step of productizing your offering. Producing Productization lists will give you the content—keywords and key phrases—to create branding and advertising campaigns that promote the best, most unique things about your offering. While it is optimal to perform Productization before developing your offering, it is better to do it now than never. Performing the steps of the Productization process, will enable you to tightly target your campaigns on specific groups of people likely to find benefit in what you've created, for the greatest response and conversion rates on all your marketing efforts.

Describe Your Potential Offering

When writing a strategic marketing plan, we begin by defining the objective of the plan. Generally, the goal of the plan is to make the company more money by generating sales of the offering. However, it often isn't possible to sell a product or service, or even a message, directly, especially with expensive items or complex software. Instead, we create branding campaigns, which helps build brand awareness of the offering and company, to motivate the audience we targeted with these branding efforts down the line on purchasing our stuff.

It is imperative that we have a framework for the marketing efforts we hope to create, to meet the objective of our marketing plan. Like getting organized, without a specific, clear description, we don't have a path to follow that will lead us to our stated objective.

Don't get too hung up on making this description perfect. Engaging in the Productization process ,will help you align your offering to effectively brand it and market it to specific people, who'll likely find value in it down the line. This brief description is meant to keep you on track, to producing the offering you have in mind. It is important to note, once you've initiated productizing your offering, you will very likely have to change your original idea, or even developed product, to fulfill the desires of your target audience. But don't despair. Most every startup changes their original idea or complete offering before launch, or even after launch when their product doesn't sell much.

Performing the complete Productization process, will give you an intimate view of what you plan to sell, as well as help you define 'product/market fit,' and a target audience to sell it to. This initial description of your potential offering is a loose outline of what you *think* you have, whether an idea you'd like to actualize, or a fully developed product you want to market for profit.

It's time to describe your offering! Make sure to put these documents in your MY IDEA folder, the top folder in your STARTUP HIERARCHY.

Step 1: Write a <u>brief</u> description of the idea, or developed offering, you plan to market throughout the LSE series. This description should focus on the *best bits* about your potential offering—what problem it solves, or desire it may fulfill if produced and sold. This first draft description, write as much as you'd like, to accurately describe the product, service or message you'd like to sell.

This brief description of your potential offering is NOT an Elevator Pitch. We'll get to that later in this workbook, as an effective Elevator Pitch can only be executed once you are intimate with the offering you hope to sell.

Step 2: **Read your description out loud to yourself** multiple times. Underline or highlight the words and phrases that best describe the offering you plan to market. Cross out (but do not delete) words, phrases, even sentences that are confusing or too generic to be clearly and easily understood.

Step 3: On a separate document, **edit the description** of your projected offering, or completed product, to less than 50 words.

Step 4: **Edit your description to fit on a small post-it note**, with the sticky back. A post-it note will ensure your description is short because the post-it is small. Additionally, once you get a short, clear, *specific* description of your idea down on the post-it, stick it on the frame of your computer screen. A post-it describing the offering you are hoping to actualize and market within eye-shot, will continually remind you to keep your efforts focused on doing so.

Remember, once the process of Productization is implemented, you may discover you must iterate your original idea to make it marketable. With every iteration of your potential (or existing) offering, rewrite your brief product description on a new post-it note. Take down the old post-it, and stick the most current on your computer monitor's frame while working the steps of the RAF Marketing Method.

-

-

-PRODUCTIZATION 101-

Step 1 of the 3-Step RAF Marketing Method

We begin the RAF Marketing Method of turning an idea into a *marketable* offering for profit (even non-profits), by taking the first step:

Step 1—Get Ready, and productize a potential product, service, or nonprofit message (or even developed product) into an offering of *value*.

Productization is the process of getting to know your offering, and identifying where it fits in the marketplace of sellable items. It's likely you *think* you already know what you plan to create or sell. It's even more likely if your offering is already developed, maybe even selling, you are *sure* you know all there is to know about your product and business. *Prove it!*

As CEO of your idea, or developed product, your #1 job is to sell it. You must be able to market—pitch, write about, advertise—your projected offering clearly, concisely, knowledgeably. Performing the Productization process will help you get to know what you are planning to sell, or currently selling, *intimately*, which will allow you to create branding and advertising campaigns that get greater response, and ultimately sales of your valued offering.

In the startup marketing process, it is important to perform Productization *before branding*, or creating any campaigns to market your offering. You must take this *first step* to get your offering ready to brand and market for several reasons. First, you must have a thorough understanding of what you plan to sell—the characteristics, or **features** of our potential or complete offering. You must understand how these features translate into **benefits**, and identify **who** will likely benefit, or find value in the features of our upcoming product or service.

During the Productization process, you'll learn to implement bullet lists of features, benefits and solutions, as well as how to identify and list potential target markets and users for your offering. Initializing and performing the Productization steps will give you the ability to talk about your projected offering with knowledge. Initializing Productization will also provide you copy content of keywords and key phrases for your advertising and marketing campaigns in the branding process down the line.

This module provides an overview of the Productization process. You will engage in productizing *your* offering next. **Module 5: Productizing Software**, will give you the steps of the Productization process, next. Whether you are producing software, or cupcakes, consulting services, or nonprofit message, the steps of Productization are the same, for any offering you have now, or will have in the future. Remember, Productization is like a math equation. Plug in the idea or developed offering, follow the steps, *in order*, and you will produce a marketable offering of value, for profit.

Productize Your Offering for Startup Success

As previously mentioned, the Productization process is not rocket science, but it is the first place most startups fail. It's much more entertaining to design and build our product idea, as your projected or completed offering is likely related to something you enjoy doing, or are currently engage in, such as software development, or cooking for your family. Productizing an idea into an offering of value means a lot of research. *Blah!* And most every entrepreneur finds out stuff we really don't want to know anyway, like our great idea for the *next big thing* has already been done by someone else. And if we invest all the required time in performing the Productization process correctly, we won't have time to produce our fantastic idea, *and* keep our day jobs.

These are some of the excuses I've heard repeated by many of the CEOs and the marketing pros I've worked with over the years. At best, neglecting to implement the Productization process, this *first step*, you'll likely waste a lot of time, energy and money with misdirected product development, as well as marketing efforts that generate little response, and slow, to few sales. At worst, ignoring Productization leads to startup failure. The Productization process is time consuming and detail oriented, but *necessary* to implement, *in order*, for startup success at launch, and throughout the life-cycle of your business.

To begin, let's examine the first few steps in the process of Productization. To productize an idea, or a developed offering, into a product or service (even a nonprofit's message) that will likely make money, requires clear, concise, *specific* answers to the first three questions in the Productization process:

1. **What IS it?**
2. **What does it DO?**
3. **WHO does it serve?**

Answer these three questions in *specific* detail with any product, service, or message you envision selling. This is the *first step*, the beginning of the math-like equation of marketing any business idea.

Giving Birth to Your Offering

To actualize a thought or concept, product in development, or market an existing offering, we must *first* describe its characteristics—what marketing calls its **features**. If it's a physical product, how big is it? What color? Weight? Dimensions? What ingredients, or materials is it made of? If it's software, what are the key **functions** the software performs?

Once we've defined some key **features** or **functions** of our idea, we identify the **benefits**, or a solution our projected offering will likely provide for a specific group (or groups) of people. These groups are considered our *broad* **target markets**. Next, we drill down on who these people *are*. We get to know them as individuals, find out what these **target users** like and don't like, where to find them, and how to reach them.

We develop the first draft of an **Elevator Pitch**, *after* we've initialized the Productization process, so we can concisely chat up the benefits our offering provides the projected target audience. We draft a 2nd pitch, a 3rd, 4th, 5th and so on, always refining our messaging to entice, engage, and motivate our audience to take the *action* our CTAs directs. (Yes, even an Elevator Pitch has a call-to-action. ALL effective marketing efforts have a CTA.)

After we productize what we *think* we have, we search for our **competition**—anyone, anywhere, producing a similar offering to ours. There will *always* be *someone*, *somewhere*, marketing a potential offering, or already producing and currently selling (or attempting to sell) a product or service (even vaguely) similar to what each of us may conceive. We study what our competitors have. This will either force us to iterate our original offering, and/or help us define what makes our offering different, *better*, than theirs. And we note, our competition's target markets and users, to perhaps adopt as ours down the line.

We stay ahead of our competitors by employing **horizontal and vertical**

marketing models to help guide us to new target markets and users. We also use horizontal and vertical modeling for new product development, to come up with future offerings, that will keep our startup in front of our competition in the race for market share, i.e. new customers.

The notion that all we need to build and grow a company is to increase our *reach* —the people who 'view' our marketing efforts—is a fallacy. It is imperative we assign a **profit model** at the launch of our offering, to make money with our startup, or get money to support it, as with nonprofit organizations. As our business grows, increasing in both users and offerings, it is equally important that we introduce profit models that will keep the customers we have, draw in additionally customers, but also increase our profit margins.

Productization is a powerful tool used to turn your offering into a marketable product, service or message of value, for profit. But only if it is implemented IN ORDER. In this module, we examine the foundation of Productization, and each of its components, using an existing product we all know. In the modules that follow, we'll engage in the Productization process step-by-step, by actualizing each step, *in order*, to productize a **SaaS** (**software-as-a-service**) application I conceived ages back, but have never actualized.

Through the process of productizing my SaaS idea, you'll learn how to create Productization lists and charts for *your* product, service, or message, that you'll use as guidance and direction in developing, branding and marketing your offering, as well as copy content for the advertising and marketing campaigns you'll learn to produce in LSB Workbook 2: Branding.

Productization Step-by-Step

As stated, to market an idea (or produced offering) into an offering of *value*, that someone besides you actually wants, begin by answering, in *specific detail*, the following three questions:

What IS it? What does it DO? And For WHO?

While this may seem rather broad, with any marketing endeavor we start wide, and drill down to the most likely *people* (not markets) who will benefit from the specific features or functions of our offering.

Let's pretend you are a **product manager** (**PM**) for an art supply manufacturer. Your development team is considering producing, or is in the process of developing, some very cool new colored pencils. A team member came up with the idea for these colored pencils because the pencils she was using from another manufacturer didn't draw radiantly, and dulled her presentations.

As a *smart* PM, you take this new colored pencil product idea, and get it ready for marketing. You begin with a brief description of your team member's idea: *New, radiant, colored pencils*, and put these words on a post-it note on the frame of your computer monitor.

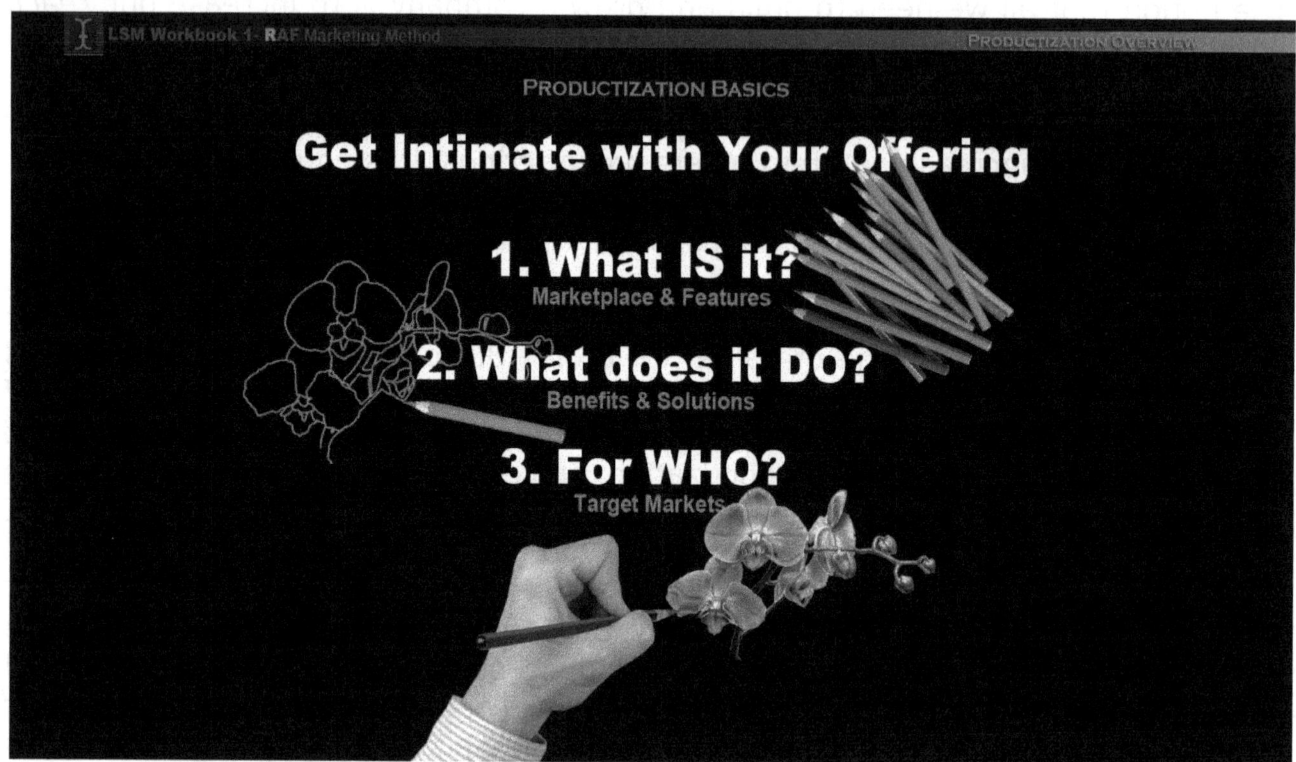

Next, you being the Productization process, which starts by asking, and then answering, the first three Productization questions about these new colored pencils:

1. **What IS it?** Colored pencils. 240 colors. High wax content. Opaque application.

2. **What does it DO?** They draw, in radiant colors, the high wax content making the colors opaque.

3. **For Who?** I assume (project) for kids, to professional-level artists.

Easy, right? While the above example is extremely simplified for clarity, you must implement the Productization process with *every offering you envision*, whether trying to realize an idea, or market a product or service you've already developed. Asking yourself: **What IS it? What does it DO?** and **For Who?** will give you a framework to actualize what you conceive. This will help you focus your development efforts on designing and implementing features and functions of your offering, that are likely to benefit specific people.

Fit Your Offering into a Marketplace

To simplify the Productization process, let's take something that we all know—a chainsaw. Why a chainsaw? Why not! We'll use this chainsaw to model the steps in productizing *any* idea, or developed offering, as a chainsaw is already developed by many manufacturers. We'll move on to productizing software, next.

As previously stated, it really doesn't matter if you are productizing a new version of a known product, or inventing a new product, or service, or even message. Performing Productization will help you identify what you have, what purpose it serves, and for who, to begin marketing it effectively.

I'll rewrite the definition of a chainsaw as our product description for my post-it note. This is the same type of description you should write on a post-it note about *your* projected offering.

Description of my *new* chainsaw: *Ultra high-powered, light-weight chainsaw with diamond-tipped teeth on the chain that moves around a titanium blade*.

This description stemmed from *Google's* description of a 'chainsaw.' I simply added features that I want to put into the new, improved chainsaw I'm considering developing. I'll put this short description on a post-it note, and stick it on my computer monitor's frame, so that every time I work on my new chainsaw idea, this brief description will keep me on the path to creating it.

Now, let's answer the three key Productization questions about my new chainsaw in *specific* detail.

We begin the process of Productization by *categorizing our idea* in the broadest of senses. Remember, marketing starts wide and drills down. **What IS it** begins broad, and first identifies the overall scope of our offering—where it fits in the marketplace of sellable items.

IS it a PRODUCT—meaning a physical object, like a new fashion line, or draft beer? Or a program that performs a function, like *Photoshop* or *MSWord*, or a virtual experience, like an ebook or online class? Though online products have no physical features, they still must be produced, unlike repackaging content as a service, like *Facebook*, or *Instagram*. A novel must be *written* to produce an ebook. The novel is the *product*. *Amazon* selling it for your tablet is the 'delivery' *service*.

IS your offering a SERVICE? A human service like a mechanic, or a real estate broker, or a teacher. Perhaps your idea is **software as a service** (**SaaS**)—a **peer-to-peer** (**P2P**) SaaS application, like *Uber* or *AirBnB*, or maybe a social media platform like *Twitter* or *SnapChat*?

IS your idea a MESSAGE, such as a political position like global warming? Or a religion, or religious-based mission? In this first part of Productization, you are simply *categorizing your idea*, NOT marketing branded messaging, like in an ad campaign. We'll get to building brand awareness with messaging in LSB Workbook 2, once Productization is underway. To categorize your idea as a message, it must fall under things like politics, a social cause, or religion—[generally] nonprofit organizations.

Using this marketplace model, I've identified my new chainsaw as a PRODUCT.

This first step in the Productization process is <u>defining the category of the marketplace in which your idea fits</u>. Is it a product, a service, or a message?

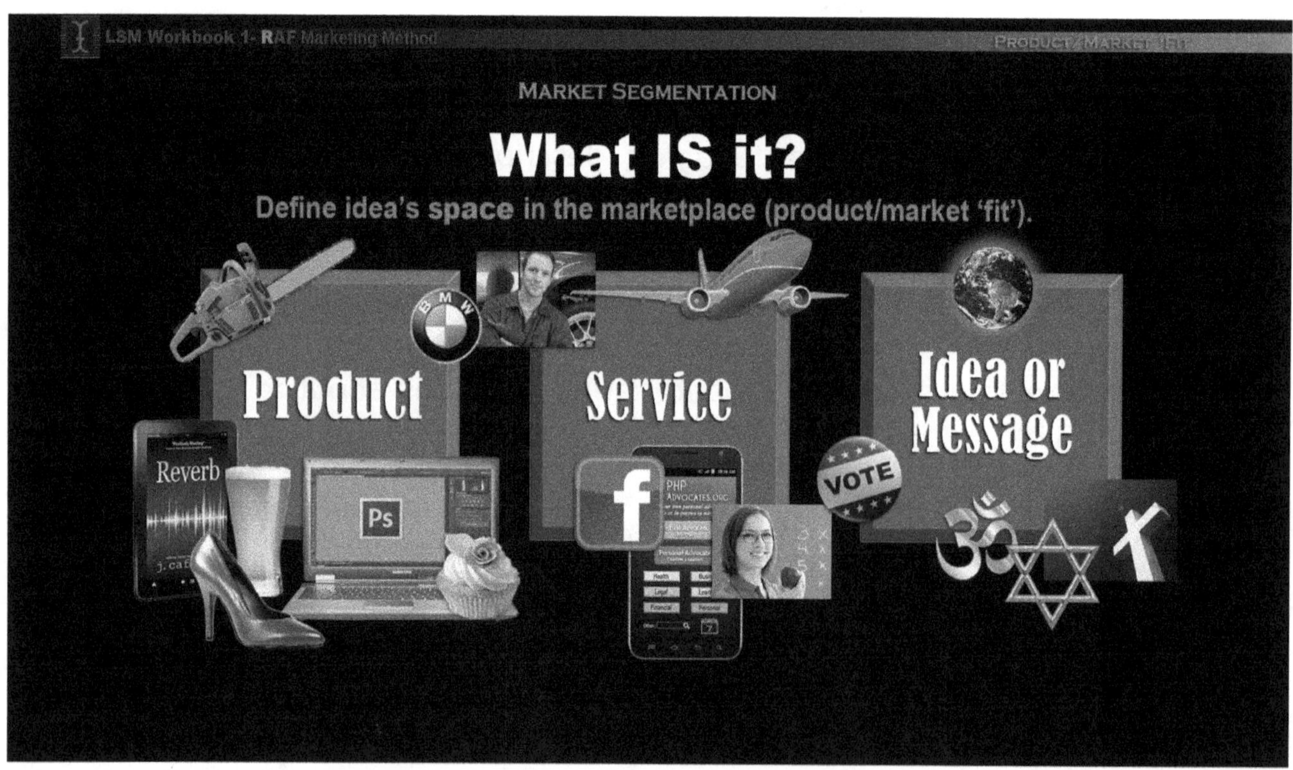

To keep you on track to producing the offering you envision, add the word, PRODUCT, SERVICE, or MESSAGE to the bottom of the post-it note with your description, to remind yourself of exactly what your offering is, and where it fits in the marketplace of sellable items. Marketing a message is very different from marketing a product. So, be sure to categorize, then label your offering correctly.

Step 1: Describe the FEATURES of Your Offering

What IS it? Once you've established a foundation for where your idea fits in the marketplace, you still must define what your idea, or developed product IS—literally. What are the *specific* FEATURES or FUNCTIONS (in software) that define or describe your projected offering?

Beyond your brief post-it note descriptor, you must identify what, *exactly*, you are hoping to create, are in the process of creating, or would like to sell more of?

The next step in the Productization process is to describe the features/ functions of your potential offering. In other words, asking yourself "What Is it?" is the process of defining the *specific characteristics* of your idea.

To illustrate this next step, let's continue to productize my new chainsaw idea. We've already broadly categorized it as a PRODUCT. Next, we simply describe its features. Right now, we're not too concerned with the benefits of this chainsaw. We'll get to those next. For now, let's just examine its features.

FEATURES of my potential new chainsaw:

- 10,000 rpm engine
- 1/4" thick plastic body
- Diamond-toothed chain
- 8 hours of fuel capacity
- Titanium blade
- Shuts off automatically
- Chain can rotate forward and backwards

These are some of the *specific* features of my new chainsaw, describing what I envision this product will be.

SPECIFIC means: directly describing the *particular* characteristics—the features or actual functions of your offering, as in the chainsaw example above. I did *not* populate the **FEATURE list** with phrases like: "*Powerful* engine. *Solid* grip. *Strong* blade. *Huge* fuel capacity. *Tough* frame." These phrases are all *fluff* terms. The italicized words are basically meaningless adjectives that give no useful information. **Do NOT use fluff terms** or words in your Productization lists. BE SPECIFIC when populating all your lists.

Detail features specific to your offering. *Powerful*, which, undoubtedly, the chainsaw is, becomes: *10,000 rpm engine*. With this description of exactly how powerful our chainsaw is, we now have content to tout down the line in our marketing efforts. We also have exact data that illuminates how much faster our chainsaw is over our competitors. Instead of '*Solid grip*,' 1/4" plastic clearly describes *exactly* how thick the body of our chainsaw is. Again, we can use this data down the line in our marketing efforts, but also to help us identify a target market for our chainsaw in which light-weight, durable plastic may be important.

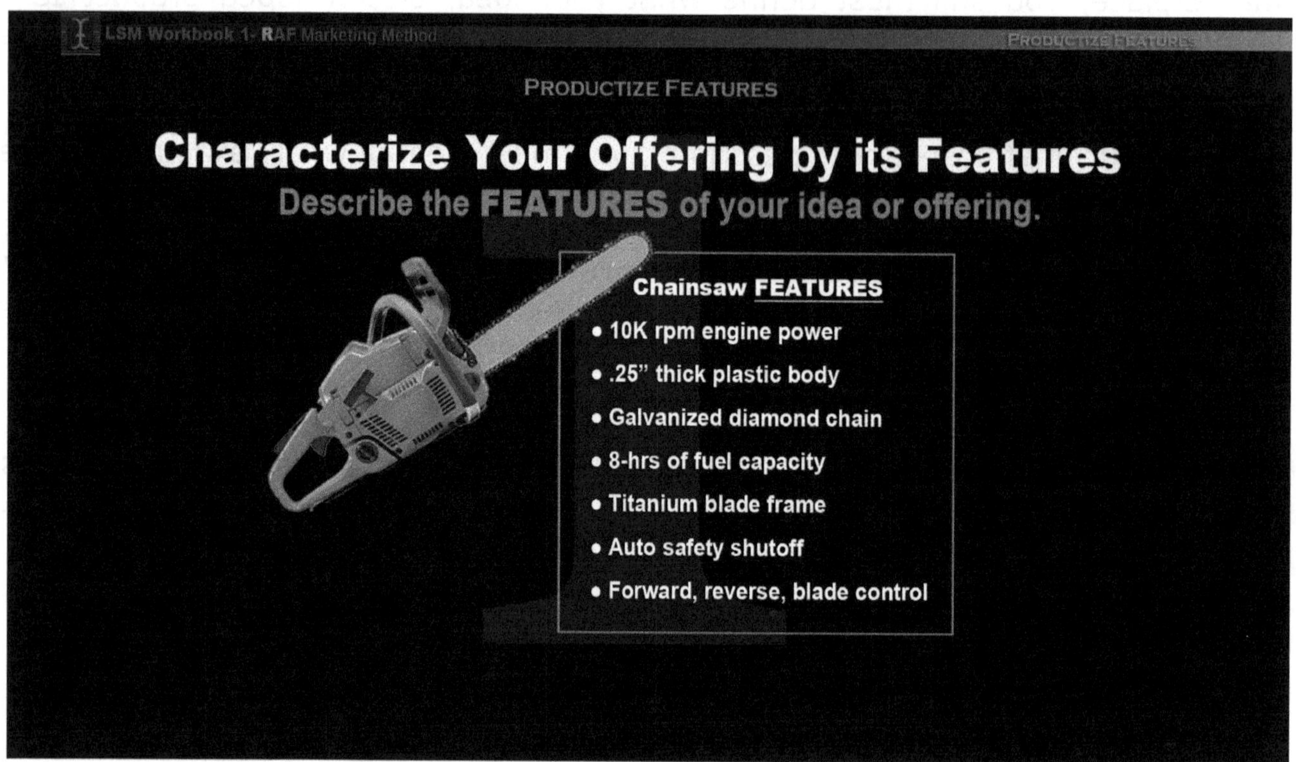

The process of identifying features is not complicated, but often lengthy. And it's not a one shot and done, but a *continual process*. You will be adding to your FEATURE list throughout the life cycle of your business. Doing so, not only helps you *intimately* understand what your potential offering IS, it also helps keep the development of your offering on track. Additionally, the Productization lists you produce in this process will give you **content**—keywords and phrases—to use in your marketing and advertising campaigns in the branding process.

To begin designing and marketing your idea, or product in development, take this first step in the Productization process:

1. Define your idea's space in the marketplace, aka "product/market fit."
2. Describe, in *specific* detail, the FEATURES or FUNCTIONS of your idea, offering in development, or actualized product.

-
-

STOP! Do CHALLENGE #7 before moving on.

◆◆◆

CHALLENGE #7: Engage in Real-World Productization

FEATURES and FUNCTIONS are used every day in real-world marketing. You'll find them on labels, as in the ingredients on food products. You'll see them in digital and print marketing efforts touting the best things about an offering. You'll notice them in reviews of products, even books and movies—"an epic romance," as 'romance' is a particular feature or category of storytelling.

Seeing is Believing, as the colloquialism goes. So, it's time to check out the first step of Productization in real-world marketing.

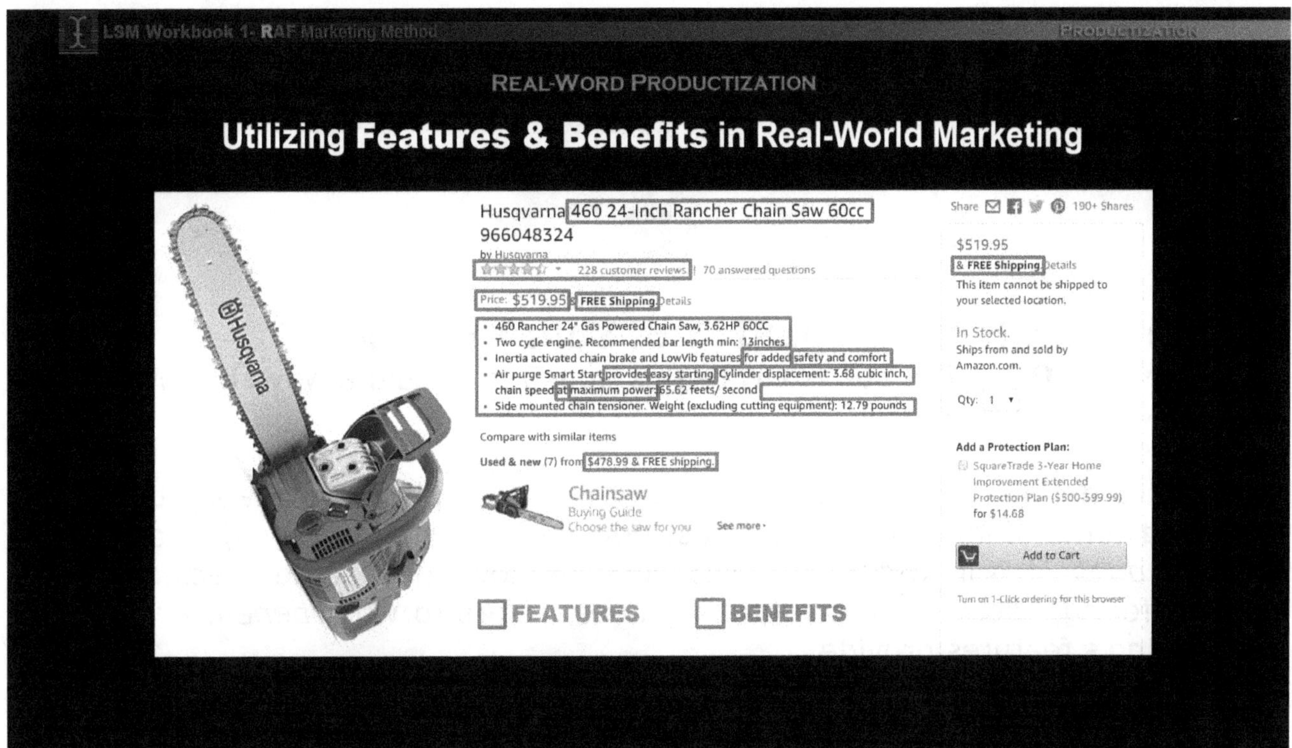

1. **Go to Amazon.com.**

2. **Choose a CONSUMER product you know** (preferably use).
   Suggestions:
   - Tech device (cellphones; tablets; computers; printers)
   - Home/Garden/Sports (décor; tools; supplies and equipment)
   - Food/Health/Beauty (groceries; wine; vitamins; makeup)

3. **Go to the PRODUCT PAGE of your chosen offering, and find the FEATURES of the product.** (Also look at *Product Specifications;*

Information; or *From the Manufacturer* sections for additional features.)

4. **Title your document with the name of the product, and its PRODUCT PAGE URL. List all the FEATURES you find.** List ONLY features. Do *not* include the product's benefits. Just list the FEATURES or FUNCTIONS of the offering.

As stated, it is important to *write down* what you find, in this case, LIST THE FEATURES of the offering you chose. Even copying the list of FEATURES off Amazon's product page will give you an intimate understanding of the process of identifying the FEATURES of any offering. Discovering how the FEATURES of an offering are used in real-world marketing, will show you why it is necessary to perform this first step of the Productization process with every idea, or offering you develop.

◆◆◆

Step 2: Identify the BENEFITS of Your Offering

What does it DO? (The subtext with this question should always be "What does it do for your target user?")

After we've defined where our idea fits in the marketplace of sellable items, and described some of its features, we must now identify what our idea, or developed offering, *does*. It is important to note, since we now know some *specific* features of our offering, listing what our offering *does,* refers to what *benefit* or solutions our offering's features provide.

It is likely, when you conceived of your offering, you thought of some benefits that it would deliver. It's reasonable to assume, when you originally considered your offering, you considered its features and benefits as the same thing. They are not. Many benefits can be derived from one particular feature of an offering, so be sure to follow the steps of the Productization process exactly, *in order*, and begin productizing your offering by its specific features *first*.

We derive our BENEFITS list, including solutions to a problem our offering provides, by transposing our list of features into projected benefits.

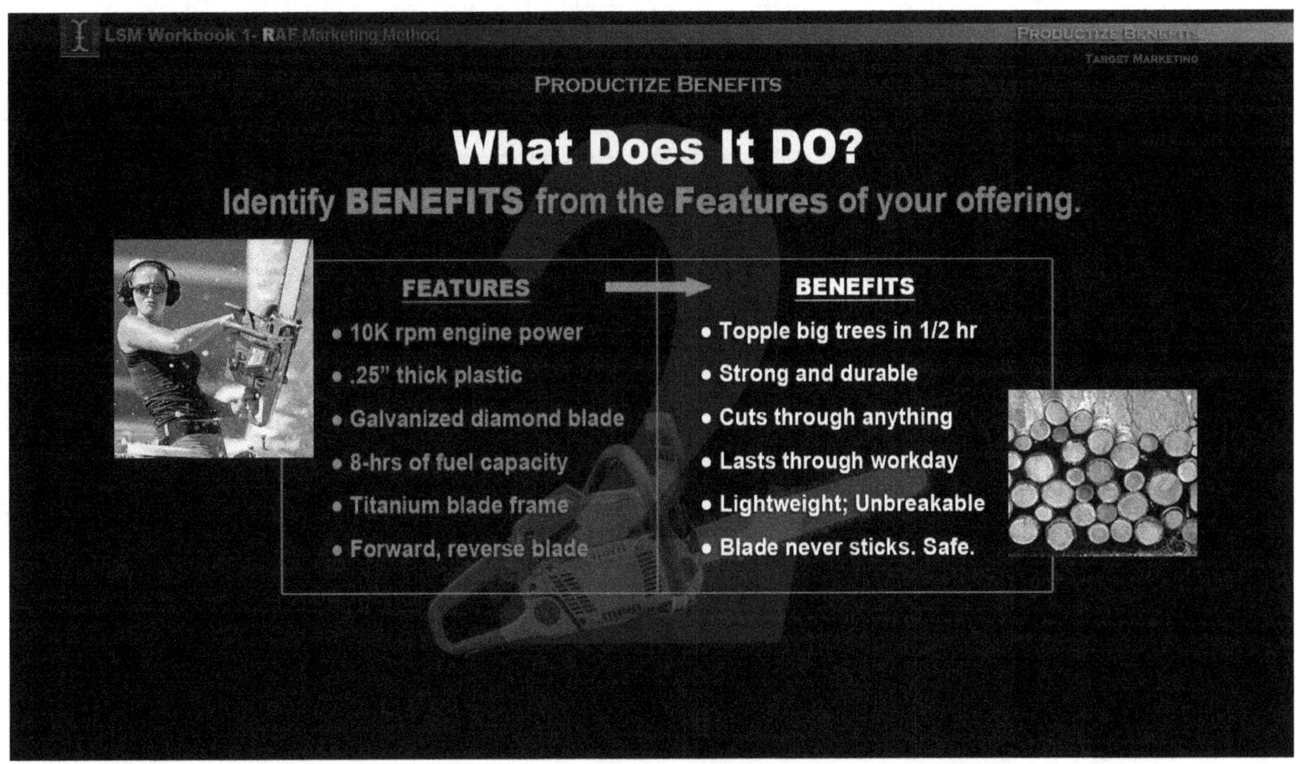

Still using my new chainsaw as a model, I've taken the FEATURES list we just created, and transposed these characteristics of my offering into benefits.

- FEATURE: What can a 10,000 rpm motor do?
- **BENEFIT**: *It can topple mature trees in half an hour.*

- FEATURE: Why is ¼" thick plastic body important?
- **BENEFIT**: *It's strong and unbreakable.*

- FEATURE: Why does a diamond-toothed chain matter?
- **BENEFIT**: *It can cut through metal or hardwood with ease*

- FEATURE: Why does 8 hours of fuel capacity matter?
- **BENEFIT**: *The chainsaw can operate throughout the workday without stopping, saving time, and money in fuel costs.*

- FEATURE: Why is a titanium blade important?
- **BENEFIT**: *It's lightweight and virtually indestructible.*

- FEATURE: Why does it matter that my chainsaw shuts off automatically?
- **BENEFIT**: *It makes it safe to use if it is dropped or left unattended.*

- FEATURE: What advantage does the chain's variable rotation provide?
- **BENEFIT**: *The blade won't get stuck in the material it is cutting.*

All these features of my chainsaw simply translate into benefits. And by answering the second Productization question, **What does it DO**, we are defining the *benefits* the *features* of our offering provide.

Just like your FEATURES list, avoid fluff words and phrases in your BENEFITS list. *Be specific*, and list actual advantages your offering's features deliver. Detailing benefits, will also provide you with great copy content of keywords and phrases, directly related to your specific offering, for your advertising and marketing campaigns. The more benefits you can define, the easier it'll be to sell your offering down the line!

Identifying benefits also helps us find the people most likely interested in the features of our offering. If I am a single man, it is unlikely I'll be interested in women's menstrual products. It's unlikely I'll find a need for an insulin tester if I'm not diabetic. And I'm probably not interested in downloading a mobile application if I don't have a smartphone, or internet service available on my cellphone.

Any given product or service, or even message, will have a limited group of people likely to find utility in it. No matter what the product or service, the offering's benefits, often couched as solutions, will not satisfy every human being on the planet. Regardless of how great our chainsaw is, only limited groups of people, likely in construction or landscaping, have any interest in chainsaws. Identifying benefits helps us narrow everyone on Earth down to those most likely to find benefit from the features of our offering.

Step two, in the Productization process is identifying the benefits or solutions the features of your offering provide.

Step 3: Project WHO Will BENEFIT from Your Offering

TARGET MARKETING is a method of identifying the *groups of people* mostly likely interested in our offering or message. As stated, **tightly-targeted marketing efforts get the greatest response and conversion**. But it's important to note, we are *never* selling to markets. We are *always* selling to individual people.

We must productize our potential offering's features, as well as the benefits those features provide, *before* beginning the target marketing process. We can't possibly predict *who* our product or service will benefit ,until we know *what* our offering *is*. Once some features and benefits of our offering are defined, we project *who* will find value—a benefit or solution—in the features our product, service, or even message, offers.

Step three, we hypothesize, speculate, project what *types of people* will benefit from our idea, or developed product.

Utilizing the BENEFITS list we previously derived from our offering's list of FEATURES, we follow the same protocol, and derive a list of potential TARGET MARKETS from our BENEFITS list. These are not exact target markets because right now, we're just projecting who these people might be, considering WHO the features of our offering will serve.

These are *broad* markets, grouping people with similar characteristics, like demographic traits—their age, sex, race...etc.—but also by their particular personality traits, also known as **psychographics**—what they like, and don't, and why. *Remember*, psychology is at the foundation of marketing. We must get into our target customer's head, understand what motivates them as individuals, to get them to do what we want. We'll drill down on turning target markets into targeted users, or potential customers, in Module 5: Productizing Software, next, as we are *always selling to individual people*.

Target marketing begins with what marketing pros calls the "lowest hanging fruit," or the *most likely groups of people* who will find interest in our offering. Since chainsaws are a known commodity, with others already producing similar products, our most likely target markets are groups of people already using a chainsaw. Obviously.

Many of you will likely be looking to improve on an already existing offering, like my new, improved chainsaw. From *Uber* came *Lyft*. From *Amazon* came *Google Play*. From *Netflix* came *Hulu*. An easy way to find a few initial projected markets, is to look at your competitor's targets. (We'll get into **Competitive Analysis**, and how to utilize your competitors for a variety of marketing endeavors further along in this workbook.)

Assuming your offering is unique to itself, and does not have any known or direct competition, like a new clothing line or software application, the process of target marketing remains the same as offerings that improve on existing products.

We follow the same paradigm to identify our target markets as we did identifying our BENEFITS from our FEATURES lists. We transpose our BENEFITS list into WHO will likely benefit from using our offering. To identify some target markets for my new chainsaw, I'll begin with my "lowest hanging fruit."

- BENEFIT: *My chainsaw can topple mature trees in half an hour.*

- BENEFIT: *It can cut through metal or hardwood with ease.*
- **[Potential] TARGET MARKETS**: *Tree removal specialists. Landscapers. Professional gardeners.*

My new chainsaw would definitely benefit landscapers, both professional and serious home gardeners. Many still use clippers and hand saws to groom yards, build fences or retaining walls. Some are still using just an ax to chop tree limbs, and my chainsaw would be so much faster and easier.

Tree removal specialists use chainsaws. From power companies to construction prep, there are quite a few groups of people using chainsaws to cut trees. Utility companies have large crews that require chainsaws, but they generally have a corporate culture slower than molasses, and they'll be a harder sell, unlikely to switch to my unknown brand. I project one of my most likely targets to market my new chainsaw, will be professional gardeners and landscapers that thought they were saving money buying the cheap chainsaw they're using, but it's not nearly as powerful, or economical as mine! For a nominal price difference, this particular group of people—one of my target markets—could get my rippin' fast chainsaw that would help them cut more trees and make more money.

- BENEFIT: *The chainsaw can operate throughout the workday without stopping, saving time, and money in fuel costs.*
- **[Potential] TARGET MARKETS**: Construction Workers. Fire Fighters.

Construction is a very broad target market, and should be narrowed a bit to *types* of construction, as most don't construct an office tower with a chainsaw. Roofers, foundation, floor and building framers, often cut the wood required to do their job with a chainsaw. Stopping throughout their day to refill the fuel in their chainsaws cost them time and money. My new, improved chainsaw can solve this issue for them. Fire fighters are an important target market as well, as they need to be able to operate without stopping to create fire breaks while fighting forest fires.

- BENEFIT: *My chainsaw is lightweight, durable, and virtually indestructible.*
- BENEFIT: *My chainsaw is safe to use.*
- **[Potential] TARGET MARKET**: Single mothers.

In this process of identifying groups of people that will benefits from my new chainsaw, we've uncovered another potential market for my offering. The single mom. She is likely young, 20s to early 40s, low to middle income, lives in a rural location. She doesn't have a partner to cut firewood for her and her kids, and can't afford to hire someone, so she has to do it herself. This woman can use my improved chainsaw because its lightweight and durable. It's safe, and easy to use. Additionally, because titanium is virtually indestructible, she won't have to replace my chainsaw for a long long time, and this women needs to be conservative with her money. So, we've identified a group of single woman, low to moderate income, likely a parent, who is yet another target market for my offering.

- BENEFIT: *My chainsaw is safe to use.*
- BENEFIT: *My chainsaw is lightweight, durable, and virtually indestructible.*
- BENEFIT: *The blade won't get stuck in the material it's cutting.*
- **[Potential] TARGET MARKETS**: Baby Boomers. Millennial Vintners. Home Remodelers.

Then, of course, there are the Baby Boomers and Millennial vintners that made money on tech stock and go up to Napa Valley (just north of San Francisco) to start a vineyard. They are generally older, mid 40s to mid-60s, and can't lift or operate heavy, commercial-grade chainsaws. They'd likely use my new chainsaw, if they knew how much simpler, and more efficient it is than doing everything by hand, as so many Boomers of the hippie era try to do.

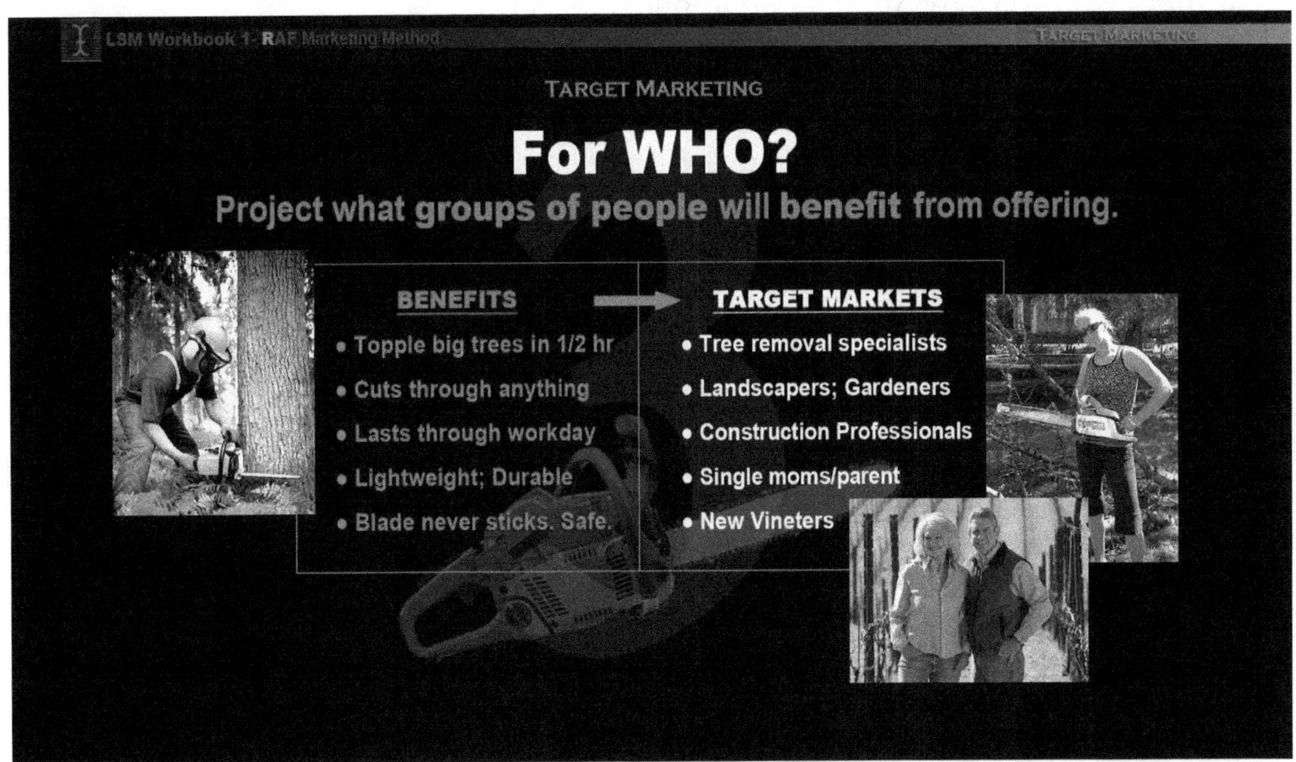

Home remodeling is done by professionals, but also homeowners of moderate to high income, since owning your own home is generally an expensive purchase.

High income homeowners generally pay a pro for remodeling, so we'll target middle income homeowners with my new chainsaw. Of course they'll need a safe, lightweight, durable chainsaw. And one that lasts, as well. Additionally, adding a room, to building retaining walls, to constructing fences, they need to cut through many different types of materials, and the blade on my chainsaw won't get stuck cutting into any material because it can reverse.

Vintners and home remodelers are smaller markets than construction or landscaping, to be sure, but, with these two target markets we can market to both men and women, and **NICHE markets** get greater response.

We'll drill down on who these broad target markets are in the Target Marketing module, to discover our target users—the actual *people* we'll target with our campaigns to get the greatest response on our marketing efforts.

Target Marketing Through Productization

To identify potential target customers—the *people* we project will find value in our offering—we align the features of our product, service, or message, to the benefits our features deliver, and then align those benefits to potential groups of customers who will likely find value in our offering.

Even if you have a particular target market in mind when you came up with your idea, or you have targets you are currently selling your developed offering to, we always need *more customers*. To grow and sustain any company you will always need more people to buy your product, sign-up for your service, or into your message. Implement the first three steps of the Productization process, and utilize them to identify target markets throughout the life-cycle of your business.

Remember, target marketing, like all marketing, starts broad and drills down. In this initial phase of identifying potential markets—groupings of likely customers who'll buy our offering or into our message—we define broad markets, like 'construction,' or 'single moms.' However, these broad markets have limited utility in terms of tightly targeting our advertising and marketing efforts for greater response. To achieve the greatest response, target your campaigns to *individual people*.

Never forget that we are always selling to *people*, not markets. We must target individuals for the greatest return on our marketing investment. Using **common sense**, psychology, and the massive amount of data available today, getting intimate with your target audience is totally doable. These are the people you want to reach, and engage with your advertising and marketing campaigns, as they are most likely to purchase, or buy into your message.

The following modules will take you step-by-step in identifying the features and benefits, target markets and users of a software idea that has yet to be actualized. We'll explore how to find competition, and define what makes an offering unique, desirable. We'll project additional target markets and users through horizontal and vertical marketing models, as well as potential new offerings to keep your startup relevant a year and five down the line.

Now that you have an overall understanding of the process of Productization, it's time for *you* to implement Step 1 in the RAF Marketing Method. **Get Ready** and productize your offering, or developed product, service or nonprofit message into an offering of value, for profit.

MODULE 4: PRODUCTIZATION 101 REVIEW

- To **productize** an idea, or developed offering, we begin by giving clear, concise, and *specific* answers to the following three questions:
    1. **What IS it?**
    2. **What does it DO?**
    3. **For WHO?**

- **Productization** begins with identifying our offering's '**Product/Market Fit**', defining our idea by where it 'fits' in the marketplace of sellable items. Is our offering a **Product**, a **Service**, or **Message**?

- Once we've defined our offering's 'fit' in the marketplace, we must describe what it IS—its characteristics, or FEATURES, in software known as FUNCTIONS.

- When we have a lengthy list of the FEATURES of our potential offering, we align them to BENEFITS or solutions that the FEATURES of our offering will provide.

- And finally, we project WHO—the potential MARKETS and PEOPLE, in software also known as USERS, that will benefit from the FEATURES/FUNCTIONS of our upcoming offering.

- To create branding and marketing campaigns that get the greatest response, get your offering **READY** by performing the Productization process *first*, and turn your idea into a product, service or message of *value* for a specific group of people.

-

-

STOP! Do CHALLENGE #8 before moving on.

◆◆◆

CHALLENGE #8: Engage in Target Marketing

1. **Pick a favorite book <u>or</u> movie.**
   Example: "An Inconvenient Truth" (2006)

2. **Describe the audience <u>originally targeted</u> with the** [book or] **movie's marketing efforts.**
   Example (for "An Inconvenient Truth"): Male/Female. 20 – 75 yrs old. College educated. White-collar career path. $$$ - $$$$ income. Democrats. Liberal. Reformed Christian or Jew, to no religious affiliation. Single/Married/Divorced. Parents of tween, teens or adult kids. City/Suburb of major city (but not rural or remote). Energy-efficient. Healthy lifestyle. Reads or works at night, or watches PBS and late night talk shows...

3. **Write a brief REVIEW of the** [book or] **film, marketing to the <u>original target audience</u>.**
   Example: Vice-President Al Gore uses data analysis, science and time-lapse photography to show us how humanity is negatively impacting the environment on Earth, and inadvertently creating Global Warming. He closes the film with practical calls to action we can all take in our daily lives to conserve energy and help stop our destructive impact on our planet.

4. **Describe a <u>NEW TARGET MARKET</u> you'd like to motivate to see the film.**
   Example: Male over Female 2 : 1. 15 – 75 yrs old. White. Religious conservatives. High school educated. Blue-collar or civil service career path. $ - $$$ income. Republicans. Married with two or more kids. Military, manufacturing or repetitive job functions. Living in rural or remote areas of the U.S. Large, gas-powered SUVs and/or trucks. Overweight or obese, fast food consumers. Binge-watches series, reality TV and game shows...

5. **REWRITE the TITLE of the** [book or] **film, to attract your <u>NEW TARGET AUDIENCE</u>.**
   Example: "The Next Great Flood is Coming" (2006)

6. **Write a NEW brief REVIEW of the** [book or] **movie that pays off the NEW TITLE, to get your <u>NEW TARGET MARKET</u> to see the film.**
   Example: Dystopian look at a future where weather is out of control, and eventually destroys everything on the face of the Earth, with earthquakes, tornadoes, and global flooding. Shameless support for renewable energy, while

dissing traditional American industries like coal and oil. Witness Vice President Al Gore's dark and foreboding vision of tomorrow.

Targeting your advertising and marketing efforts to address the desires or issues of a *specific group of people* (**target markets**) will garner greater response on your campaigns. I can not stress this enough. We are *never* marketing to the world. A typical rejoinder of most entrepreneurs I've worked with is, "most everyone on the planet can use it." Wrong! Most everyone on Earth will *not* find benefits in your offering, regardless how great you think it is. Utilize the **Productization process** to get intimate with what you plan to sell, as well as *who* you plan to sell your product, service, or message to.

◆◆◆

Productizing Software or Cupcakes

Since many of you want to learn how to actualize, or sell, software ideas, in the next module, we'll go through the process of productizing a **peer-2-peer** (**P2P**), **software-as-a-service** (**SaaS**) application.

The process of Productization—the steps you must take to create an offering someone will want—are the same whether developing chainsaws, cupcakes, or SaaS. To productize a software application into a mobile service for profit, we'll follow the exact same paradigm shown with the chainsaw. We'll answer the same three primary questions: **What IS it? What does it DO? And for WHO?** And we'll perform the step-by-step process of productizing a software idea into an offering of value, for profit.

◆◆◆◆◆

MODULE 5: PRODUCTIZING SOFTWARE

Step 1. Get Ready: PRODUCTIZE Your Software

The chainsaw example in the previous module illustrated what Productization *is*. But between concept and reality is the Grand Canyon.

In this module, we repeat the steps we took with the chainsaw—the first phase of Productization, and ask the same three question we did about the chainsaw:

1. **What IS it?**
2. **What does it DO?**
3. **For WHO?**

In Module 5, instead of a physical product, we're going to identify the characteristics of a software idea, and complete Step 1 of the 3-step RAF Marketing Method, to bring a software application, program, or platform, to fruition.

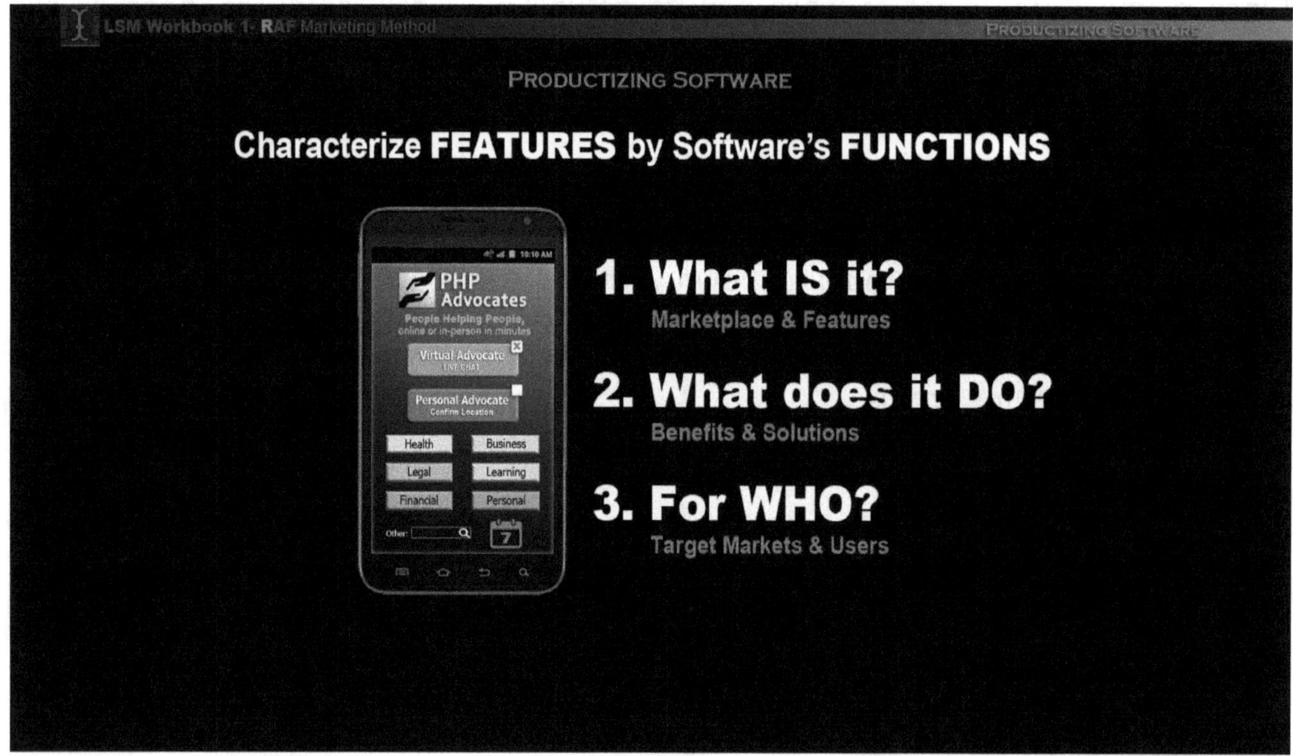

We'll begin, as we did with the chainsaw, by categorizing my software idea's space in the marketplace, also known as, my software app's product/market 'fit.' Next, we'll identify some features and benefits of my software service. With my **Startup Hierarchy** already set up, I'll have a place—my Productization folders—to put the first two of the eight required Productization lists we'll create in this module, beginning the process of getting my new venture **Ready** for marketing.

In **List 1A**, we'll define my software's **FEATURES** or **FUNCTIONS** (which are the same thing). **List 1B** will identify the **BENEFITS** of my software idea—the solutions, or value my offering provides. List 2A will define who will find benefits in my software's functions, but we'll get to identifying target markets for my software in the next module.

Again, in this module we'll only be filling List 1A and 1B with the functions and benefits of my software idea. Regardless if your offering is a software application, cupcakes, a dental practice, or even a nonprofit message, follow the steps presented in this module to begin productizing *your* idea! Even with fully developed offerings, initializing this *first phase*, and all phases of the Productization process, will enable you to create branding and marketing campaigns that get the greatest response.

Productize Software from Idea to Marketable Offering

To illustrate the process of Productizing software, I've chosen an idea I thought of a while back, but, to date, have never actualized:

> *A peer-to-peer (P2P) mobile app that connects people with experts to help them, both in-person and online.*

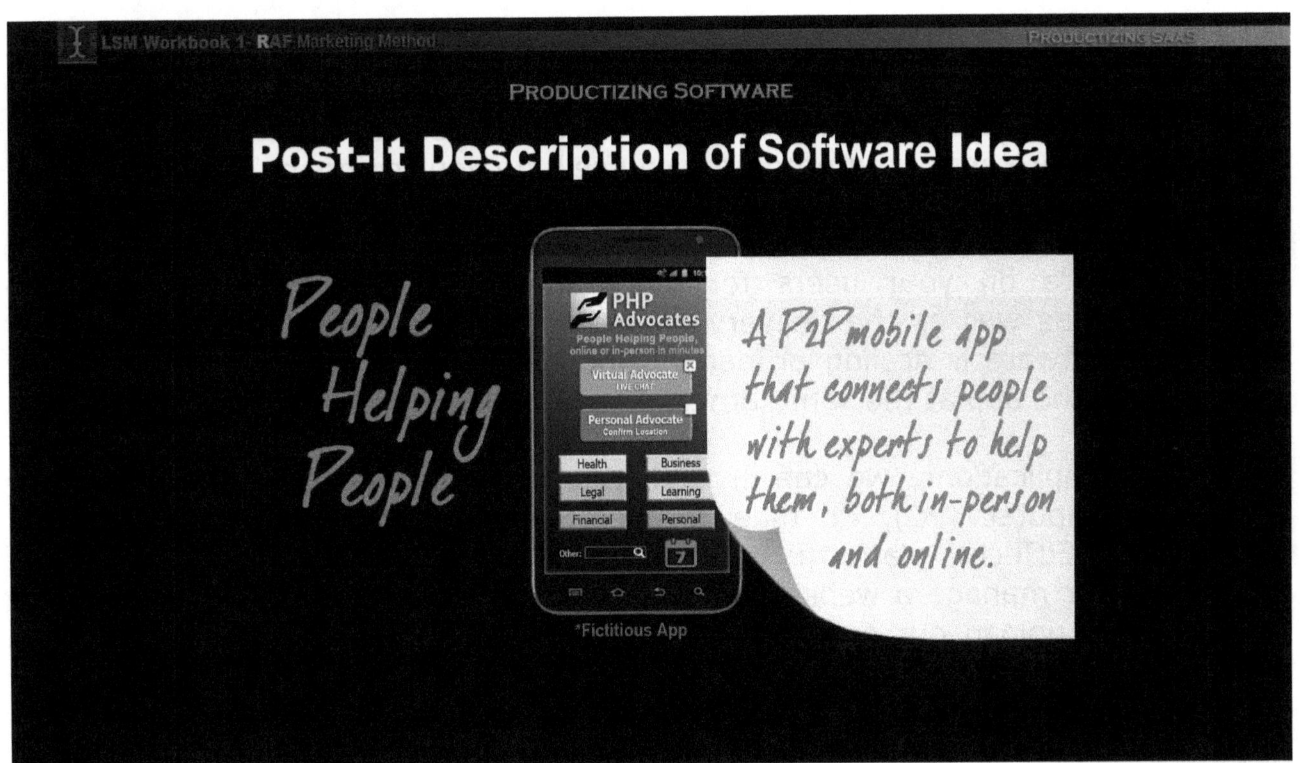

This is the original, brief, post-it note description of my idea. I've given my idea a name, *PHP Advocates*, to more easily identify it throughout this workbook, but it's likely you do not have a name for your idea, if it has yet to be developed. We will get into naming conventions for your offering *and* startup in LSB Workbook 2.

PHP stands for *People Helping People*. I'm using my *PHP Advocates* idea as the Productization example, since many of you are likely designing software-as-a-service (SaaS) applications, programs, or social, peer-to-peer (P2P) platforms.

Unlike the chainsaw example, software has no physical characteristics, so describing its functions becomes a bit more challenging. But we begin with the same first question about my software idea: **What IS it?**

Identify Software Fit Through Market Segmentation

We categorize our offering into specific industry segments, to help us more effectively identify broad marketplaces in which the features of our software idea fit. Identifying 'product/market fit' is essential to finding potential target markets and users in which to sell our projected offering. We examine industries, and job functions within industries, to find the *people* who will likely benefit from what our software does. 'Product/market fit' is the very beginning of the Productization process.

Much of today's software applications are delivered via the 'cloud'—meaning the software is stored in a centralized location that is easily accessed through a mobile phone, a laptop, a tablet, or other electronic device. It's smart business to run your software apps, and programs you sell, on your company's cloud. A cloud is a bank of computer servers which store and deliver the application when requested from an electronic device, like your smartphone. First, you can collect a ton of data on your users for later analysis. Second, *you* control the functionality, as well as the delivery of updates for your application, and make sure your software is scaling properly—functioning correctly, even with a lot of clients using the app at the same time.

With SaaS applications, we can create stunning imagery in *Photoshop* on our personal computer (PC), or take a photography course from an education technology (EdTech) platform on our mobile phone. We can develop an application, or manage a website with online tools we access through our tablet or laptop, or upload our creations to social media platforms from *Facebook* to *Snapchat* in real time.

If you are creating a program or application you hope to run on a cloud, so it is easily accessible by most electronic devices, begin the segmentation process by identifying the type of cloud software you plan to create.

Software is [generally] parsed into three commonly used segments:

- **IaaS**—Infrastructure as a Service
- **PaaS**—Platform as a Service
- **SaaS**—Software as a Service

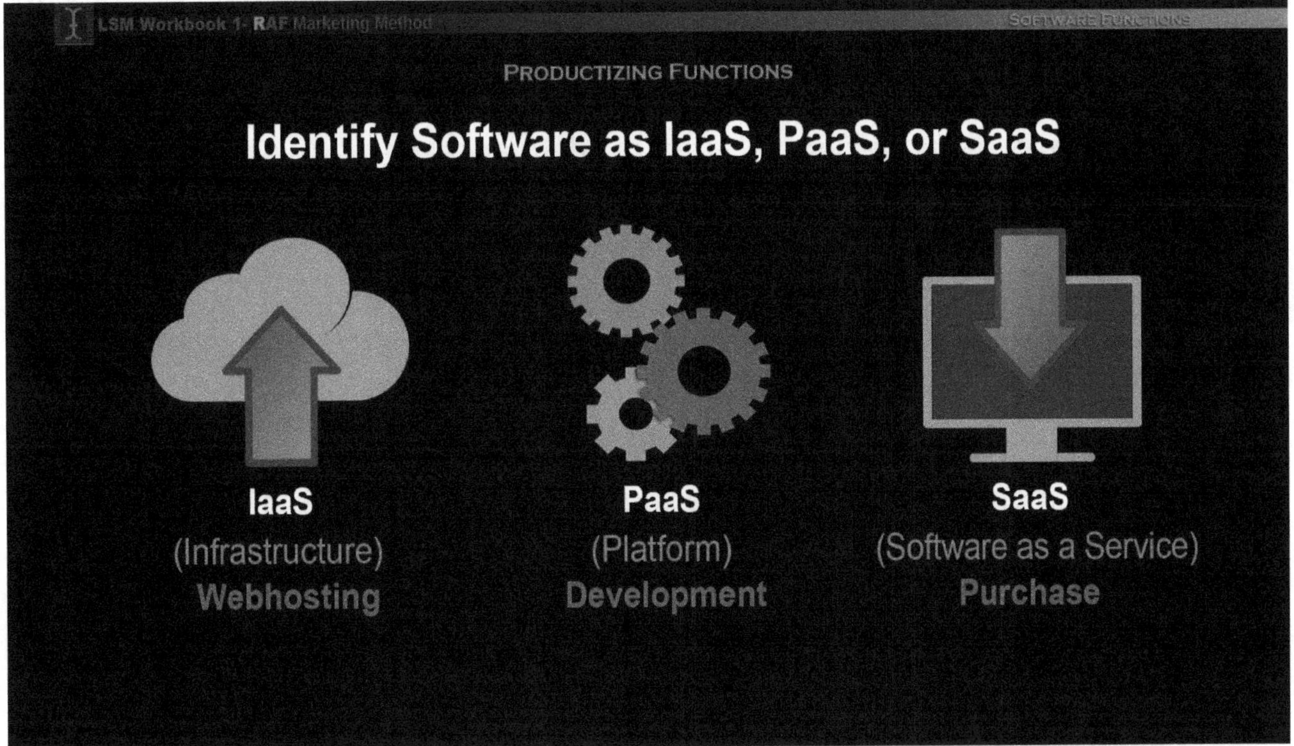

IaaS—Infrastructure as a Service, is the foundation of 'cloud computing.' It is the infrastructure housing applications and programs, such as webhosting services, virtual networks, storage and servers. It's also operating systems, CPU operations, memory and backup services. If you are creating a IaaS offering, you are building hardware, or software that manages and delivers networks, apps and programs.

Who are target markets for a IaaS offering? Systems managers, hardware engineers, OS and CPU developers, IT specialists. These techies manage and create platforms from QA (quality assurance) testing, to development environments, to integration and deployment of infrastructure programs. *Amazon Web Services* (*AWS*) is one of the most widely recognized companies selling an array of IaaS offerings.

PaaS—Platform as a Service, gives users a platform and environment to develop, manage and run applications over the internet. *Red Hat* is one of the better known PaaS providers, providing an open-source software platform for developers to create enterprise applications—complex programs to help corporate operations as opposed to individual users. PaaS is where developers create, integrate and deploy applications for end-users—individuals like you and me.

Who are target markets for PaaS offerings? Computer engineers. Software developers. Data scientists.

SaaS—Software as a Service, is tightly defined as *a software licensing and delivery model in which software is licensed on a subscription basis and is centrally hosted* (*Wikipedia*).

The Lean Startup series uses a *loose* definition of SaaS, as *a distribution model in which a company hosts software applications, and makes them available to customers over the internet* (*TechTarget*).

Subscriptions are certainly a great profit model for SaaS, but there are other ways to make money with a SaaS offering, which we'll explore in the last module of this workbook.

Google is essentially a SaaS offering. Their product is *Search-as-a-Service*. When you input a query into *Google's* search bar, your query runs through *Google's* servers, on *Google's* cloud. *Google* then utilizes their proprietary software to 'crawl' the internet and return answers.

Social media tools that help you manage your social content, and platforms from the job site, *LinkedIn,* to the video sharing site *Vimeo*, are SaaS. **Content management systems** (**CMS**) that help you manage your online content, and **CRM** (**customer relationship management**) systems, give corporations and individuals tools to manage their content and customers. MMORPGs (massive multi-player online role-playing [video] games), to the full *Adobe Creative Cloud* with *Photoshop, Acrobat, After Effects,* and other tools for graphic designers, (now only available through subscription), are just few of the wide variety of today's SaaS offerings.

Target markets for SaaS largely depends on the potential user's job function. Most of you developing software are likely developing SaaS offerings. Recommendation engines to database analytic tools, developers are creating the next generation of great SaaS products. To *market* them, you must first productize them, identify what your SaaS *is*—its functions; what it *does*—its benefits or solutions; and *who*—target industries, markets, and people—likely interested in your offering/s.

The Market Segmentation Process

Market segmentation does not begin and end with IaaS, PaaS, and SaaS. We are always looking for more target markets, and to do this we must define what our offering *is*, and *does*, to figure out *who* will find value in it.

If you are planning to sell, or already selling a physical product, like a baked good, or a draft beer, you must segment your offering in the same way we'll segment my *PHP Advocates* software idea. In other words, you still must go through all the steps of Productization to help you determine your target markets and users.

While software segmentation might seem more complicated then selling a fashion line, it really is the same process. You must determine where your clothing fits in the marketplace of fashion. The fashion industry has many 'branches.' Clothing for young, or older, or ethnic like an African style, or Punk. It is also made with various materials like sustainable cottons, or hemp, or manufactured threads like polyester...etc. Each will suit a different type of person, and breaking down your offering with a market segmentation model will help you find these people. And remember, tightly-targeted marketing gets the greatest response!

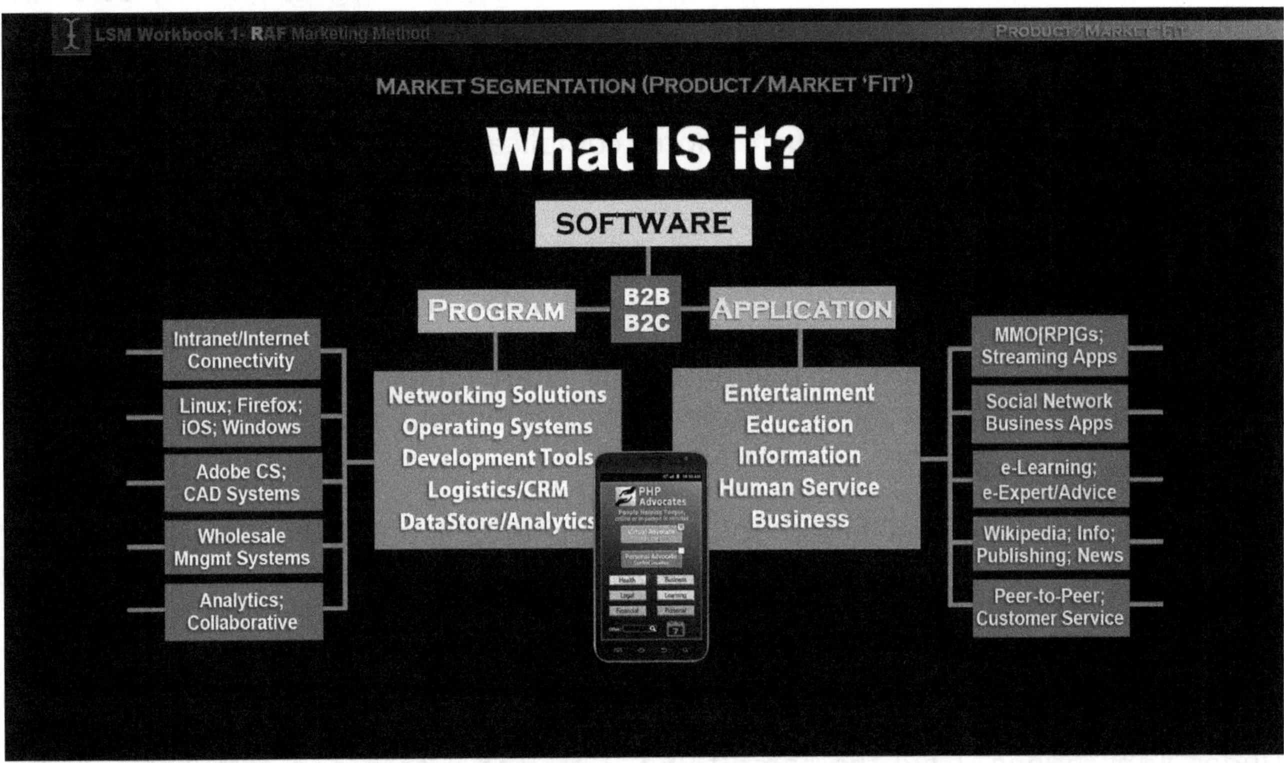

To illustrate the *software* segmentation process, I've created a simplified industry segmentation model, specifically for software, to help me define my idea—find its *space* in the marketplace, or 'product/market fit.' But how did I create an effective model that helps me meet this objective?

First, I *thought* about the types of software out there, and made a mental list of the software categories I imagine my application idea might fit. Then I *Google* "software categories." *Google* returns nearly half a million links that show dozens to hundreds of software categories, many in convenient bullet lists.

Software is *PHP Advocates* overall *space* in the marketplace. What IS it? It's software. And that's very general, which is where we begin. As with all marketing, segmentation starts broad and drills down as tightly as possible to *fit* within specific industry segments.

I created a schematic chart using several of the main software categories, also known as '**topic classifiers**' that I found through *Google's* returns. Then I break down these categories/classifiers into segments, or broad grouping of similar software types.

To make it easier for me to find *PHP Advocates* 'product/market fit,' I began by segmented software into two commonly used terms: Programs (also called Systems), and Applications. At the top of my chart I've segmented my software under these two common classifiers.

These labels are often used interchangeably, but when we think of programs, we're usually referring to much more complicated systems, like networking solutions or operating systems, or complex development tools like *Photoshop* or CAD systems.

When we talk about applications, we're usually referring to simpler programs, like mobile apps that are customer facing, user friendly, and deal with industries like entertainment or education. I populated my chart under both the Programs and Applications classifiers, filling each with additional, more specific industry segments.

Under Programs, I listed broad software segments I got from *Google*, such as *Networking Solutions, Operating Systems,* and *Development Tools.* From these classifiers, I further refined my industry segments to include *specific* programs, such as *Adobe Creative Cloud*, and operating systems like *Linux*, as well as *customer relationship management (CRM) systems,* and *data analysis* programs.

Under Applications, I did the same thing. I started with broad software industry classifiers such as *Entertainment, Information,* and *Human Services*. Beyond these categories, I further refined my list to include more specific software application types. *Entertainment* further segmented to *MMOG video games, online education*, and even *social networks*. These classifiers will break down even further to *FPS (first person shooter) video games*, or *entrepreneurship courses* under *online education*.

Market segmentation modeling enables you to identify your offering's 'product/market fit' simply and effectively. Include as many industry segments in *your* segmentation model as you can thing of, to flush out specific industries where your offering fits. Performing market segmentation will also help you identify features of your offering, and target markets in specific job functions that will likely find benefit or value in your offering, enabling you to produce tightly targeted marketing down the line.

To identify not only specific industry segments, but features, i.e. functions, of my *PHP Advocates* idea, I pick *characteristics* of my software out of the segmentation model I created. I've identified my idea as an application, not a program, as my software won't let you create things, like *Photoshop*, but it will connect you with assistance, more like *Uber* on steroids. *PHP's* primary use is not entertainment, but aide—physically showing up to take someone to a doctor's appointment, or physical therapy session, and waiting, in the waiting room, like a trusted family member, to take them home again.

The more classifiers you identify in *your* model, the easier it is to align the features/functions of your offering with specific industry segments that will likely benefit from using your offering. Tightly segmenting industries, gives you insight into the *people*, through their job function, that are likely target markets for your software program or application.

Using this segmentation modeling technique, I've determined that *PHP Advocates* space in the broad, overall marketplace of sellable items, is software. More fine grain, I've begun the classification process of taking my original idea, the one in my head, and formed it into a potential **business-to-consumer** (**B2C**), **peer-to-peer** (**P2P**), human services, **software as a service** (**SaaS**) application.

Question 1: What IS It?

Utilizing the Market Segmentation model, we've already begun to define some of the features/functions of my *PHP Advocates* idea. We've figured out its space in the marketplace of sellable software, and we've identified specific industry segments, like *human service*, possibly *education,* and *business services*, with experts available to give aide when needed.

Just like the chainsaw example, to understand, and communicate what my application *is*, we begin by creating a list of my software's functions. I simply, succinctly and *specifically* describe each feature/function I put on my list.

I'm a visual learner, so I created a 'working' **user interface** (**UI**) for my *PHP Advocates* idea, to visually understand how to identify the software's functions. It is highly unlikely I'll use this crude UI in the final version of the launch product. I've created it simply to *view* my idea—take it out of my head and *see* it in front of me.

Visualization is a powerful tool for actualizing ideas, to be sure, but if you do not have a UI designed for your software application, which most of you likely won't, yet, *no worries!* We'll get on to **User Interface** (**UI/UX**) design in LSB Workbook 2. For now, if you are a visual learner, like me, you can draw a 'working' UI on a napkin, or create one on your laptop, or wait until you come up with a substantive list of functions before conceiving how your users will access them.

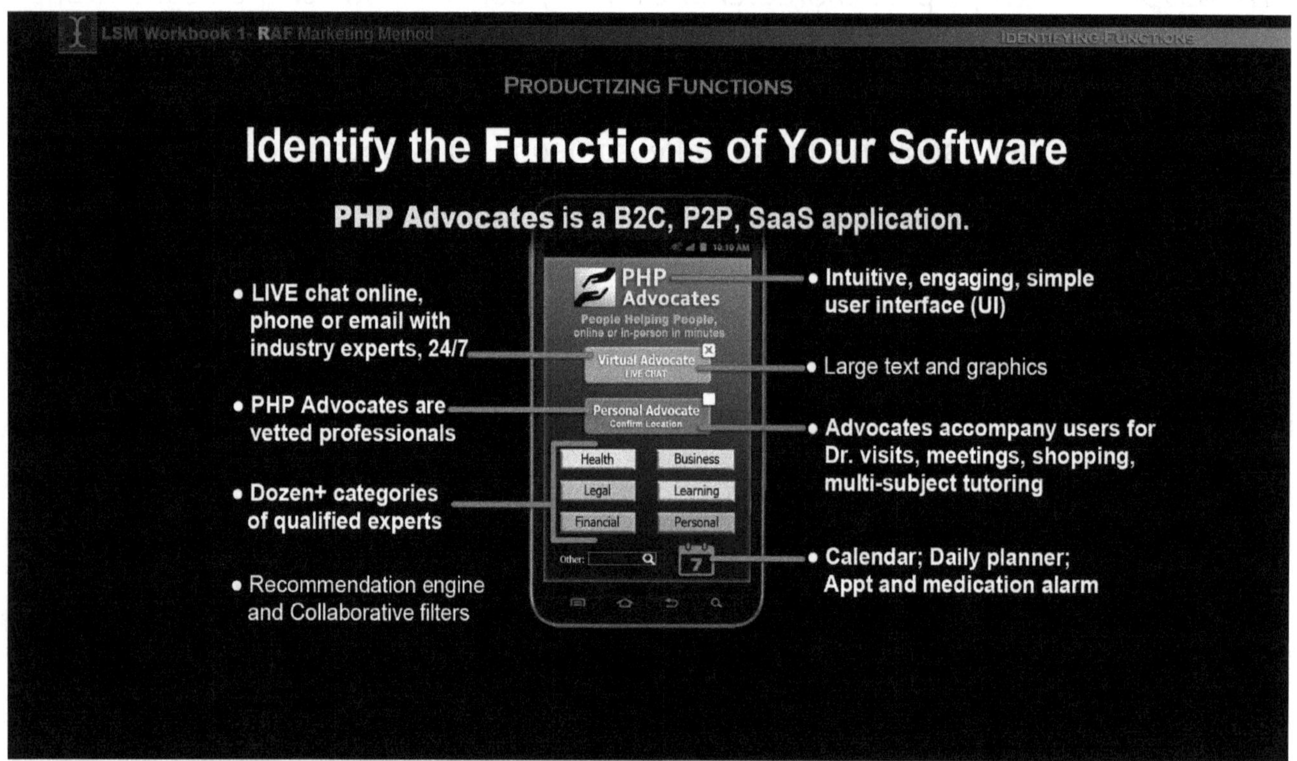

Begin **Productization List 1A**, and actualize your projected offering's features/functions by simply listing as many as you can imagine. We'll use my *PHP Advocate's* idea as an example of how to construct the first of the eight (8) required Productization lists, to create a *marketable* product, service, or nonprofit message.

List 1A: FEATURES of Your Idea

We've identified *PHP Advocates* as a **business-to-consumer** (**B2C**), **peer-to-peer** (**P2P**), human services, **software as a service** (**SaaS**) application from my segmentation model. From the same model we've also identified *education*, and *business*, as potential industries in which *PHP* fits. More fine grain, we've further projected *education technology (EdTech),* then drilling even deeper, we've pinpointed *e-experts, e-learning,* possibly *business tools* as additional functions for my *PHP Advocates* application, all of which fit my offering into multiple SaaS industry segments. The more industries, and job functions *your* offering serves, the more likely you are to grow a sustainable company.

I limit this *first list*, List 1A to only my projected offering's functions. I'll get to benefits, and potential users of my software in a minute.

Productization List 1A: FUNCTIONS of *PHP Advocates:*

- Expert advocates, actual *people* come to help you, or a loved one, *in-person,* anytime, anywhere.
- Online, live video chat with professionals.
- Over a dozen categories of experts online, or in-person.
- All *PHP Advocates* are thoroughly vetted, with extensive background checks, and references.
- Calendar with Daily Planner, as well as appointments and medication reminders.
- Accurate recommendation system to match users to experts.
- Cloud platform, responsive UI, with TLS protocol for secure e-commerce.
- Etc...

I'm simply creating a **bullet list of the functions** of my projected application, just as we did with the chainsaw. I use the simplest language, *not* technical terms, to be easily understood by most people. Many stakeholders in your new venture, such as those you hire to help you produce your idea and marketing efforts, will be using your Productization lists throughout the life-cycle of your business. It is imperative that all lists are easy to understand. Fill your list with as many features/functions as you can conceive. The more functions you conceive for your application, the more benefits you can identify about your software offering.

Use bullet points, and describe each feature or function of your offering in one short, *succinct* sentence. Be very specific, *no fluff words* like "powerful." Explain *how* powerful, quote clock speeds on uploads, or render-time on graphics cards. And don't forget to use the simplest possible language for quick reading and greatest communication to the largest possible audience.

The first part of *PHP Advocates* features/functions list is the *reason* I came up with my original idea—it solved my problem, or fulfilled a desire of mine. So, my first bullet point, my #1 function in List 1A is, in fact, getting a trusted, real person to help my aging mom at doctor's appointments, or with her shopping.

The rest of the list follows the same process as productizing the chainsaw earlier. Simply list the specific features/functions of your [projected] offering.

There are *must have* functions, for any consumer software *application* to have broad appeal: Easy to learn. Simple to use. Secure. Intuitive. Responsive. Fast. These should be included in your list, (regardless that competitors all touts this), to keep everyone working on the development of the software, and the marketing of your offering on the same path to achieving a functional and engaging UI.

One of the many functions I want *PHP Advocates* to have, is an accurate recommendation system that will match users with all types of advocates that will serve their needs any time they log on to my system. To actualize this function requires **Artificial Intelligence** (**AI**), and **Behavior Driven Development** (**BDD**) algorithms. While recommendations that match users to the advocates they want quickly and easily, is clearly a benefit of *PHP Advocates*, for the functions list, we don't necessarily care what the benefit of this function is, or who this function will serve right now. List 1A simply lists that *PHP Advocates* is projected to have this particular type of functionality.

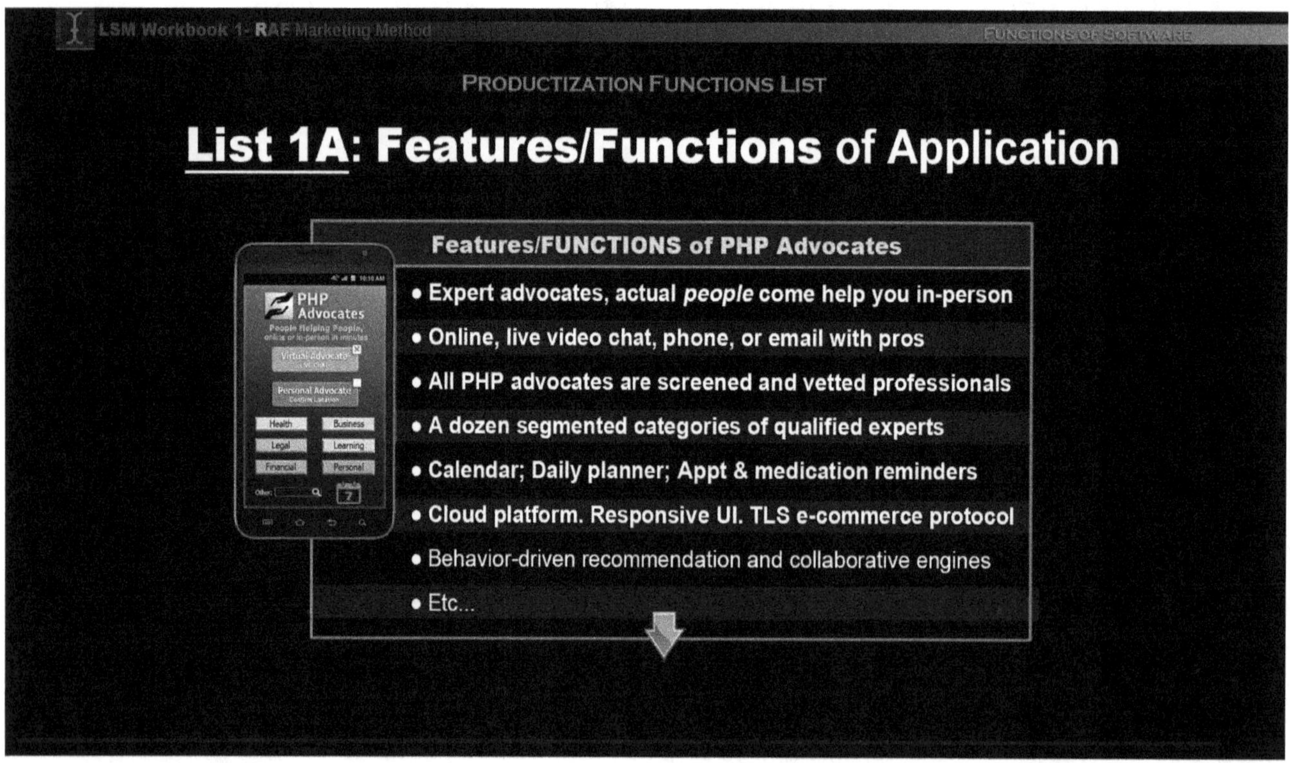

In forming my idea for *PHP Advocates*, I've imagined many functions for my application. When conceiving features/functions for *your* idea, start *broad*, and position your idea in the marketplace of sellable offerings with an industry segmentation model. Next, list the best features/functions *first*, then drill down beyond them to the required basics for broad appeal of any software application, to the *specific* functions of your software idea.

Remember to focus List 1A on just the features/functions—the characteristics of what your idea *is*. Begin with the reason you came up with your idea in the first place, the problem it solved, or desire fulfilled. Finish your features/functions list with the most obvious *must have's* for broad appeal.

The Productization process works the same for software, services, consumer products or even nonprofit messages. If it's a physical offering, like a sports drink or makeup line, describe the ingredients, or materials it's made of; its method of delivery; its construction, optional colors or designs to choose from. If it's software, simply list the functions the software performs.

Whether software, or cupcakes, list as many features/functions as you can conceive, as *specifically* as you can (no fluff words). The longer your list, the more content—keywords and phrases directly related to your offering—you'll have for your marketing efforts down the line.

Creating List 1A, the features/functions list of *your* offering will also help educate you as to the viability of turning your initial idea into an offering of value. If, in the process of creating your features/functions list, you can't think of more than a few, that likely exist in competitor's offerings, then you must iterate your idea—morph it into something else. If your features/functions list is long, with at least a couple of unique bullet points that sets your idea apart from similar offerings, it's likely you have a solid foundation for actualizing your idea (or developed offering) into a marketable product, service or message for profit.

This first part of the Productization process—defining some the features/functions of your idea, lets you actualize it, give it shape, context, components, both real and sometimes virtual 'parts,' that coalesce, and turn your idea into more than just a vague notion or passing thought. But more than that, your features/functions list clearly shows you what you have, and don't, and what you need to add to your idea to turn it into a product or service someone besides you wants. Even better, the words on your features/functions list can be used as direction and content for your branding and advertising campaigns, whether you create them, or hire someone else to create your marketing efforts for your new venture.

And don't forget, as with *all* Productization lists, the features/functions list is dynamic. **List 1A should be added to all the time**, with every new characteristic uncovered, and every update or upgrade released. Be sure to put this first list in your FEATURES and BENEFITS folder in your Startup Hierarchy, for easy access by you, or any stakeholders who may need it in the future.

Question 2: What Does It DO?

Now that we know where my software idea fits in the marketplace of sellable items, and some of the functions of my offering, it is taking shape, becoming something, other than just an idea in my head. It is important to remember, even if your idea is already developed into a product or service, performing Productization, each and every step, *in order*, will give you a list of content—keywords and phrases about your offering to use in your marketing efforts.

As an example of the process required to implement **Question 2: What does it DO**, we'll continue productizing *PHP Advocates*. Just like with the chainsaw example, where we took its features and transposed them into benefits, we're going to do the same thing with my software application. To identify the benefits of *PHP Advocates*, I'll take the functions of my software idea from List 1A, and transpose them into **benefits** and **solutions**.

Features/Functions and benefits are often interchangeable. A feature of ice cream is that it is cold. Sometimes, eating something cold is beneficial, but no one focuses on the fact that ice cream is cold. Most of us don't associate this feature of ice cream as a benefit. The benefit derived from cold ice cream, is it cools you off when you feel hot.

It is important to categorize features and benefits separately, and in this bullet list fashion, so you, and those you hire, have content for your marketing material —features, benefits and solutions—to tout in the branding and advertising process. You will use the words and phrases on List 1B, noting the benefits of your offering again and again in your ad campaigns and marketing material for pre-launch, roll-out launch, and beyond.

You will likely promote the benefits of your offering/s, software or cupcakes, with most all of your marketing efforts for the life-cycle of your business. **Productization List 1B** gives you, and those you hire, effective content to create branded marketing campaigns that tout the *best bits* of your unique product. The longer your list of benefits, the more likely you are to find target markets and users to sell your offering, and create *brand advocates* of your products, services, and, eventually, your company.

List 1B: List the BENEFITS of Your Offering

As with the chainsaw example, the benefits of my *PHP Advocates* application are derived—transposed—from its FUNCTIONS—Productization List 1A.

I've identified many benefits from my features/functions list. *PHP Advocates* primary function, the reason I thought of the idea in the first place, was a platform to connect those in need with professionals who can provide expert aid. This primary function of my application is also an obvious benefit, but I'm going to reword this function into a benefit for List 1B, to populate this list with **content** to use in my marketing efforts when I begin creating campaigns.

- FUNCTION: Expert advocates, actual *people* come to help you, or a loved one, *in-person,* anytime, anywhere.
- **BENEFIT**: *Get the help you need for you or loved ones for doctor visits, help with shopping, and in-home care, 24/7.*

- FUNCTION: Online, live video chat with professionals.
- **BENEFIT**: *Get professional tutoring, or expert business advice and guidance you need in minutes by a qualified industry professional in a variety of subjects, live, online.*

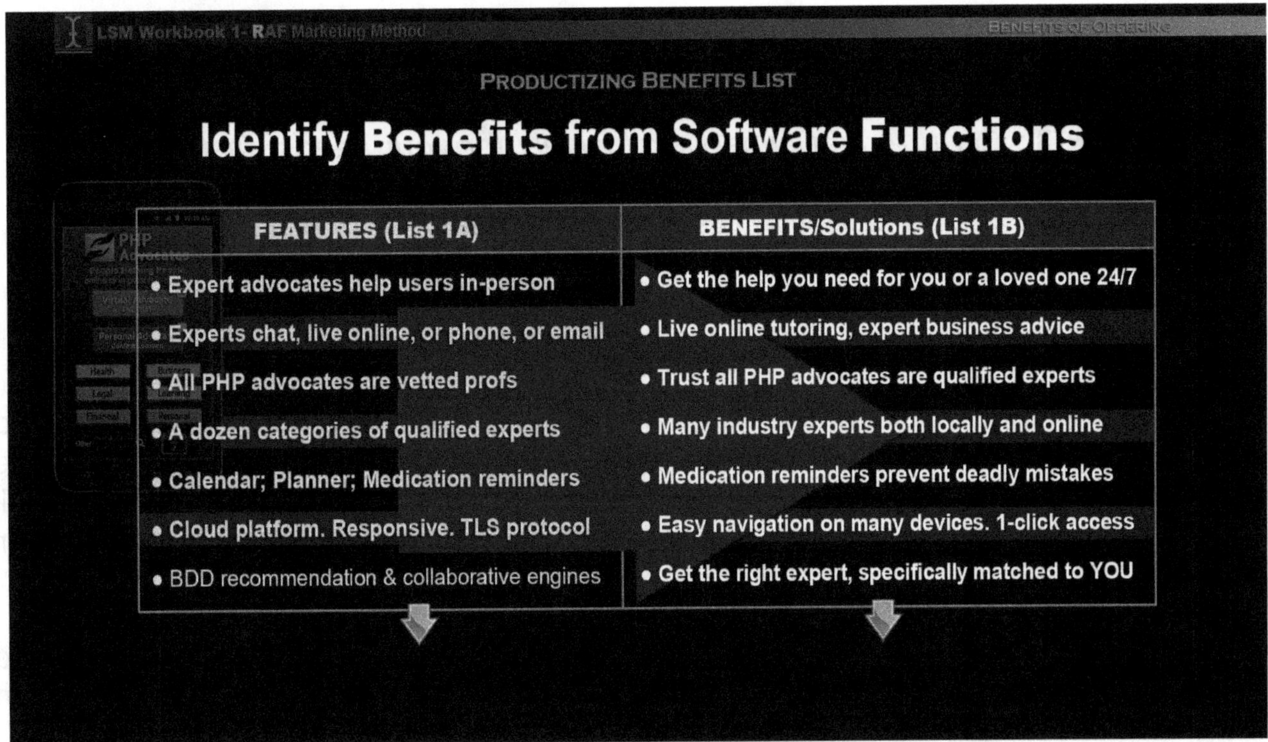

- FUNCTION: Over a dozen categories of experts online, or in-person.
- **BENEFIT**: *Get an RN to pick-up and take your aging mom to her medical appointments, and talk with her doctor about medications, as well as interactions, then relay this information directly back to you.*
- **BENEFIT**: *Or get a math teacher to come to your home for your teen, or teach him face-to-face online with weekly tutoring sessions.*

- **BENEFIT**: *Or find a dog-walker for your pooch, or talk to a veterinarian online to find out what medication your dog needs for his arthritic hips in seconds.*
- **BENEFIT**: *Or find an online or in-person workout partner, a physical therapist, in-home chef, or party caterer.*

- FUNCTION: All PHP Advocates are thoroughly vetted, with extensive background checks, and references.
- **BENEFIT**: *You can trust that all PHP Advocates will be qualified professionals in their area of expertise.*

- FUNCTION: Calendar with daily planner, as well as appointment and medication reminders.
- **BENEFIT**: *Medication reminders for you or a loved one help prevent deadly mistakes of under or over medicating.*
- **BENEFIT**: *Appointment reminders help you monitor your loved one's medical appointments, or tutoring lessons, to be sure they get where they need to be on time.*

- FUNCTION: Accurate recommendation system to match users to experts.
- **BENEFIT**: *Get the right expert exclusively for your needs, fast.*

- FUNCTION: Cloud platform, responsive UI, with TLS protocol for secure e-commerce.
- **BENEFIT**: *Simple to navigate across many devices, with one-click access. Easy payment method through application's secure platform.*

Just like the chainsaw example, I took my features/functions list, and determined what benefit each function of my software provides. At this stage in the Productization process, don't be too concerned about *who* your offering will benefit right now. We'll get to that next. For List 1B, just focus on aligning your features/functions with the benefits they provide.

As mentioned, there will be a lot of crossover between the features/functions and benefits of your offering. At times, they will seem one and the same. While an "Intuitive and engaging UI" are functions of most software with broad appeal, even *PHP Advocates*, these functions are also benefits. I can promote the functions of my software with the words: *Intuitive and Engaging UI,* in my marketing material targeted to developers or engineers. But I'll translate the functions into benefits, and add them to my 1B bullet list with words like *Easy to Learn, Simple to Use* when marketing to older, less tech-savvy targets.

After listing some of *your* offering's features/functions in List 1A, you must stop to consider how these features will likely benefit someone. Simply take your FEATURES list, and transpose them into BENEFITS, just like we did with the chainsaw, and my *PHP Advocates* application.

Even if you designed your offering with a direct benefit or solution for a specific target market, remember, you always need more customers, or users, to sell to. And each group of people you target with your offering, will find a different value or benefit in your product, service or message. So, be sure to be as thorough with List 1B, BENEFITS, of your offering, as you were with your features/functions list!

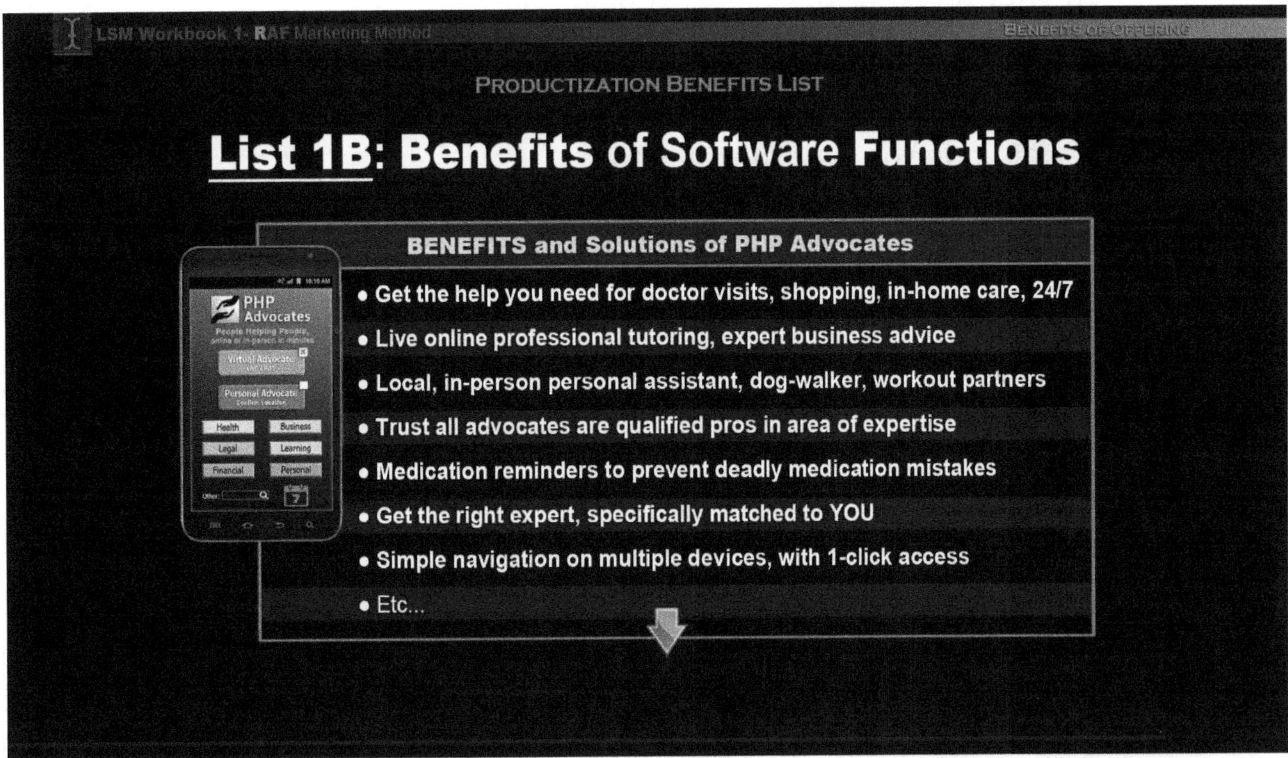

It's important to note that benefits and solutions are virtually the same. A benefit of *PHP Advocates* is that the app allows you to build teams of pros for your needs. This benefit can also be couched as a solution. Entrepreneurs are often solopreneurs—people who work on their own, usually out of their home. Working on their own, they lack the resources to employ needed personnel. With *PHP Advocates*, users can create a team of on-call consultants to help them anytime, 24/7 in fact.

Couching benefits as solutions requires at least *some* projection of who your target market is. *PHP Advocates* provides entrepreneurs (which is a target market) a solution to their lack of personnel and resources. We'll closely examine Target Marketing and Targeting Users in the following modules, but for List 1B:

BENEFITS, if you've no target market in mind yet, no problem. Focus your list on just the benefits your offering's features/functions provide.

List 1B: Benefits of *PHP Advocates*:

- Get help from an expert advocate for you or loved ones for doctor visits, help with shopping, in-home care.
- Get live, online professional tutoring, or the expert business advice and guidance you need in minutes, from a qualified industry professional.
- Local tutors, dog-walkers, workout partners, or personal assistants come to your home or business, to help you.
- You can trust that all PHP Advocates will be qualified professionals in their area of expertise.
- Medication reminders for you or a loved one help prevent deadly mistakes of under or over medicating.
- Get the right expert exclusively for your needs, fast.
- Simple to navigate across many devices, with one-click access.
- Easy payment method through application's secure platform.
- Etc...

Just like List 1A—my features/functions of *PHP Advocates*—for List 1B, I simply list as many benefits as I can conceive, that the functions of my SaaS app provides.

Once you've filled the benefits list with an initial set of bullet points of benefits and solutions that your offering's features/functions provide, be sure to save it in the F & B folder, under Productization lists inside your main GREAT IDEA folder. Make sure to adhere to your Startup Hierarchy, and put files in their specified locations to find files, documents and imagery fast and easily.

And remember, like all Productization lists, your offering's benefits, List 1B, should be added to continually. Every time a new benefit or solution is uncovered, a bullet point describing it should be added to Productization List 1B. Grow your benefits list over time, by consistently updating and upgrading the features/functions of your product or service. Don't forget, the third place startups fail is by not investing in R & D (research and development) of new offerings beyond their first success.

Access to all Productization lists should reside on your company's networked cloud, so they are available to the appropriate stakeholders as the need arises. From product development to marketing, Productization lists set up a foundation, a structure to your organization, that keeps everyone focused on selling the same thing—the *best bits*—benefits and solutions—of your offering and company.

MODULE 5: PRODUCTIZING SOFTWARE REVIEW

- To **productize software**, first, we segment it to fit in one of three marketable software categories: IaaS, PaaS, and SaaS.
    - **IaaS**—Infrastructure as a Service
    - **PaaS**—Platform as a Service
    - **SaaS**—Software as a Service

- The process of **Market Segmentation** helps us determine our software's '**Product/Market Fit**'—the specific type of program or application we are planning to market and sell.

- To determine software's '**Product/Market Fit**,' create a **software segmentation** schematic chart. Begin the schematic by parsing software into two commonly used segments: **Programs** and **Applications**.

- **Programs** are generally complex development tools, or graphic design tools like *Photoshop*, and generally utilized as **business to business** (**B2B**) tools.

- **Applications** usually refer to simpler programs, such as customer-facing mobile apps that are less expensive and easy-to-use. Applications can be B2B or **B2C** (**business to consumer**).

- Software FEATURES are [generally] called FUNCTIONS. In software, **Productization List 1A** is an ongoing bullet list of the FUNCTIONS of your potential offering.

- **Productization List 1B** are the BENEFITS potential users will derive from your software's FUNCTIONS.

- Whether selling software or cupcakes, or marketing your law practice or homeless advocates organization, **Productization Lists 1A and 1B** will give you **content—keywords and phrases** directly related to your offering—for your marketing campaigns *after* productizing your product, service, or nonprofit message.

- **Productization List 1A: FEATURES/FUNCTIONS**, and **Productization List 1B: BENEFITS/Solutions** of your offering, should be implemented *before* moving on to Target Marketing, targeting users, or creating marketing campaigns to promote and sell it.

-

-

STOP! Do CHALLENGE #9 before moving on.

CHALLENGE #9: Identify Real-World Productized Software

1. Go to Google Play: play.google(dot)com/store/apps

2. Find a SOFTWARE application (preferably one you use).
Suggestions:
- Music (*Spotify; Rock Hero; Dance*)
- Entertainment (*Netflix*; *Amazon Prime*; MMO Gaming)
- Education (required, or interest-based courses)
- Business (CMS*; CRM‡; Networking; Data Analytics)
- Peer-to-Peer (P2P) services (How-To; Experiences; Advise)

(*Content Management Systems; ‡Customer Relationship Management)

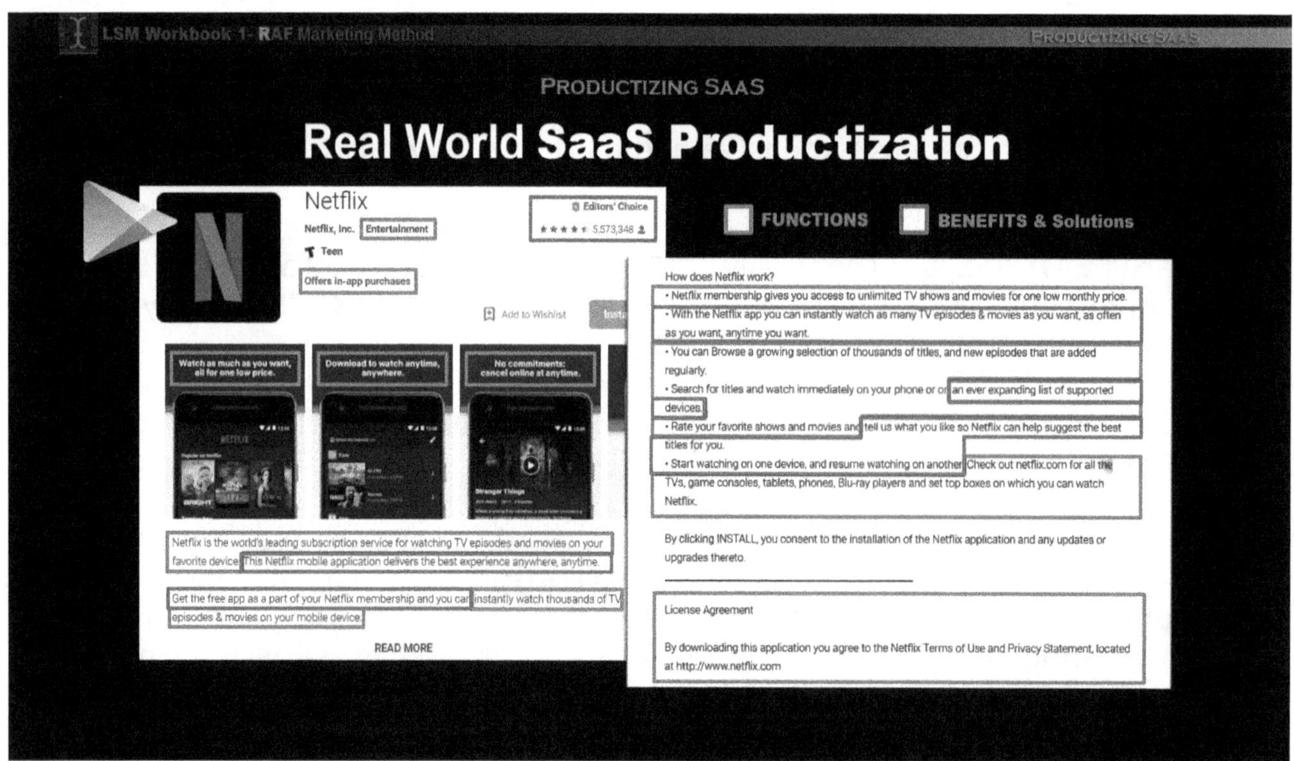

3. Study the sales page and find the BENEFITS of the software offering. They may be combined with functions, or separate, under READ MORE, or in the WHAT'S NEW section towards the bottom of the web page. If you read carefully, you will be able to discern the function from the benefit that function provides.

4. **List all the BENEFITS you find of your chosen application.** Make sure to write down the name of the software application you are using for this CHALLENGE, as well as the URL of the offering. Create a **bullet list of the benefits** you find, as the writing process will accelerate your learning! List ONLY benefits. Do *not* include the software's features/functions.

Examining how **features/functions**, **benefits** and **solutions** of a fully developed software application are used in real-world marketing, will give you insight into producing *your* offering's benefits' list. Produce **List 1B**: the **benefits** of your offering *after* completing this CHALLENGE!

Once the Productization process is implemented (because it is never 'complete,' since you will be adding to your lists all the time), you'll learn to take the **content** from List 1B, and create *your* branding and marketing campaigns. These will be used to promote the **benefits** and **solutions** that your offering provides, in LSB Workbook 2.

◆◆◆

WHO Will Find Benefit in the Features of Your Offering

Once you've created the first two of the eight required Productization lists to marketing your idea, or developed offering, you're ready to explore *who* your great new offering will serve. Walking the process of constructing List 1A: FEATURES, and 1B: FUNCTIONS, gives you insight into what you *think* you have to sell. If you come up with only a couple of features/functions for your projected offering, that have only a few benefits, it's likely you'll have to go back to the drawing board, and iterate your original idea, or even complete offering, and add more features/functions to derive more benefits that will serve a greater number of people. The more unique features your product, service, or message has, the more likely a large number of people will find benefits, or value in your offering.

At this point, you should have answered the first two of the three primary Productization questions:

1. **What IS it?** FEATURES/FUNCTIONS list.
2. **What does it DO?** BENEFITS/Solutions list.

Once you have a fairly extensive list of FEATURES and BENEFITS, you must determine WHO will likely benefit from the specific features of your offering. Discover how to find the *people* who will find interest and value in your offering, then identify what they like, and don't, where they hang out, and how to reach them with your marketing efforts, in the following module.

3. For WHO? (WHO will benefit from your offering?) TARGET MARKETS and USERS—Productization List 2A and 2B, next.

◆◆◆◆◆

MODULE 6: TARGET MARKETING

Why Typical Response Rates are So Low

Target Marketing is regarded as one of the most difficult bits of the Productization process. It's hard to figure out what people want, especially when we often don't know until we see it. You didn't know you wanted a cellphone until you were aware it existed. We often want things we know we shouldn't, like crappy snacks, or do things we know we shouldn't, like texting while driving. To complicate matters, with life events, and age, our desires are constantly changing, so even with the big data analytics of today, marketing, like psychology, is still more art than a science.

Humans are complicated. We're self-interested—involved with our jobs, our family and friends, our hobbies, our cellphones, which is why most marketing efforts go unnoticed. We must perform the Target Marketing process with every product, service, or message we conceive, to focus our branding and marketing campaigns at the most likely people who will find value in our offering. But even armed with today's behavioral data tracking, individual credit card purchases, mobile and internet usage—what sites we visit, what ads we click on—marketers still won't know ,what we will do next, what we *want* next, or even *why* we made the decisions we have.

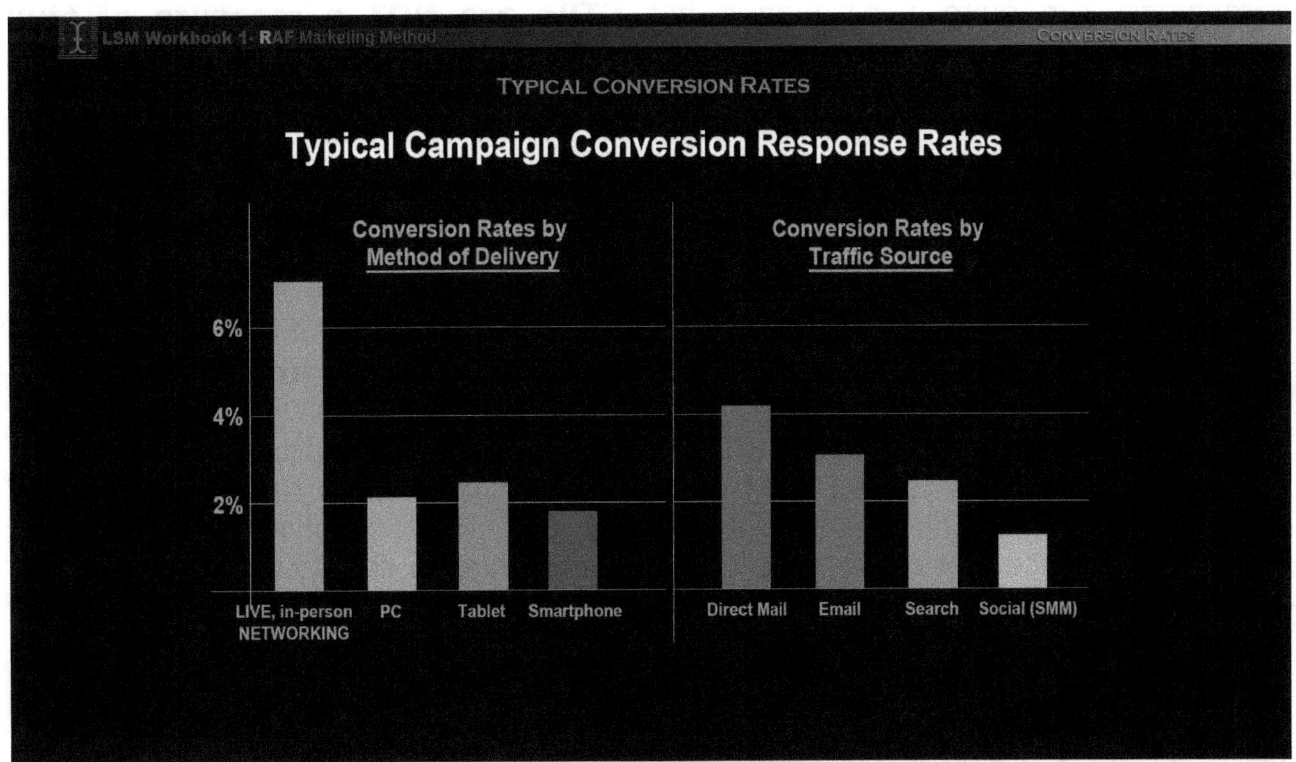

Response rates—the ACTIONS taken by the viewer in response to our branding and advertising campaigns—are surprisingly low, even with all the big data tracking and analysis going on. Additionally, response rates vary, depending on the industry, and the medium—whether it's a print, or digital campaign. Method of delivery—an *iPhone* verses a laptop—also plays a role in conversion rates.

Tightly targeting your marketing efforts will yield the greatest response rates, whatever the medium or method of delivery.

Typical response rates of conversion—getting someone to try, or buy our offering, or take the *action* our CTAs direct, like sign up for our company newsletter, typically run between **0.1 – 3%**.

Good response rates on any given campaign usually are between **3 - 7%**.

Great response rates on any given marketing effort are anything *above* the **5 – 7%** range. It's important to note—the best ROI on your marketing investment is not necessarily with digital campaigns. In particular, direct (snail) mail usually has good to great response rates, if targeted correctly. And it is a fact, the **best response rates come from networking in-person**, stepping out, shaking hands, delivering your elevator pitch to one or a group of people in front of you.

Click-Through [response] Rates (CTR)—getting clicks on your digital campaigns—run quite a bit higher, but **CTRs are NOT a measure of true conversion**. *Actual* conversion is getting the viewer to *act* on the specific directive of the campaign, take the *action* (beyond clicking on the button or link in the ad or post) that your CTA directs, like getting sign-ups, or trial downloads, or even purchases of your offering/s.

The Target Marketing Process

We've turned our idea, or developed product into an offering of *value* once we've identified: **What our offering IS, what our offering DOES, and for WHO?**

Target Marketing is the second phase of the Productization process. We use the features and benefits (phase one) of our offering, and align them to groups of potential users who will have a desire fulfilled, or a problem solved from using our product or service. For many people, giving money to a charity, or their religious organization, helps them feel magnanimous, benevolent, which is the benefit or value of giving charitable donations.

So far, we've defined my *PHP Advocates* offering by a few of its features and benefits, therefore effectively turning it into a *potential* product or service, assuming we haven't produced the actual offering yet. However, to make it into an offering of *value*, we must project *who* will find a purpose, or worth, in the offering we hope to market and sell.

If your offering is already produced, and you don't know who, *specifically*, will find value in your product, service, or message, figuring out your target audiences *now* (as opposed to not doing it at all), is better late than never! If you are only targeting one group of people for your offering, the target marketing process will help you identify many more users to market it to. And remember, **tightly targeted branding and marketing campaigns have the best conversion rates**—getting people to *act* on your CTAs—buy; sign-up; subscribe.

Remember the Conversion Funnel in Module 2: Marketing 101? Before the conversion process begins, we must determine *who* we are trying to convert, or sell to. No matter what we *think* our product, service, or message has to offer the *world*, everyone on the planet is not going to find value in our offering. Planet Earth is NOT a target market.

Branding, advertising, and marketing dollars should be spent on attracting the *most likely* groups of people who may be interested in what we are selling. These likely groups are called our **target markets**.

The Target Marketing process begins with **market segmentation**, or identifying potential markets, or *broad groupings of people* for our offering. Remember, marketing starts wide and drills down to the individual. And it's important to keep in mind, we are *never* selling to target MARKETS. We are always selling to PEOPLE, or a particular target audience/user. Even if we are selling to many groups of people, we must categorize, or segment them separately, then target our marketing to each group differently, with what excites or may interest them.

Social media platforms, like *Instagram*, *Pinterest* or *Facebook*, often have a broad cross-section of users, but even so, not *everyone* on the planet uses them. Their enormous base of users grew organically, but also, strategically. When *Facebook* first came online, their target market was Harvard students only, then universities across the U.S., then they opened their platform to universities beyond the U.S. After that, they invited high school students to log on, then expanded their user-base to employees of several companies, including *Apple* and *Microsoft*. In all cases, *Facebook* went after *specific groups of people*—target markets—to sell their offering, and initiate the conversion/sales process.

Step 1: The Market Segmentation Process

To identify potential target markets for *your* offering, begin by segmenting people using four main data sources:

- **Demographic data**, meaning age, sex, race, education level, income level, marital status, occupation, religion. Think of demographics as the features of a person.

- **Geographic data** is location, urban/rural, ethnicity, climate, environmental conditions. Geographics is where we live, the communities we exist in, live and online.

- **Psychographic data** is psychological data, such as personality traits, values, religion, political orientation, attitudes, interests, and lifestyles. Since psychology is the foundation of marketing—manipulating people to *act* on our CTAs (calls-to-action)—it is extremely important that we think about who these people *are*—what they like and don't, what they buy, where they hang out, with who, and why.

- **Behavioral data** is the *next big [Silicon Valley] thing*. Actually, it's here! We are all being tracked around the internet, as well as offline when we make purchases with our credit cards, or write a check, or even open a bank or mobile account. We *are* the product, regardless if we are buying an offering, or just internet surfing. **Affiliate marketing** (which we'll examine in the last module of this workbook) pays billions annually for our information, to advertise to you what their data analysis determines you want.

Our purchase data, web-surfing habits, clicks on links, our tweets, mobile texts, social updates and posts are being mined, collected and analyzed to help marketers figure out what each of us wants to buy, (or what we will buy into), what we're likely to give a try, believe in, and even think about at any given point in the day. We know you are more likely to think about coffee in the morning, and a sugary treat in mid-afternoon. We know you are more likely to purchase something frivolous on the weekends, or a Friday, than any other day of the week.

The privacy train has left the station, and there is no going back. Beyond just our personal behavior, *Google, Facebook, Instagram...etc.,* also tracks the behavior of the family and friends we are connected to online. Then, they correlate *your* behavior with your connections, because it is more likely you'll influence, or *be* influenced to purchase or view the same, or similar offerings by those you know. In fact, **correlation engines** are more powerful than data mining and analysis of individuals.

In our globalized marketplace, where I can get cupcakes made in L.A. delivered to my office in Beijing in 24 hours, geographic data is less significant than ever, as is much of the demographic data, like gender, age, race...etc. In most cases this data is too broad to use for effective targeting. We can't motivate an entire race, or age group, or gender to do what we want them to.

The two most popular data sources today are Psychographic and Behavioral, to *'get inside our head,'* and find out what we are likely to do next, and want next. Never forget, you are *always* marketing to people, *not* markets. The more we learn about the *individual*, the more likely we are to, first, find them—identify the places they hang out, online, and in-person—and then *sell* them on our offerings.

Find and Target Your Lowest Hanging Fruit

We'll get to creating **Productization List 2A: Target Markets** for your offering in a minute, but first, let's find out how to bring the Target Marketing process beyond market segmentation, which, as discussed, has limited utility. To identify our initial target markets, we start with a lot of guesswork on *who* these broad groupings of people might be. We'll drill down to the individual, once we've identified broad markets that we project our offering will serve.

Begin by thinking back to when you conceived, or heard of the original idea that you're in the process of marketing. It's likely your idea was sparked by a desire—yours, or maybe someone you know.

I came up with the idea for *PHP Advocates* when I was visiting with a friend at her mother's retirement home near Sacramento, California. My friend lamented that living so far away, it was impossible to assist her mother at doctor's appointments, or even to get her mom to the physical therapist she needed for her new hip replacement. My friend is a well-paid Hollywood executive, and can easily afford to hire help for her mom, if she "just knew someone qualified" she could trust, she told me. On my drive back to San Francisco that evening, I mulled over the types of mobile applications that would help my friend get qualified, trusted assistance for her aging mother. That's when my fictitious application, *PHP Advocates,* began forming inside my head.

Wherever your idea comes from, there is a *reason* you thought of it. Likely, you became aware of a problem, as I did when I thought up *PHP Advocates*. The fact is, even if you thought of an idea to fulfill a desire that, as far as you know, only *you* have, you've just identified at least one target market. YOU are a specific type of person, with specific characteristics, that put you in a social class, or group of people with similar characteristics, and therefore likely have some of the same desires as you have.

'Top-down' marketing is when we already have an idea of who our projected audience might be. In my case, it's me, and my friend, and mid-life women like us with aging parents. My most likely target market for *PHP Advocate* is already defined. Thing is, I need a *lot* more people to sell to, than just the group like me if I want to create a sustainable business.

If you have no clue who your target market may be, use *you!* Identify characteristics in *you* that will find value in your offering, to begin the Target Marketing process for your projected product, service, or message. The more markets you come up with, that will likely have *some* interest in what you are selling, the greater the response will be to your marketing efforts.

I start a list of potential target markets for *PHP Advocates*. I begin my list with the most obvious markets for my offering, also known as the "lowest hanging fruit." This includes the groups of people I originally thought would benefit from my offering, as well as groups of people like me. I continue listing potential markets for my app, populating the rest of my list with groups that seem less likely to use it, at least for the initial launch of my software.

As stated, I already had a target market in mind, when I came up with *PHP Advocates*. *Children of Aging Parents* are my most likely broad target market for my fictitious application. When I originally conceived the idea for the app, I was trying to solve the problem my friend had articulated, as the *mid-life child of an aging parent*.

Since my friend and I both have aging parents, I first considered what features/functions *I'd* want in a mobile application that could help *my* folks? My imagination played with the idea of this mobile app, and considered other functions that could benefit people with related issues. Beyond helping my parents, what kind of help did I consistently need? What kind of assistance do I want from vetted industry experts, both in-person *and* online?

These types of question are essential to ask yourself, when projecting the initial target markets for your offering. But marketing a new offering isn't exclusive to *your* needs, or people just like you. In fact, if there are not a *lot* of others who'll probably find value in your product, service or message, you likely don't have a sellable/marketable product, yet.

While the process of Target Marketing helps us identify groups of people to market our offering to, it also gives us insight into the strength *and* weaknesses of the features and functions of what we plan to sell. If our offering has limited value for most people, or benefits only one small group, we must iterate our product or service, if we plan to realize a sustainable startup. Create more features/functions that will benefit more people. (If, however, you simply want to sell your software in a licensing agreement to a technology company, iterating your very tightly targeted offering may be unnecessary, as long as your product or service fulfills a direct need of your specific target user).

Let's imagine the idea for your offering was conceived to solve a problem or fulfill a desire of your initial 'top down' *low hanging* target market, as my application, *PHP Advocates,* was. You've begun your first two Productization lists, and identified many features and benefits your projected offering will have that will likely serve your initial market. This particular target market is the "size of Texas," (a popular marketing colloquialism), and your product aligns perfectly, i.e., has great 'product/market fit,' without changing it, as *PHP*. *Children of aging parents* are currently a huge percentage of the population, with the Baby Boomer generation becoming parental caretakers. While this target market is easily large enough to provide a healthy launch for my software application without having to iterate it much, I'm going to continually need *more* markets, that translate into users, to sell to, to support the growth of my business.

If you want to build a *sustainable* startup, you too will continually need to find more people who will likely find value in your offering/s to sell to.

How do we find these mythical target markets and user for our offering/s, beyond just us, or people like us? Well, we can build a prototype of our idea, and test-market it. But that would take a lot of time, and may be rather expensive. We can put together an **MVP** (**minimum viable product**), and do a test launch, get our target users to download it, then wait for them to point out, i.e., cuss us out, when they find bugs. MVP may be a trending launch model, but it is a *bad* marketing strategy. The initial offering from any startup must be as great as their pre-launch and launch marketing promises, to initiate a successful launch, and build a sustainable company. Remember, the second place startups fail is *launching without infrastructure to support brand, or fulfillment* of the offering functioning as promised.

Psychographic and Behavioral data analysis are useful tools to help us more tightly align the features of our offerings with *who* will find benefit from using them. However, collecting the amount of data required to have any significant impact on conversion rates requires tracking our user's behavior over time. At this stage in your startup development, you likely have no users, or the number of users you need to utilize the data you collect effectively, *yet*.

An easy path to discover our most likely target markets for our pre-launch, and launch marketing efforts beyond our small circle of friends and family, is to transpose Productization List 1A, the FEATURES, and List 1B, the BENEFITS of our offering into *who* will likely find value in using it.

The benefits of your projected offering were derived from its features. You'll derive your target markets from your benefits list, in much the same way. You'll find target users, the actual *people* likely to purchase your offering from your target markets list. First, let's focus on populating List 2A with your offering's list of potential target markets.

LIST 2A: Identify your Target MARKETS

The initial Target Marketing process follows the same paradigm as populating your benefits lists. Start with List 1B—the BENEFITS of your offering, and align each bullet point on your list, to groups of people who will likely find value in your product, service or message.

Begin by asking yourself what *groups of people*—target markets—will find benefits in the features/functions of your offering? Break these targets down demographically and geographically, i.e. women (as opposed to men), their age range, race, income level, where they live...etc. Remember, marketing starts wide and drills down to target customers/users. We'll get on to identifying their psychographic and behavioral characteristics, after we've identified some broad target markets.

Each of your offering's features and benefits serves *some* group of people. Target Marketing *begins* with projecting, essentially *guessing*, segmented groups of people that will likely be interested in the benefits of your offering.

Still using my *PHP Advocates* application as the example to illustrate the Target Marketing process, each of my application's benefits translates into someone, somewhere, who will likely find utility in them. Let's consider who these groups of people—*PHP Advocate's* target markets—may be.

I begin with the first bullet entry on my BENEFITS list, List 1B:

- BENEFIT: *Get help from an expert advocate for you or loved ones for doctor visits, help with shopping, in-home care.*

I align this benefit of my application with broad groupings of people who can likely use it:

- **TARGET MARKET**: *Women (over men 2 : 1) of Elderly Parents. 45 – 70 yrs old. Upper income. Caucasian. Asian. College degree.*
- **TARGET MARKET**: *Temporarily injured, or permanently disabled. 21 – 75 yrs old. Mid-upper income.*

Since I designed my application to aide people like my friend and me, the lowest hanging fruit for my software is *Children with Elderly Parents*. *Women* is a very broad target market, but an important distinction in the Target Marketing process. Sociologically, women are usually the primary caretakers of aging parents, whether their own folks, or their husband's parents. *Upper-income* is also very broad, but important to note, since one of the best functions of my application is people helping people *in-person*, which can get very expensive, depending on the advocate's expertise, and the user's needs. Hiring a registered nurse (RN) to help my mom at her doctor visits would be costly. *Caucasian* and *Asian* women are likely to have more money than other ethnic groups, which is why this race distinction is made. Additionally, women are more likely to ask for help over men 2:1, so *women* are one of the "low hanging fruits" I'll approach with *PHP Advocate's* marketing efforts. Marketing to women is usually different, requires different words and images, than marketing to men.

The age range of *45 – 70* is demographic data, and gives me a good idea who this group of women is, likely Baby Boomers born in the 1950s to 1960s, with attitudes and viewpoints typical of that generation. This data also gives me direction in designing my app's **user interface** (**UI**). The UI navigation needs to be easy to read for aging adults—simple buttons with large text—since many older adults have poor vision.

My second target market entry: *Temporarily injured, or permanently disabled*, is one I'd not considered when I first came up with *PHP Advocates*. But, of course, my application is made for them as well, as often people with recent injuries are can not drive, or even get to public transportation. Sure they could call *Uber* or *Lyft*, or some other car service, but they could not get the personalized service I project my app will have. My advocates can run into the pharmacy to pick up their prescriptions, or in just a few clicks on my user-friendly UI, *PHP Advocates* can get them a registered physical therapist, or a professional exercise trainer to come to their home.

I align the next bullet point on my benefits list with a potential market:

- BENEFIT: Get the live, online professional tutoring, or expert business advice and guidance you need in minutes by a qualified industry professional in a variety of subjects.

- **TARGET MARKETS**: *Entrepreneurs. Solopreneurs. Home office pros. 21- 65. Mid-upper income.*
- **TARGET MARKETS**: *Students. Male/Female. 21- 70. Low – upper income.*

People who work on their own often need a wide variety of expert resources to conduct business on a competitive level. One of *PHP Advocates* projected functions is to have experts across multiple disciplines, so entrepreneurs, and work-at-home pros become additional target markets I hadn't originally considered, when I thought of an application to help my aging parents.

The age range of 21 – 65 is far too broad to have any real significance, but it gives me some ideas on who these people may be. Recent college graduates looking to start their own gig, or older adults who have aged out of the job market and must make their own job to pay the never-ending bills are additional targets to consider marketing my *PHP Advocates* application.

Students has no real significance either, since anyone, at any time, can be a student, especially with online courses. But I project a feature of my app will be professional tutoring, or even online courses down the line. Recognizing this market, reminds me of this projected feature, and therefore benefit, of my software. I've added *Male/Female* and *Low – upper income* for reference only. When the projected target market has no specific distinction, such as either sex, any income or any race is applicable, it is unnecessary to include it in your bullet list.

I align the next bullet point, and the next, and so on, from my benefits list with other potential markets:

- BENEFIT: You can trust that all PHP Advocates will be qualified professionals in their area of expertise.

- **TARGET MARKETS**: *Child of aging parents. 45 – 70. Upper income. Caucasian. Asian. College degree.*
- **TARGET MARKETS**: *Parent of tweens, teens, or newborns. 25 – 65. Mid - upper income.*
- **TARGET MARKETS**: *Students, and business pros. 18 – 70.*

It is fine to repeat a target market in this initial Target Marketing process. In fact, it's preferable, as it gives you a good idea who your strongest targets may be.

As a child of an aging parent, I want to be sure that whoever I hire to take care of my parents will be vetted, qualified pros. Beyond this already identified target market, *Parents* want to make sure that their child is safe, when bringing a tutor into their home, or even face-to-face online. We'll drill down on who these parents are, what they like, and don't, next. But first, I need a *lot* more broad markets than these to derive a long list of potential users. I align my next BENEFIT bullet point.

- BENEFIT: Medication reminders for you or a loved one help prevent deadly mistakes of under or over medicating.

- **TARGET MARKETS**: *Children of aging parents on medication.*
- **TARGET MARKETS**: *Parent or loved one of child on medication. 25 – 70. Middle – upper income.*
- **TARGET MARKETS**: *Prescription drug takers. 21 – 70. Middle – upper income.*

Children and/or adults on prescription medication can use this benefit of *PHP Advocates* to assure they take the proper amount at the proper times of day. Additionally, this function/benefit of my software has extended my target markets to middle-income users, since they are on medication just as much as upper-income folks. I align my next BENEFIT bullet point.

- BENEFIT: Simple to navigate across many devices, with one-click access.
- BENEFIT: Easy payment method through application's secure platform.

- **TARGET MARKETS**: *Older, mobile users of P2P services. 40 – 70. Prescription glasses. Mid - upper income.*

Older mobile users who conduct business or personal transactions, like online purchases or banking, are a broad, and rapidly growing demographic of the global population. What these tech-savvy adults *do* online will be far more useful behavioral data for targeting potential *users*, but, as with all marketing, the Target Marketing process starts with very broad groupings of people, and drills down to the individual.

Productization List 2A: TARGET MARKETS for *PHP Advocates:*
- Women of aging parents (over men 2 : 1). 40 – 70 yrs old. $$$$. Caucasian. Asian. College degree.
- Temporarily injured, or permanently disabled. 21 – 75. $$- $$$$. Caucasian. Asian. College degree.
- Entrepreneurs. Solopreneurs. Home office pros. 21- 65. $$ - $$$$.
- Students. Business professionals. 18 – 70. $ – $$$$.

- Parent of tweens or teens. New mom or dad. 25 – 65. $$ - $$$$.
- Children of aging parents on medication. 40 – 70 yrs old. $$ - $$$$.
- Parent of child or loved one on medication. 25 – 70. $$ - $$$$.
- Prescription drug takers. 21 – 70. $$ - $$$$.
- Older, mobile users of P2P services. 40 – 65. $$ - $$$$.
- ...Etc.

Each of *PHP Advocates* features, benefits and solutions, taken directly from their Productization lists I created earlier, solves a problem, an issue, fulfills a desire or adds value to someone's life. Targeting Marketing—creating broad groupings of people who will likely find value in our offering—is how we *begin* to identify who these people are. But to really get to know them, what they like, and don't, what attracts them, how to reach them, and effectively manipulate them to do what *we* want, requires getting *personal* with the individual.

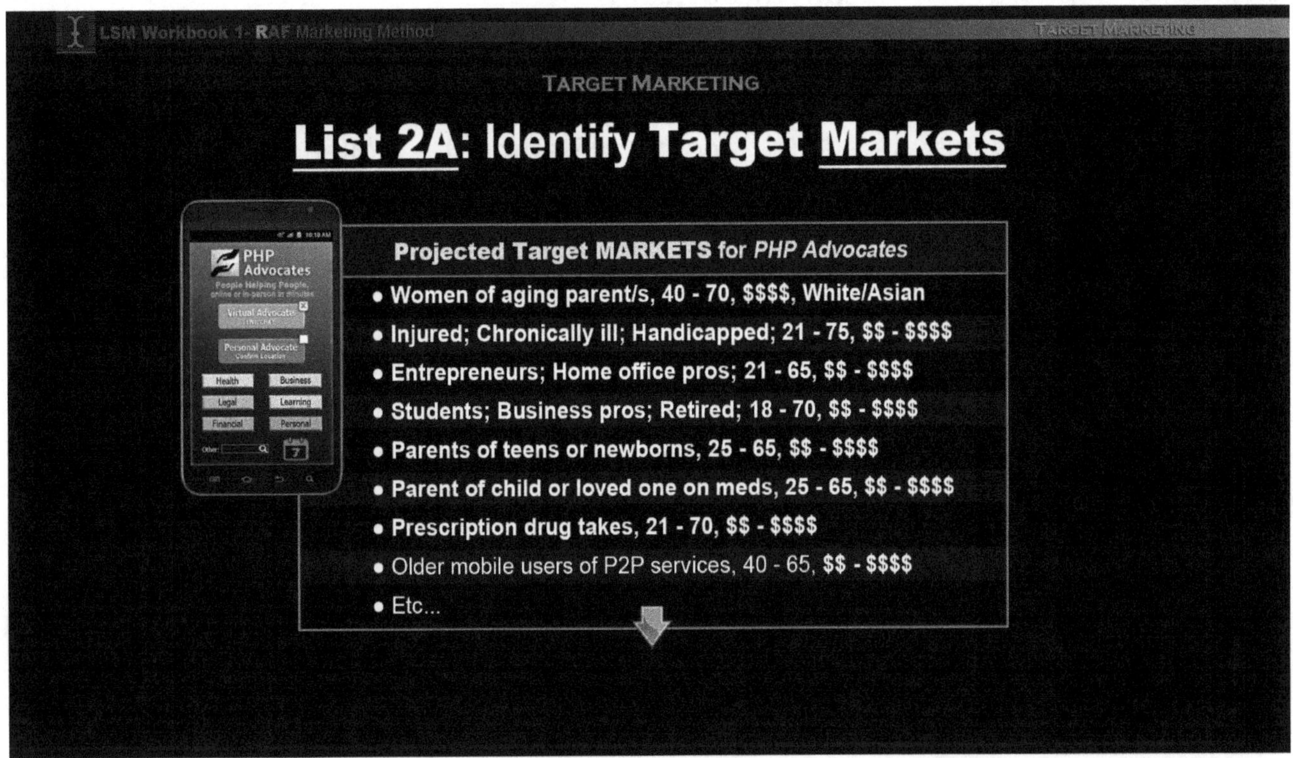

Remember, we are *never* selling, or even marketing to markets. We are always trying to reach individual people, hoping to trigger each person that views our campaigns, to act on our CTAs.

-

-

STOP! Do CHALLENGE #10 before moving on.

◆◆◆

CHALLENGE #10: Engage in Target Marketing

1. **Pick a popular product, service, or brand you do NOT use.** (I don't use *Uber*, or *Sephora*. I have my own car, and I don't wear make-up.) Review their website, as well as some of their marketing efforts, which you can find with a *Google* search, "X-company advertising," as well as campaigns that you see in print, or online.

2. **List Demographic, Geographic, Psychographic, and Behavioral characteristics** of the lowest hanging fruit, or the *most likely* **target market** for the offering you chose. (This group of people may or may not be the target audience the company is already targeting with their marketing.)

Example: *Sephora*; www.sephora(dot)com

Projected Target Market (lowest hanging fruit)

- **Demographics**: Female. 15 – 55. Single. Dating. Newly Married/Divorced. New mom, or no kids, yet. $$ - $$$$ income. HS student – College educated. White-collar career, admin to c-level executive.

- **Geographics**: City or suburb dweller, within 40 mi of major east or west coast metropolis. Trending or 'good' (expensive) neighborhoods.

- **Psychographics**: She likes to be noticed, even envied for her appearance. She rarely leaves the house without putting on makeup, which she believes she needs to look acceptable. She consistently feels judged by others, and worries about the impression she's made in business and social events. Makeup is often her 'mask' of confidence.

- **Behavioral**: She has both professional, and weekend/play attire. She bought seven pairs of heels the last year, and wears them to work and dating (according to her *Facebook* post—a selfie before her date last week). She frequents trendy eateries, dance and music venues, and is on her iPhone from waking till sleeping. She's on most popular social media platforms, from *Instagram* to *Pinterest*. Most of her electronic devices, from her phone to laptop, are *Apple* products. Much of her disposal income is spent on entertainment and fashion, with most purchases made though her mobile.

This is the process of **Target Marketing**—finding groups of people who will likely find benefits in your offering's features/functions. Identifying target markets for a product, service or brand you do NOT use, will demand you step outside of *your* desires, and examine the characteristics and psychology of people who are different from you.

◆◆◆

Visual Targeting

As stated, I am a visual learner. Most sighted people are. While our Productization lists can be translated into many languages, subtle complexities in communication get lost in translation. It would take many words to describe a complex story, that one visual can often express without any text at all. It is extremely important that you, and those you hire, have a clear understanding of your target markets and users, as all your marketing efforts must be tightly targeted to get greater response, and eventually more sales.

Visual targeting is a way of mitigating miscommunication between you and those you hire, in any country, and most any language. To produce tightly targeted marketing for your new venture, every stakeholder involved in creating campaigns for your company must know *who* will likely find value—both real and perceived benefits—from the features/functions of your offering/s.

Engaging in the visual targeting process is similar to translating features to benefits, or benefits to target markets. Since I now have some target markets in mind for *PHP Advocates*—Productization List 2A, I use them as broad topic classifiers to search *Google* and *Bing* for imagery that visually identifies these broad target markets, or groups of people with similar tastes and characteristics who will likely find value in my app.

To create a visual targeting graphic, simply take List 2A, and use your bullet points of keywords and phrases as search terms to find and collect pictures of the types of people for each target market you've identified on your list. Pay close attention to details like race, sex, age, and other apparent demographic characteristics, when picking images to add to your collection of potential target markets. Many stakeholders will be using this graphic for direction, on how to position your marketing efforts to tightly target potential users. It must be as graphically specific, as unambiguous as possible, to clearly identify who these people are.

It is very important to focus each marketing effort on **only one target market per campaign**. (The step-by-step process of creating tightly targeted branding and advertising will be closely examined in LSB Workbook 2.) Remember, the more tightly we target our marketing efforts, the more likely we are to motivate potential users to *act* on the CTAs in our campaigns.

Using my *PHP Advocates* app as the example, I create a visual Target Marketing graphic. This graphic will help me, and those I hire, to remember the groups of people I've already identified (Productization List 2A), to tightly target all my marketing efforts directly at each group. I'll add to this graphic when additional target markets reveal themselves through the response to my initial pre-launch and launch campaigns.

In the case of *PHP Advocates*, my most obvious target market is *Children of Aging Parents*. My largest pictures, my lowest hanging fruit, will be of *mid-life, stylish White and Asian women, 45 – 65*, in their executive office, or with their aging parent. I place less likely target images smaller, like pictures of 20-something *entrepreneurs*, and *college students*. I put a very small image of a *grandma* on her mobile on my graphic of target markets. Cellphone use among older adults is a rapidly growing market.

The visual Targeting Marketing graphic for your offering should be one, or several slides, not only to simplify communication on who your target markets are, but also as part of your pitch presentation, to demonstrate that you have a variety of markets in which to sell your offering/s. The largest images on your slide should be your lowest hanging fruit, your most likely target markets.

Continue this process of aligning each target market in List 2A, with images of the types of people you've identified in your bullet point text. Populate each slide of your visual targeting graphic with 4 – 7 (max.) specific pictures of your projected markets, for every offering you actualize. Since you are always selling to actual people, not markets, you'll describe these people in Targeting Users next, and it's much easier to describe something with its image in front of you.

Put Productization List 2A, and your visual Target Marketing slides, in your Target Markets folder of your Startup Hierarchy, for easy access by you, and all stakeholder involved in the marketing of your new venture.

MODULE 6: TARGET MARKETING REVIEW

- **TARGET MARKETING** is the second phase of the Productization process, because we use the features and benefits (phase one) of our product, service, or message, and align them to *groups* of potential users likely to find value in our offering.

- **Target markets** are broad groupings of people with similar characteristics and desires, that will likely find benefits or solutions in the features of our offering.

- To identify potential **target markets** for our offering, we segment people using **four main data sources**:
    - **Demographic** data—age, sex, race, education level, income level, marital status, occupation, religion.
    - **Geographic** data—location, ethnicity, climate, and environmental conditions of potential customers.
    - **Psychographic** data—psychological data, such as personality traits, values, attitudes, political orientation, interests, religion, beliefs, and lifestyles.
    - **Behavioral** data—purchase data, customer loyalty, web-surfing habits, clicks on links, social media posts and updates, search keywords and phrases, etc., virtually anything you do, or post on the internet. Even live purchases, like restaurant meals, are tracked, correlated and sold to affiliate networks.

- To find **target markets**, begin with the "lowest hanging fruit"—the most obvious broad group of people likely to benefit from the features in your offering. Briefly describe each **market** in **List 2A** (even if it's just you, as *you* are a *type of person*), using the **four main data sources** marketing uses to broadly segment people.

- We derive **target markets** from the benefits the features of our offering provide for particular broad groupings of people.

- Creating a **visual Target Marketing graphic** is an effective way to communicate the target markets you have in mind, that will benefit from the features of your offering.

- The **Target Marketing process** is imperative to implement during Productization for startup success, because it identifies likely groups of people who will find value in our offering to focus our marketing efforts.

-

-

-TARGETING USERS-

Get Intimate With Your Target Markets

At this point, you should have initiated Productization Lists 1A: FEATURES, and 1B: BENEFITS of your offering, and begun Productization List 2A, the initial projected TARGET MARKETS for your product, service, message, or application. But you must remember, you are *never* selling to target *markets*. Every campaign you create, branding or advertising, must be directed at a tightly targeted audience of actual *people*, to get them to act as your marketing directs.

Targeting users, or the actual people likely to be interested in what we have to offer, are derived from List 2A, our TARGET MARKETS list. To identify target users for our offering, we drill down to individuals within our broad markets, to help us define who these people actually *are*. Through behavioral data of purchases, our clicks on ads, social posts and the emojis we use, our likes and shares, location (GPS) tracking on our cellphones, to the sites we visit and engage with frequently, marketers now know a LOT about us. They know where most of us live and work, what we're doing at any given point during the day, what we buy, watch, listen to, and talk about. They know what we do for a living, how much we earn, what we believe in, or don't, how old we are, our race, religion, political affiliation. We know quite a bit about the individual these days. And with machine learning algorithms, establishing correlations between what *you* do, and those you are connected to do, we're learning more about you, your friends and family by the day, hour, minute, second.

Most all major corporations are collecting big-data these days, because data analysis can and does increase conversion rates, with the *right data*. However, much of today's analytics is "*garbage in >> garbage out,*" so be mindful not to rely too heavily on statistics. THINK about the types of people who will benefit from the features/functions of your offering. Use the four main data sources as prompts to clearly, and specifically, segment your potential target markets *and* users.

Still using my *PHP Advocates* as the Productization example, we know from my target markets list, that *Women* are a primary market for my application. Though men will probably be a good percentage of the experts on the site, women will more likely be the users, since women are more inclined to ask for help, for their parents and themselves, than men. But women are close to half the population on Earth...And it's impossible to effectively market to half the planet. So, we need to get more intimate with the individual women *PHP* will likely serve.

Take any two women of the same race, religion, socioeconomic background—grew up in a typical U.S. middle-class home—even living in the same general location. One of the women is 63. The other woman is 23. This age difference makes virtually everything else about them quite different. Much of their demographic data is different, from their marital status, to their education, job title and current income level. Most of their Psychographic and Behavioral data, from what they like to do, read, watch, as well as who they interact with, both in-person and online, is radically different. They both may be located in the Seattle area, but the younger woman likely lives in the city, or is a campus dweller, while the older woman is living in the suburbs, so their geographic data may have subtle differences. They both are avid cellphone users, though they visit different sites, and utilize different mobile applications and platforms.

The *actions*, known as *'events'* in data science, these two women take, will categorize them as individuals through analysis of their behavioral data, from their purchases, to the websites they visit, to their credit rating.

It is important to note, "data," that gives us insights into our target users, is not only derived through big-data aggregation and analysis. THINK about your offering, the features/functions, benefits and solution of what you've conceived, and the characteristics of the people most likely to use your offering. Psychographic and Behavioral data can be derived from analyzing your family, friends, and colleagues behavior. OBSERVE what people *really* do, not what we *say* we'll do. Consider *why* people take the actions we do. Categorize behavior by *actions*, even if it's just *vocalizing* an ideology, like a political viewpoint, or their standpoint on immunizing children, or global warming.

We'll drill down on finding and communicating with your target users throughout all three LSE Workbooks. But what is the purpose of extensively researching, then segmenting all this data, to create lists of potential target markets and users?

To create a *sustainable* business, you need a constant stream of different people who'll find value in what you are selling. And, of course, the tighter your marketing efforts target *individual behavior*—their likes, dislikes, concerns, issues, desires—the more likely you are to sell your offering. But beyond these previously discussed factors, figuring out who your target users *are* will give you clues about where to find them, and how to manipulate them with your marketing efforts. While a 21 year old woman will be engaged with social media, it's likely she's on *SnapChat*, or *YouTube*, as opposed to the 60 year old woman sharing pictures of her new grandchild on *Facebook*. Getting *intimate* with your target markets is essential to reaching your target users with your marketing efforts.

Targeting users is the process of identifying patterns of behavior in broadly segmented groups of people—our target markets. Effective marketing finds the triggers that get *individuals* to act, and then develops advertising and marketing with primers that manipulate/motivate us to purchase, sign-up, subscribe, or buy.

List 2B. Targeting Actual PEOPLE

Target USERS are the actual *people* within a specific target market.

It is likely that you can't afford access to big-data collection and analytics during the startup process. No worries! You can still identify and even *reach* the people who'll likely find value in your offering, by simply translating your target markets into target users. In much the same way we derived our BENEFITS (List 1B) from our FEATURES (List 1A), identifying target USERS (List 2B) requires honing in on the members in each of the broadly segmented target MARKETS (List 2A), and further refining their characteristics to project the *types of people* who will likely find value in our offering/s.

Still using my *PHP Advocates* app as the example, I can identify specific characteristics about my potential users from my target markets list.

I begin with the first bullet point entry on my TARGET MARKETS list, List 2A, and align this target with the *individuals* most likely to use it:

- TARGET MARKET: Women of aging parents (over men 2 : 1). 40 – 70 yrs old. Upper income. Caucasian. Asian.

- **TARGET USER:** *Female Baby Boomer. Parent of teens or grown children. Grandparent. Working mom. Management or C-level executive (CEO, CTO, COO). 150,000+ income. College degree. Home owner, in good to excellent suburb of a major city on the east or west coast. Family oriented. Christian, Jewish, or other religious orientation. Active in community through church, temple, kids/grandkids, school and/or sports activities. Local gym member. Volvo, Subaru, or SUV vehicle owner. Shops at Whole Foods. Frequents hair salons/beauty parlors and day spas.*

Baby Boomers (born between 1946 – 1964) is still too broad to have any real significance, but gives me a specific age range to focus my marketing efforts, between 50 – 70 years old. I can now narrow this broad, but focused target down to characteristics of individual behavior, to more tightly target them as potential users.

To utilize the best bits of *PHP Advocates*, most of these *Baby Boomer* women will have to be upper-income—*$150K annually* (minimum), to be able to afford the personalized services my application provides. Women making over *$150K annually* are likely *college educated—Bachelors degree or higher*, and have achieved a *management-level career-track*, assuming they are still in the workforce at their 'advanced' age. My *White* or *Asian upper-income women* are likely *homeowners, living in a wealthy suburb near a major city*.

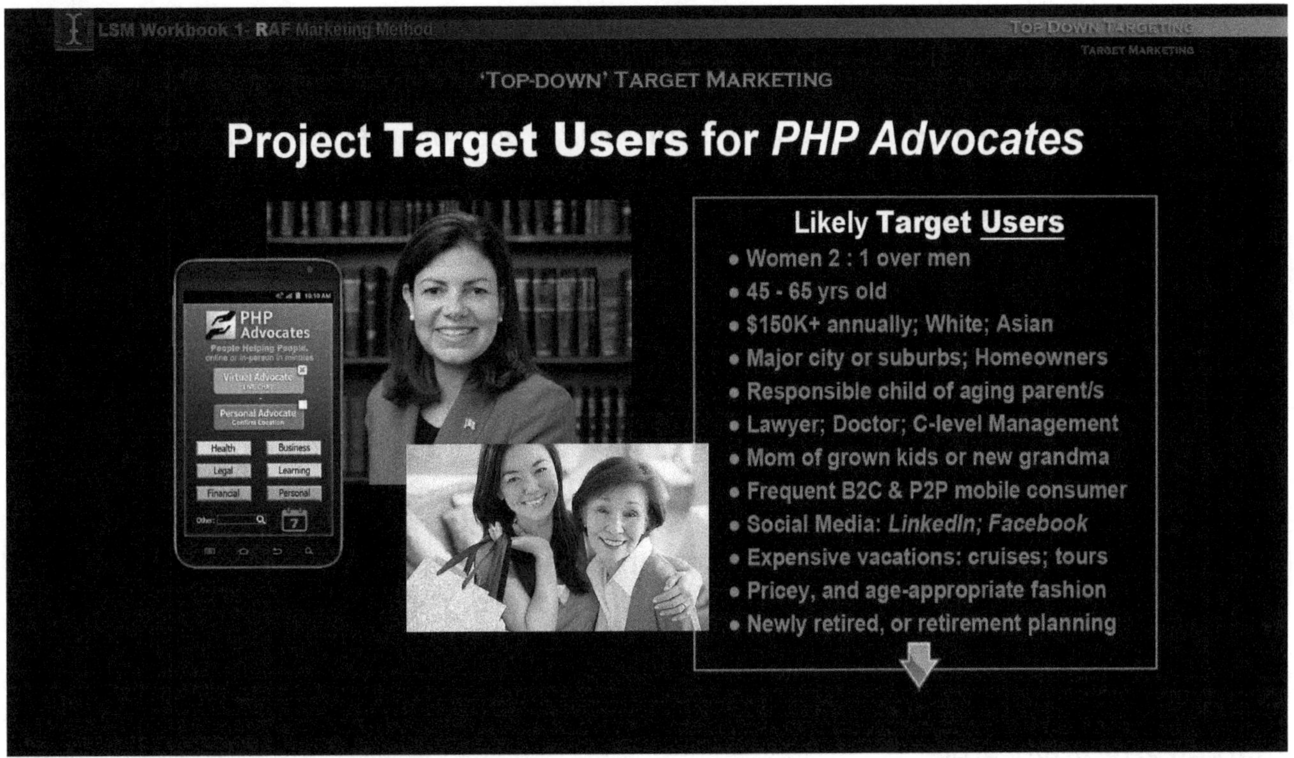

It is *bad marketing* to ignore known data simply to be politically correct. Marketers must use legitimate statistics and observations of repeated behavior as data sources, to market our offering to the most likely adopters, for the greatest possible response to our marketing efforts.

One quick *Google* search shows me that only 15% of women over 40 are childless, so it's likely my *affluent female Baby Boomer* is a *mom*. *Women* born in the late 1940s through early 1960s generally had kids earlier than today, so it's reasonable to assume her kids are grown, either *teens*, or in college, or on their own with their own kids by now, potentially making my most obvious target user a *grandmother*.

Armed with data I've compiled using the four major data sources, utilizing my visual target marketing slides, and considering common sense, of course, I've narrowed my 'lowest hanging fruit,' my primary, but broad target market of *Women of Aging Parents*, to my most obvious target *users*. Each descriptive characteristic I list tells me not only what this target user likes, and will likely respond to, but also where to find them, and how to reach them with my marketing efforts.

PHP Advocate's primary **target users**: *Affluent, mid-life, college educated, family-oriented, mobile-savvy, White/Asian Baby Boomer moms* can be found through a variety of family and industry associations. If they are still working, they are likely to attend pricey, industry-specific conferences, networking events and other business engagements, both live, and online, such as webinars, virtual conferences and talks. I can attend these events to network in-person, which will yield my best response, or post ads on *Ted Talk* forums, or related websites, and/or engage with high-income industry groups on *LinkedIn* or in-person, in finance, pharmaceuticals, or insurance, to market my application.

My *50 – 70 year old* target user's daughter just graduated college, or got married, or had kids, and *mom/grandma* is all over her social media pages posting pictures of these milestone family events. I can reach this particular primary target user through wedding and event planning businesses, or invitation printers, and other associated online groups and forums. Her college reunion may be coming up, and even if I don't know her specific college, I can still get her attention, placing ads in popular college alumni publications. She's likely retirement planning, and there are tons of websites and even print publications of financial institutions, where I can put my marketing efforts. Our target user is getting, or just got divorced, which half the population over 50 has. She may frequent online therapy apps, or possibly an online group for divorced moms, or a networking Meetup of divorced women, all of which I can place posts, or ads to market *PHP Advocates*.

My primary target user is likely on social media platforms, even if just *LinkedIn* for her career, and *Facebook* as a touch-point to her family, *Amazon* to buy stuff, and *Netflix*, which she watches on the weekends. If she has aging parents suffering from Alzheimer's or cancer, she may be frequenting medical sites such as *WebMD*, or *MayoClinic.com.* **Social Media Marketing** (**SMM**) has many hashtags for categorizing my primary target user, from #cancer, #memoryloss, #mompreneur, #momlife, #workingmom #motherhood #parenting, to #proudgrandma, to #divorcerecovery and #divorcedmom.

We'll do an in-depth review of finding trending hashtags in LSB Workbook 2, when we create posts and SMM ads in the Branding process. For now, to find relevant hashtags, go on to *Twitter*, and use their search box. Input the # symbol in front of the word you want to research, to check if it is a trending hashtag, to more effectively reach your target users in your social media posts and digital ad campaigns.

Identifying detailed characteristics of my most likely target *users* for *PHP Advocates*, I now have *some* ideas about where to find her and how to reach her, and *attract* her with my marketing efforts. She's likely to realize the most utility—get the most benefits—from my application, since she can get trusted caretakers for her aging parent, and/or qualified tutors for her teens, college to wedding consultants for her kids, retirement or divorce counseling and more, all on my secure, easy-to-use application! My initial campaigns for *PHP Advocates* will directly address the desires, and/or the perceived needs of this particular subset of women. I'll extensively research her behavioral data, and *Google* questions on percentages and trends of these particular target users to define their aggregate behavior as tightly as possible from the data I gather and observe. I may even set up an affiliate marketing campaign on *Facebook,* or *LinkedIn*, with campaigns where *I get to choose* from their broad selection of targets who will likely be interested in my application.

My primary market—*Women of Aging Parents*—for *PHP Advocates,* is "the size of Texas," which is good, an assurance my original idea is solid, and can be marketed into a sustainable company. But I need more than *one* market, or group of users to sell to. Other, secondary potential target users of *PHP Advocates*, below my primary 'low hanging fruit,' are discovered by continually refining my TARGET MARKETS, List 2A, into TARGET USERS, List 2B.

- TARGET MARKETS: Temporarily injured, or permanently disabled. 21 – 75. $$- $$$$.
- **TARGET USER:** *Cancer patients, or sports injured who usually drive themselves, or use public transportation, but now need an advocate for doctor's appointments or weekly treatments. Patients that need in-home care or physical therapy. Type 2 diabetics, or clinically obese with recurring health issues, that need a nutrition expert, and/or regular exercise regiment, and want an in-home or online workout advocate.*

These secondary target users are also a substantial swath of the population. With over 60% of the U.S. currently classified as obese—25 pounds or more overweight—Type 2 Diabetics are a growing group of potential users for *PHP Advocates*. Many of these target users can be middle income, since they may receive 'worker's compensation' from their employer or the government, during their temporary illness or injury. I'll market my app to these potential users on diet sites, online exercise platforms, heath and wellness applications, as well as print magazines that are popular in doctor's offices, such as *Fitness*, or *Real Simple*. I continue transposing my TARGET MARKETS bullet list into bullet points of TARGET USERS.

- TARGET MARKETS: Entrepreneurs. Solopreneurs. Home office pros. 21- 65. Male/Female.
- **TARGET USER:** *Career-track Millennials. 18 – 45. Low to moderate income. Single. Recently married. Job-seeking college students, recent graduates, or college educated, looking to add to their skill set and/or resume. Tech-savvy who use mobile peer-to-peer (P2P) services (like Uber or AirBnB), born with a cellphone in their hand. Living with parents, or renting an apartment. City dweller.*
- **TARGET USER:** *Home-bound new mom or dad, looking for work-at-home business opportunities while the other parent has a full-time job away from the home. Renters or homeowners in suburbs of a major city. 25 – 45. $$$ - $$$$*
- **TARGET USER:** *Home schooling parents, religious conservative or ultra liberal, in sparsely populated rural areas. 25 – 45. $ - $$$$*

There are many social media platforms, and probably thousands of groups, online forums, webinars, talks, conferences, businesses, and even hashtags, focused on helping college students start careers, as well as build their skill set to get a job. I'll find them—this one tightly targeted group of potential users—and create campaigns that address the problems and desires of *job-seeking college Millennials*, to make them aware I have an application that can benefit them.

New parents are often home-bound, at least one parent staying home to take care of the children. They need a lot of help, from cooking for their baby, to baby wellness, to baby and me classes, to childcare. Traditional homemakers to home schooling parents also need help with additional academic material and classes for their kids. In most cases, to be able to afford to stay home to raise children, at least one parent must bring in a substantive income, so this group of parents will likely be high-middle to upper income. *PHP Advocates* will have classes, and a connected network of teachers to aid this group of potential target users.

To identify as many potential users to market my application to as possible, I continue transposing my TARGET MARKETS list into TARGET USERS.

- TARGET MARKETS: Students. Business professionals. Retirees. 18 – 70. $ – $$$$.
- **TARGET USER:** *Subject-specific business pros—"Learn HTML to code your website. Learn how to market your startup"...etc. Recently retired. Laid-off or fired from full-time job. Divorced/separated.*

Empty-nester parents. College educated. Looking for a job out of necessity, or to create a job out of boredom. 45 - 65. Mid to upper-income.

- **TARGET USER:** *Independent consultants such as therapists, accountants, business and marketing strategists. Seed-round financed startup founders. 30 - 65. Mid to upper income. Uses living space as office, or rents small office space.*

From my BENEFITS list, List 1B, I've identify *Students* as another broad market for my app. *All students* is too broad to have any significance, of course. So, I've drilled down to *specific characteristics* of actual students, and segmented them into target users likely to find value in the courses, taught by industry experts, I've considered implementing in *PHP Advocates*.

Much like my potential *Millennial Entrepreneur* users, *Business Pros* will also find value in my application. They can take any one of the industry-specific courses my app will offer, to help them advance in their careers. *Newly wealthy* with stock from an IPO (Initial Public Offering), or the sale of a business, or *recently retired*, or lifestyle changes like *divorce* creates business opportunities, and often turns full-time employees, or the classic homemaker, into business pros. *Consultants* often work alone—solopreneurs—and need resources, access to information, even teams of vendors to help them be successful.

I continue finding more potential users by refining my TARGET MARKETS, List 2A, into TARGET USERS, List 2B.

- TARGET MARKETS: Parent of tweens, teens or newborns.
- **TARGET USER:** *Parents of addicted gamers, or academically challenged kids who need tutoring in-person to keep them focused on learning. They are often working parents and have little time to work with their kids, so they need to hire local teachers after school hours to help. 30 – 60. Mid to upper income. Homeowners, living in the suburbs.*
- **TARGET USER:** *New moms and dads looking for child-rearing help, with same as above profile.*

Parents of tweens or teens having a hard time academically can use *PHP Advocates* to hire live, online, or in-home tutors to help their kids succeed. These parents have tried self-administered online course with little success, but are diligent in wanting to help their kids. *PHP Advocates* could be a great resource for parents of struggling tweens and teens with live teachers online, and with qualified and vetted professionals available to come to their home and help them.

- TARGET MARKETS: Parent of child or loved one on medication.
- **TARGET USER:** *Parents of ADHD kids, or kids with disease or chronic illness. Frequent visits to therapists, doctors, medical facilities. Mom and dad are avid online medical researchers for latest updates. 25 – 60. Mid to upper income.*
- **TARGET USER:** *Spouse or live-in partner of loved one on medication. Married, or personal caretaker to diabetic, cancer patient, heart disease, recurring or systemic illness. 40 – 75. Mid to upper income.*

With competition from the EdTech (education technology) platforms of *Coursera*, *Udemy* and others offering online courses, many of the groups of target users listed above seem less likely to try *PHP Advocates* than my 'lowest hanging fruit,' *Children of Aging Parents.* However, each is still a viable target to market my application. The more detail I list about these users, the more likely I am to, first, *find* them, where they hang out, and then get their attention by addressing their specific needs and desires with my marketing efforts. Each of my potential targets for *PHP Advocates* translates into somebody, somewhere, individual *people* that can use my application. In the above examples, I've segmented these people into groups that marketers call 'likely customers,' or, in software, my potential **target users**.

Productization List 2B: TARGET USERS for *PHP Advocates:*

- Affluent, mid-life, college educated, family-oriented, mobile-savvy,

White/Asian Baby Boomer moms, 45 – 70, $$$$...
- Cancer patients. Sports injuries. Type 2 diabetics. Obese with recurring health issues, 21 – 65, $$ - $$$$...
- Career-track Millennials. Single. Recently married. Job-seeking college students. Recent graduates and subject-specific students looking to add to their skill set and/or resume, 18 – 45, $ - $$$$...
- Working parents of tweens, teens, 30- 60, $$$ - $$$$...
- Recently retired. Laid-off or fired from full-time job. Recently divorced or separated. Empty-nester parents, 40 – 65, $$ - $$$$...
- Independent consultants such as therapists, accountants, business and marketing strategists, 25 - 70...
- Parents of ADHD kids, or kids with disease or chronic illness, 25 – 60, $$ - $$$$...
- Etc..

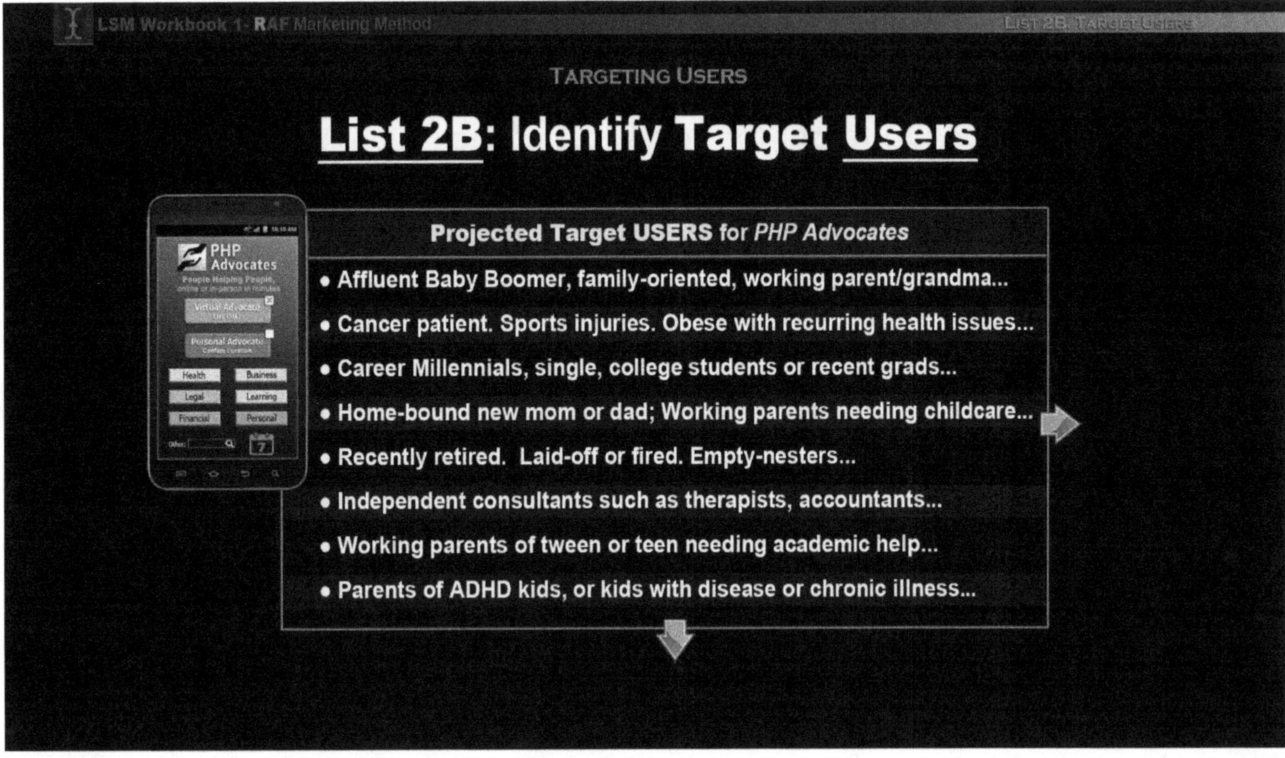

Getting intimate with your projected target markets, by identifying more specific characteristics of your target users is *required* to achieve greater response to your marketing efforts. Identifying likely target users gives us clues as to *who* these people *are*, and what **primers** and **triggers** get them to act: *buy; try; subscribe,* or even *remember* our product or company. Constructing List 2B also teaches us where to find these target users, where they hang out, both in-person and online, and how best to motivate them to *act* as our CTAs direct.

As noted, but worth noting again, businesses are gleaning more personal information than ever before. Everyone from your internet provider to *Google*, to *Facebook*, to your cellphone carrier is tracking your usage and purchase behavior now. Marketers are garnering an intimate view of our behavior. Knowing where we are, how we think and how we *feel* at any point in the day helps marketers identify the most optimal ways and *times* to manipulate us into buying their offering, or into their messaging.

I can hire an **Affiliate Marketing Network** that [ostensibly] utilizes big-data collection and analysis to place my advertising on websites and internet platforms that *they say* will likely reach my projected target users. But beware of counting on an Affiliate Networks to target users for you!

It is *your* job as the CEO of your offering to find target markets and actual people —target users—who will find value in your product or service, or believers in your message. It is imperative YOU are aware of *who* the most likely markets and users of your offering *are*. You must identify what these people like, and don't, where they hang out, and what they desire or even think they need. Don't count on *Google* or *Facebook* to target for you! Most of their algorithms suck for *tightly* targeted placement, because *Google* doesn't care if your campaign generates sales. They make money every time someone clicks on your ad, even if that someone isn't anyone real, like a 'ghost,' a fake account, or a low-wage worker at a **Click Farm**, clicking on thousands of ads an hour with no interest in any of them, simply to make **pay-per-click** (**PPC**) money for their Click Farmer.

To build a rock-solid foundation for your startup, you must get *intimate* with what you are selling, but also *who* you are planning to sell to. *Remember*, **all marketing**, regardless of what you are selling, **must fulfill a desire of a particular group of people**. It is *your* job to figure out *what* people, and how to attract them with your marketing efforts.

The Target Marketing Process

The process of Target Marketing is a combination of common sense, research, data science, and the art of psychology. We determine target markets and target users with educated guesses, based on the data we glean, and what we know and continually discover about what motivates people to act. While the target users categories may still be somewhat broad, we can initially target our advertising and marketing campaigns at these groups of individuals first, then analyze the results of our marketing efforts, and from there, further refine our target users to create a more accurate profile of the people who will benefit from our offerings.

You will dramatically increase your odds of successfully launching your product, service, or message, by tightly targeting your marketing and advertising to your most likely target users. And, you'll realize greater ROI—return on your marketing investment—with every subsequent advertising campaign, by keeping in mind you are *never* selling to target markets. You are *always* selling to potential users, actual *people* who will find value in your offering/s.

Be sure to save your TARGET USERS list to the correct folder in your Startup Hierarchy. And remember, TARGET MARKETS and TARGET USERS lists, like *all* Productization lists, should be dynamic—ongoing, and updated with every new release, upgrade, or newly identified benefit, solution, or potential target audience.

MODULE 6: TARGETING USERS REVIEW

- We are never selling to **target markets**. We are always selling to *people*. **Targeting users** means directing our advertising and marketing efforts at an individual's particular interests, issues, and/or desires.

- We derive potential **target users,** by identifying common characteristics of individual members in each of our broadly segmented **target markets**.

- One of the most effective ways to find **target users,** is to use **Psychographic** and **Behavioral data** of your **target markets,** to find patterns of behavior within groups of individual **users**. Observe, and note what people (including yourself) *really* do, not just what we *say* we'll do, to learn what truly motivates each of us.

- **Identifying characteristics of individuals—targeting users**—helps us discover what they want, what they like, and don't, where to find them, and how to reach them with our marketing efforts.

- **Big data** collection provides *some* framework for analyzing **user** behavior, but still does not tell us *why* people took an action. Analytic systems simply record that they did, then correlate individual **user** data, and the behavior of similar people, to predict future behavior of potential **target users**.

- Marketing our offering to potential **target users** tightly focuses our **marketing content,** to address *individual* desires and issues.

- You will dramatically increase the response to your marketing efforts by **tightly targeting your marketing and advertising** to your most likely target customers.

◊◊◊

-

-

STOP! Do CHALLENGE #11 before moving on.

◆◆◆

CHALLENGE #11: Get Intimate with Target Users

When was the last time you had a *real* conversation about how you *feel* about the things that matter to you? Beyond work or family related issues, how often do you tell someone, anyone, what you *really* feel and think? How well do you know your partner, spouse, best friend? Let's find out...

1. **Pick a close relative or friend** (your 'subject'), **someone you think you know well.** Title this **CHALLENGE** with the **name** of the person you'll interview, and your **relationship** to them.

2. **Profile your subject, and list their characteristics** to form a **target <u>market</u>**. Make sure to list Demographic, Geographic, Psychographic, and Behavioral characteristics of the **target <u>market</u>** to which your relative or friend belongs.

3. **Interview your subject.** Ask them the following *intimate* questions:
    - WHY do you believe in the religion you do? (If they're atheist, or agnostic, ask WHY.)
    - What scares you *the most*? Why?
    - Do you feel happy more than sad, or the other way around? Why?
    - What makes you feel happy? Why?
    - What frustrates you *the most*, or gets you angry? Why?
    - Do you think you are attractive? Why, or why not?
    - What do you like *most* about yourself? Why?
    - What do you like *least* about yourself? Why?
    - Do you like yourself? Why, or why not?
    - What was the last lie (fib, fabrication, exaggeration) you told? To who? Why?
    - Do you like people (in general)? Why, or why not?
    - What is one of your biggest regrets? Why?

Add as many intimate questions as you can think of, that reveal details about your subject. Discovering what they believe in, and don't, will give you clues to what motivates their behavior. *Be as direct as possible.* Be very careful not to judge, or comment on their answers. Simply write down your subject's response, and move on to the next question.

4. **Create a TARGET USER list** with the new information you gleaned from interviewing the subject of your broad **target market**. (Demographic and Geographic data will remain the same, but Psychographic and Behavioral data should be extensively examined for tight targeting.)

The more *intimate* we get with the individual we're trying to sell to—our **Target USER**—know what they believe in, what they like, and don't, the more likely we are to find them, attract them, and *convert* them with our marketing efforts.

◆◆◆

Create Buzz About Your Productized Offering

It's important to begin marketing your potential or completed offering as soon as you've productized it into an offering of *value*. You've done this once you answer the three primary questions about your product, service, or message:

1. **What IS it?**
2. **What does it DO?**
3. **And for WHO?**

Initializing List 1A—FEATURES, List 1B—BENEFITS of your projected offering, will answer the first two of the three questions. Initializing List 2A—TARGET MARKETS, and List 2B—TARGET USERS, answers the third question by giving us *people* likely interested in our offering to sell it to.

Set up the foundation required for startup success, at launch and beyond, by starting these first four of the eight Productization Lists. Remember, these lists are dynamic, and should be added to all the time, each time a new feature or benefit is implemented, or target audience is identified. Don't forget to put each list in their proper folder of your Startup Hierarchy. *A place for everything, and everything in its place* will save everyone in your organization, time and money, as well as keep all stakeholders on the path to achieving startup success!

Step 1, in the **RAF Marketing Method, Get Ready** and **productize** your idea, must happen *first* in the startup process. When we understand what we are selling (features and benefits of our offering), and who is likely to find value in our product, service or message (target markets and users), we dramatically increase our odds of creating advertising and marketing that converts viewers to act as our CTAs direct, and eventually sell our offering.

As the CEO of your productized offering, your #1 job is to sell it—generate excitement, buzz, even before your product or service is produced. A working draft **Elevator Pitch** begins in the Productization process, to help us define our offering better to *ourselves*, and our team, and to give us the words to chat it up, to everyone and anyone who'll listen. The greater your 'reach' to make potential users aware of your offering, the more likely you are to sell it.

Constructing the first draft of your Elevator Pitch is next.

◆◆◆◆◆

MODULE 7: THE ELEVATOR PITCH

Chat Up Your Offering to Anyone Who'll Listen

First, an **Elevator Pitch** is not the same thing as your brief post-it note description. The 'working' description you created at the beginning of this workbook, is to help you stay on track, and, not only realize your original idea, but make it *better* before launch. It's time to update your original post-it note description with an elevator pitch, specific to the *best benefits* of your offering.

Now that you started productizing your offering, you're *certain* that you have a product or service with some fantastic features, that will benefit quite a few groups of target markets and users. But do you dare chat it up before your idea is even produced, or completed? Maybe someone will rip off your idea, and make a successful company before you do. Or maybe someone already built something similar to your idea, and they didn't market it, but they will, *now* that you mentioned you're developing something like it to sell...

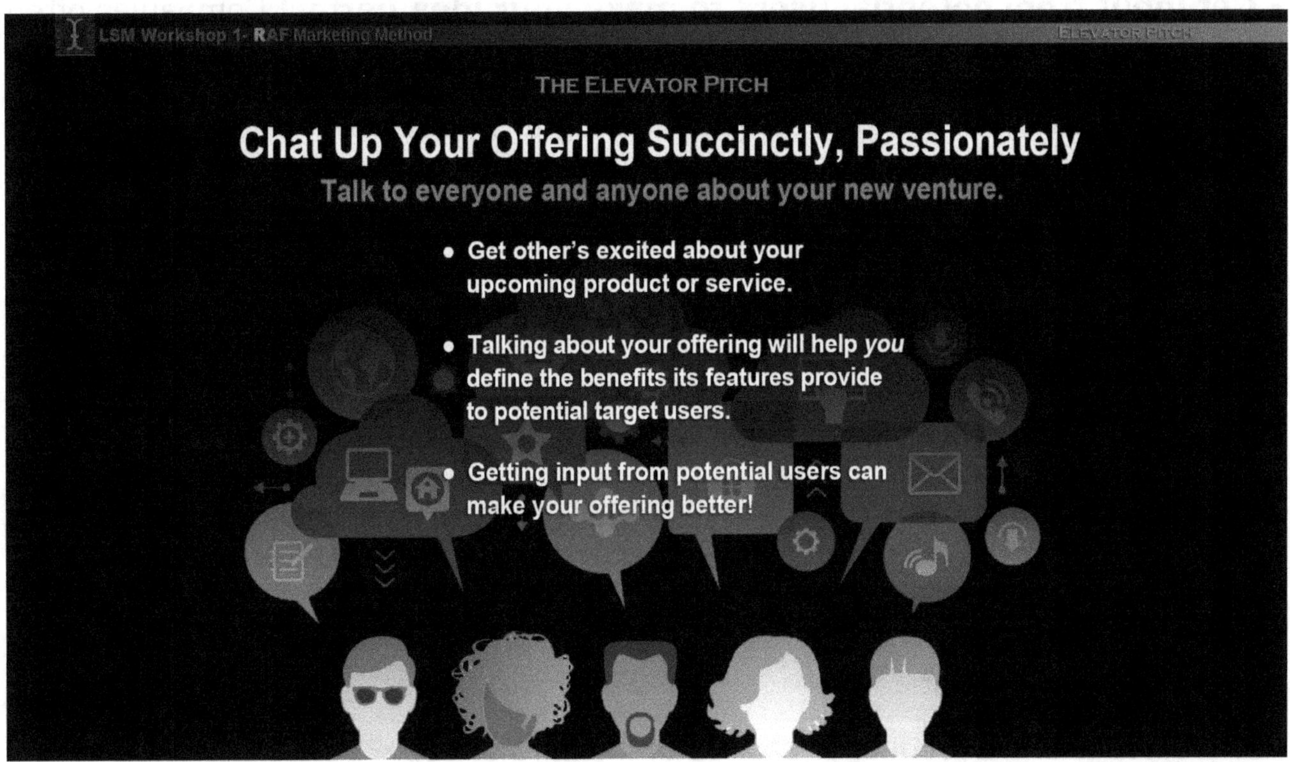

OK. Let's get it on with some truth. Stealth mode for an emerging business is NOT effective startup marketing for several reasons:

1. **As the CEO of your potential offering** (and/or emerging startup), your #1 job is to sell it, as previously mentioned, to everyone and anyone who will listen to your pitch. I'm not saying give away the algorithms to your software,

or your grandma's recipe that makes your cupcakes taste so good, but talking about your offering, even in the broadest of senses will:

- **Get others excited in it**, hopefully create some buzz, even before your offering is built. Half of the enjoyment of eating a dessert is anticipating how good it will taste. Before someone buys your product or service, or into your message, they have to become aware it exists. Your job, as CEO, is to make them aware of your great new offering, hopefully before it's produced, so when you launch, people are already salivating for it.

- **Talking about your offering will help you define it better.** Creating an elevator pitch is an intregal part of productizing your offering. The Productization process is all about getting intimate with your idea—identifying its features, benefits, and the people who will find value in your offering. Walking this process teaches you about what you *think* you have, and helps you refine your idea, or develop your product into a marketable offering.

- **Get input from potential users to make your idea better!** Companies often run market research sessions, in which they show a prototype, or a presentation in slides or video of a new product they are considering producing and/or releasing. In chatting up your offering to whoever will listen, you are effectively doing the same thing. The more you talk about your idea to people, the more feedback you'll get. Some will love it. Others will think it sucks, and serves no purpose. And though negative feedback will be hurtful, you can use it as a learning opportunity, to add features to your product or service that will benefit those who rejected your initial offering.

Still thinking someone will rip off your idea if you chat it up before it's produced? The second reason why stealth mode is bad marketing:

2. **If your idea does not have a DIFFERENTIATOR that is hard to copy within 6 months from launch, your current idea is NOT worth developing.** But *don't worry.* No problem! Iterate your initial idea, and make it harder to copy! (We'll get into how to iterate your offering to be unique in Competitive Analysis, next.)

How do you make a product or service that's hard to copy?

- If you're actualizing a software product, it should have high tech—sophisticated algorithms behind the user interface (UI), that offer unique functionality, as my fictitious app, *PHP Advocates*, does. The software should also have big-data collection and analytics to support recommendation engines, or collaborative filtering (AI software that identifies your preferences and matches them to other's preferences), for personalized target marketing.

- If you are hoping to produce consumer goods, like a bakery, a new draft beer, or maybe a fashion line, these are similar to selling 'art,' in that each has its own 'flavor,' so they are inherently unique to themselves.

- Selling Air/Media/Entertainment must be tightly targeted. An Entertainment Vlog (video blog) should be targeted to a *specific audience*, such as, *How It Should Have Ended*, aimed at young movie-goers who are also *YouTube* enthusiasts. Like consumer goods, you are basically creating 'art,' or something with your very personal signature when you create a media site.

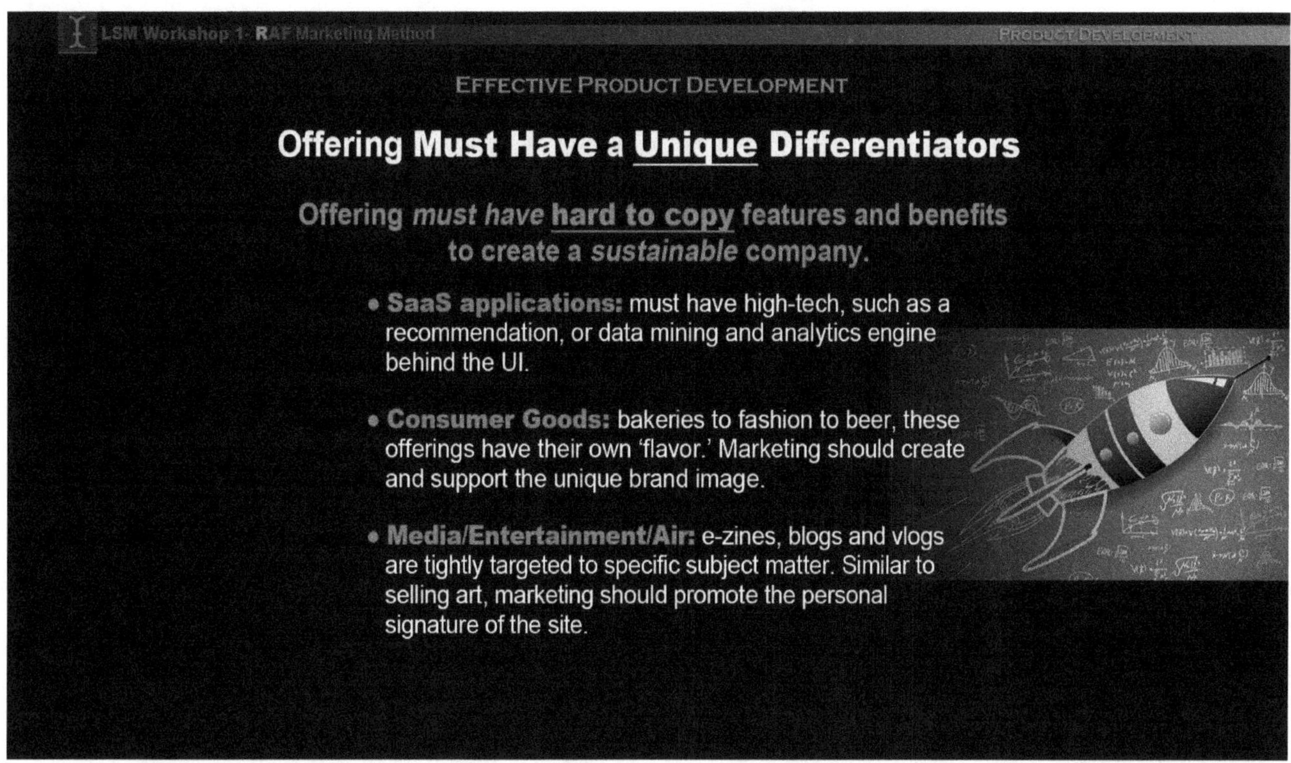

In the above three examples, the differentiator will last long enough after launch to gain market share, because each is unique to itself. Even if someone came along and copied your offering, yours has *your* particular flavor, or high tech software that isn't so easy to copy.

Are You Shy?

Do you get lost for words when asked about yourself? Do you avoid going to work-related functions, or sit at your desk nursing your drink while everyone else chats? Are you a wallflower at *Meetups* and networking events? Do you think you suck at public speaking?

A lot of us are not public people. We don't care to hang out with our work cronies, or make our jobs, our lives. But remember, if you want to launch a startup, in-person NETWORKING has the greatest return of all your marketing investments, even today! Fortunately, you don't have to change your entire personality and become gregarious and flamboyant to market effectively.

Since your #1 job as CEO of your potential offering is to sell it, you must learn to become a salesperson! We create an elevator pitch to give us the words to chat up our offering confidently, while concisely sharing the *best bits first*, the most unique features and greatest benefits about our product, service or message.

Think of an elevator pitch as an actor's script, one you study to memorize the information the pitch contains. As the primary salesperson of your emerging offering, it is your job to communicate quickly, and concisely, but also to excite potential customers, employees, and investors about what you're developing.

Utilize an elevator pitch to share your projected offering and excite potential users at business engagements, or large gatherings, from weddings to social events—when anyone asks what you're working on. Even when people don't ask, find a way to slip it into the dialog whenever possible.

Still feel apprehensive about chatting up your productized offering, because someone will rip it off? Don't be! *Everyone* has ideas, or hears about them daily. Most people won't take the time, or invest the energy to actualize them. Ideas have no intrinsic value. Only when we turn them into something real, like a product or service, or even a political or religious message, do they take on a function, a purpose, a use, something for people to interact with, believe in, act upon.

Productization is the process of marketing ideas, and even developed offerings, into real products and services that particular groups of people will find of value. And whether a message, a physical product, or a software service or platform, constructing an elevator pitch is an essential part of the Productization process, to help us more effectively promote, i.e. *market* our offering.

Checklist of Pitch Best Practices

An **Elevator Pitch** is a 5-30 second engaging speech to spark interest in you, your offering, and/or your company.

The bullet points below are tips and best practices to creating an engaging elevator pitch:

- Know who you are pitching to, and choose words and phrases that they can relate to. Since you've begun productizing your offering already, at least the first four of the eight required Productization lists, you know your offering intimately by now. You should be able to arrange your words so they directly address the audience you are pitching to.

- Describe how your target users will benefit from the features of your offering in a few short sentences. You are trying to *excite* your audience. Long explanations with too many words gets distracting. Quickly share your passion for what you envision, or have created. Keep your word choices simple, and specific to the features and benefits of your offering, to arouse interest of those you're pitching to about your great new venture.

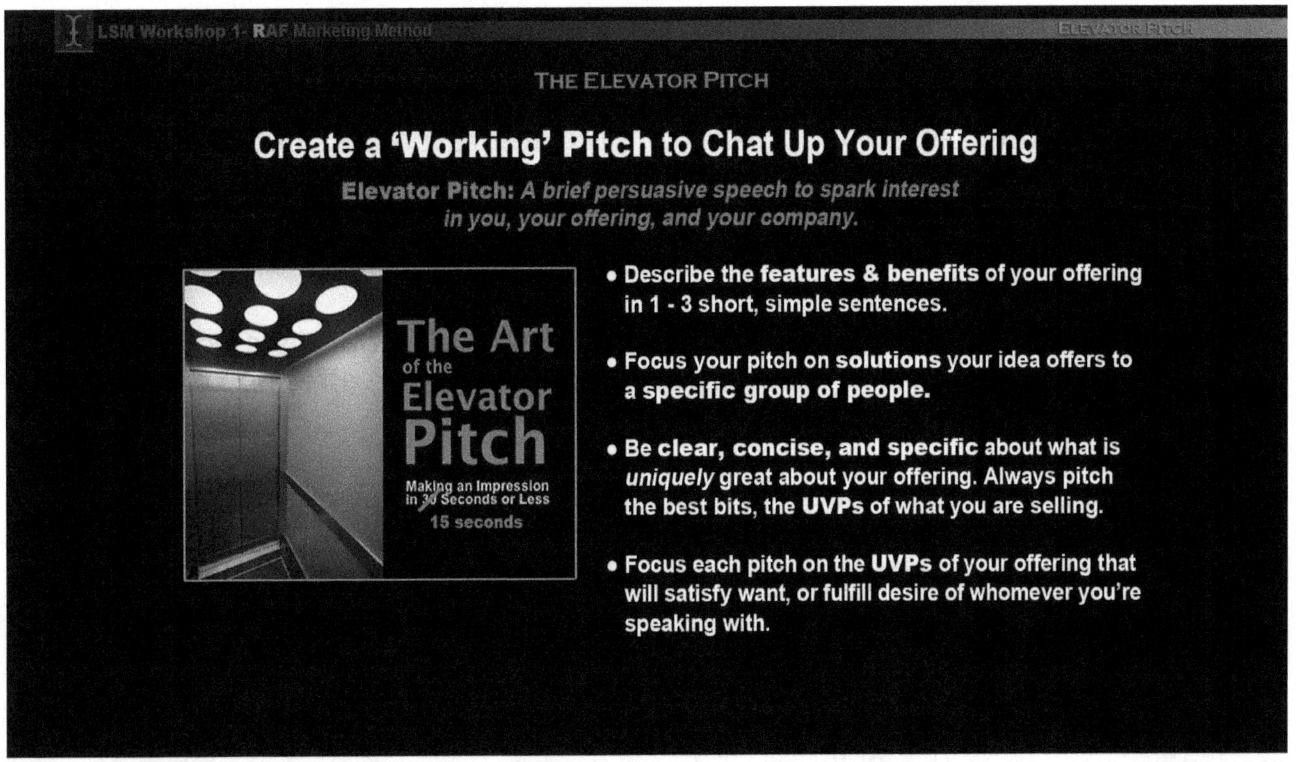

- Make sure to choose words that focus on how your offering solves a need, or fulfills a desire of a specific group of potential users, even if it's just to have more fun! Focusing your word choices on the *best bits* about your offering, shows your audience you've considered other's needs, rather than just satisfying your own.

- Be sure to be clear, concise, and very specific (no fluff words) about the best things your offering provides. Don't use words like "powerful," or "fantastic." BE SPECIFIC by stating *how* powerful, with examples of what your offering can DO. (We'll get on to doing just that—finding your **unique value proposition (UVP)**, or greatest differentiator in the next module.)

- **Beware!** If you are creating technology, software *or* hardware, do NOT use technical terms, *even when talking to technical people*. Be absolutely sure to use language that is easily understood by the average person. Do NOT try to prove how smart you are, what a great coder you are, or how adept you are in your technical prowess. Keep all pitches focused on the benefits that the features of your technology provides to specific users!

- Elevator pitches are rewritten for each particular audience, as well as refined with additional features and benefits for a variety of target audiences, throughout the life cycle of a product, service or message. They should always be based on the best UVPs, and most unique features, benefit and solutions your offering provides.

We'll review a typical elevator pitch script template, to help you put the right words in the most effective order to motivate response, but first we must examine how to recognize, and then choose the right words.

Pitching with the Right Words

We craft an **Elevator Pitch** *after* the first four Productization lists are populated, to give us the words and phrases directly related to our offering, to chat it up with confidence.

An elevator pitch should 'speak' in the voice and language of your target users, but only when they are your specific audience. While you are always pitching the *best bits* about your offering, you should change your pitch tone, tenor, and content emphasis, depending on who you are pitching to. Elevator pitch, or ad campaigns, I will use a wide variety of language to create more tightly targeted, personalized messaging. I may use the phrase, "Killer App," to viral pitch and/or market my app to *students*, but I would *not* use this phrase in pitching or marketing my app to the *Children of Aging Parents*.

If you are pitching at an event, such as a pitch competition for investor capital, and you don't know who your audience is exactly, simply focus your pitch on your offering's *unique* features, and how these features/functions will benefit various, but *specific* target markets and users. You already know who these groups and individuals are from your Productization Lists, 2A and 2B.

Using my fictitious *PHP Advocates* app as an example, I construct a *rough draft* of an elevator pitch, by transposing or outright lifting the text from my FEATURES and BENEFITS lists, Lists 1A and 1B, respectively. Of course, the specific words I choose to pitch with are predicated on *who* my projected audience is. I want to address what is important to them in my pitch, in the language they are comfortable with. If I'm pitching for funding, I may focus on the many target markets and users who will benefit from using my application, with colloquialisms like, "my lowest hanging fruit is the size of Texas," to let them know I have many people to sell to.

At this juncture in the Productization process, I want to create a *general* elevator pitch draft, to give myself a basic framework for the content I plan to pitch, regardless of the language I use when actually pitching. I have a wide range of projected customers for my application, as well as a wide variety of unique features and benefits I want to make my audiences aware of. I want my pitch language to be simple, clear, and as universal as possible to make my software's benefits quickly understood.

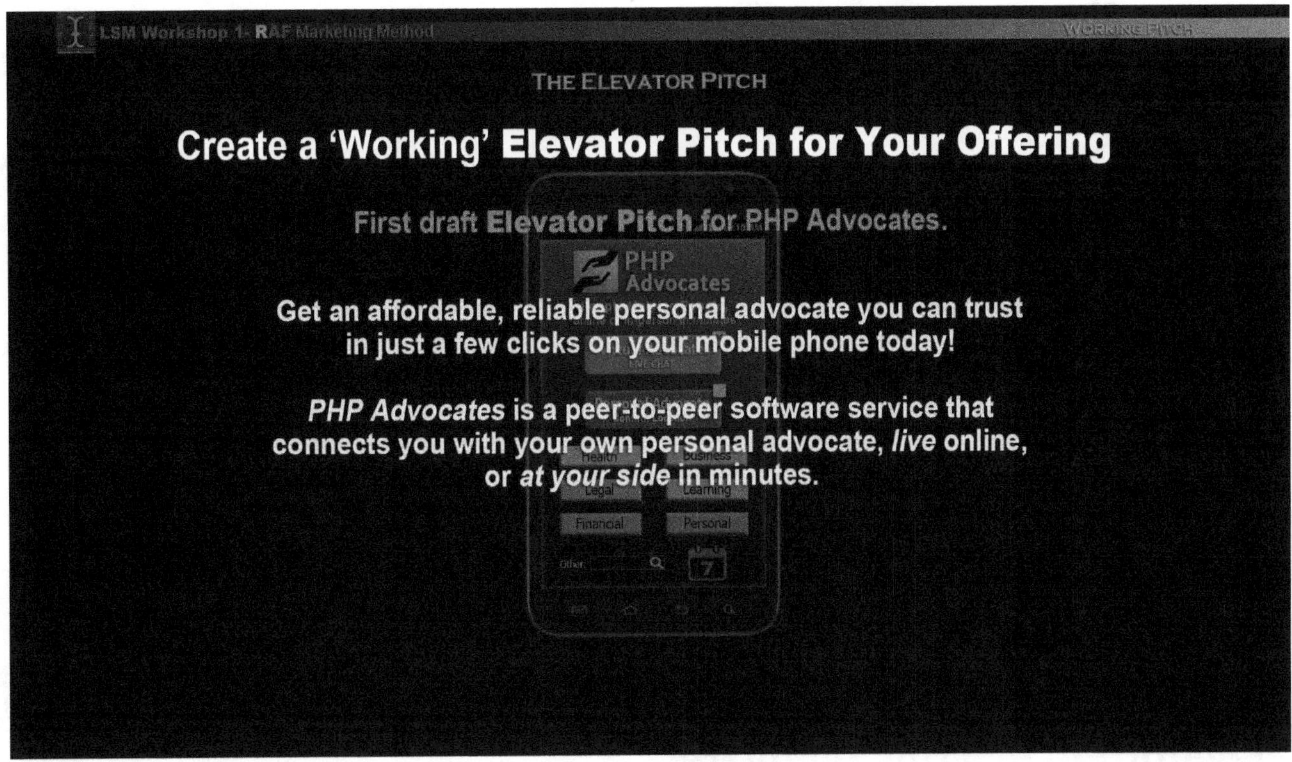

I pick the *best* functions of *PHP Advocates*, and the benefits they serve to specific groups of people, to construct my elevator pitch.

> "*Want to accompany your mom at her weekly chemo appointments, but can't afford the time off work? Need someone to go to your apartment and take your dog for a walk?*
>
> *Get an affordable, reliable personal advocate you can trust, in just a few clicks on your mobile phone today!* PHP Advocates *is a peer-to peer software service that connects you with your own personal advocate, live online, or at your side in minutes.*"

I'll change the opening questions, depending who I am talking to, and directly address how the functions of my software will benefit their individual needs and desires. If I'm pitching for funding, and don't know who my audience is exactly, I may add another question addressing another group of likely target users, but just *one* more, as I'll lose my audience, any audience, with too many opening questions.

The last two sentences are the *first draft* of the general elevator pitch I'll refine again and again throughout the life-cycle of my offering. The words and phrases come directly from my four Productization lists. This first pitch draft did not happen in the first scripting. It was originally scripted with many more words. Getting to these two, compact, clear, concise and specific statements about my software's function and utility took many iterations, but these two sentences will guide the direction and tenor of the rest of my pitch.

Writing, or in a pitch's case, *scripting*, requires editing and reediting to pare verbiage down to the right words, in the right order, to effectively excite, and engage your audience.

For *your* first pitch draft, simply take words and phrases from your four Productization lists, and string them together in a coherent fashion. At this point, you are just trying to come up with an engaging and concise way to communicate what your offering *is*, what it *does*, and *who* will likely benefit from using it.

Coming up with a clear and cohesive pitch draft, helps you define the *purpose* of your offering, to yourself, and those you talk to about your new venture. But live conversations usually lasts longer than a minute, so you are going to need more than a few sentence to pitch your offering effectively.

Elevator Pitch Script Templates

There are many **elevator pitch script templates** available online. Most of them require you have a thorough understanding of the offering you are producing, and looking to market.

To create an elevator pitch for your new venture, follow the steps below, *in order,* to confidently, and concisely chat up your potential (or produced) offering, and effectively engage your audience to ask questions, or further the discussion another time.

Say you're at a *Meetup*, or any networking opportunity, even those you create in your workout class, or singles events, or your kid's soccer games. Let's assume you are telling a story to a stranger who knows nothing about you, or anything about what you're creating.

If you already know each other, skip to Step 2.

Step 1. Who are you? Start your pitch at the beginning of your story. Stick to the basics. Keep it quick. Introduce yourself—your name, and organization, and title if you have one.

Chatting up what you are working on in business networking environments is expected. At the gym, or soccer game, find a way to casually slip in what you are up to, how excited you feel to be creating whatever you are, in your home office or garage.

Example: After her cross-fit workout class, Mary will go home and back to baking the organic desserts she hoping to launch into an online bakery.

> *"Hi. I'm Mary. Great workout."*
>
> *"Oh, hi. I'm Carly. Yeah. Hard though. Karen's a task master."*
>
> *"You're not kidding. But it's worth it for the calorie burn."*
>
> *"Touche to that!"* Carly says. *"I can have pasta for dinner, without the guilt."*
>
> *"And I can savor the double-decker cupcake filled with custard and topped with organic buttercream waiting for me at home. And the best bit, it's only like 300 calories!"*
>
> *"OMG! Where'd you find that?"*
>
> *"I make 'em. Grandma's old recipe, made* healthier," Mary adds with a smile.

Step 2. What do you have? Regardless of who you are talking to, in-person, or online, TELL, DON'T SELL your offering, or yourself. Clearly, when you originally conceived your idea, an event sparked your desire for it. *Share your story* about how you came up with your projected product or service. Share your passion for what you're creating, and why you are compelled to realize it *now*.

Pitch the features/functions that make your offering unique (UVP), something that you could not get anywhere else (that you know of)? Be sure to focus your words on the *best bit* about your offering, *the* differentiator, or UVP, also known as your offering's HOOK. In the above example with Mary, the baker, a *300 calorie cupcake* was her hook, or greatest differentiator from other bakeries. We'll review the method of identifying *your* offering's hook in the next module.

For the hook to have validity—show it's a lasting offering of value, not a fleeting eccentricity—we need *proof*. Beyond the hook, we add additional benefits and solutions unique to our offering, that will likely serve our target markets and users. Mary's proof was her cupcakes were her Grandma's recipe. This proof is an [implied] *tried and true* validation that the recipe has been tasted, and adored by many over quite a long time. Additionally, Mary included the words *double-decker* and *Healthier*, as further proof that her cupcakes were *uniquely* delicious.

Step 3. WHO will likely find benefit in your offering? Talk about who your offering will benefit, and why. When you thought of the idea, you likely had someone in mind, even if only people like you, who could use it. Share who you think will likely find value in the features/functions of your product or service.

It is important to note that original ideas for products and services often change radically, sometimes having virtually no relationship to the original idea at launch. Having many useful features, benefits and solutions for a wide variety of target markets and users, will make it easier to iterate your offering as you go through Productization, and identify *who*, if anyone but you, will find any value in your invention. Developing an *adaptable* product or service will ensure sustainability for your company over time.

Step 4. Chat up who is on your team. Including team members in your pitch may or may not be relevant to who you're speak with. Mary is likely working alone to develop her online bakery. And even if she has a great software developer putting her website together, if he isn't anyone of note, there is no need to mention him. If, however, a contributing member has a high profile, as in Bill Gates (ex-CEO of *Microsoft*) is one of the investors in your startup, well, then it might be worth mentioning—casually, of course—but you should share your excitement as well.

Step 5. A Call-to-Action (CTA) is mandatory at the end of every pitch, as it is in every marketing effort. Remember, marketing is selling—getting people to buy our product or service, or into our message. *To get people to do what we want, we must tell them what we want them to do.* Make sure to close your pitch with a CTA that will further the dialog, or spark enough interest from your audience to find out more about your offering.

In the above example, Mary gave Carly a great pitch in marketing her cupcakes, and likely sparked Carly's interest enough to ask for a sample. Mary also could have said, "If you want me to bring you one of my cupcakes next session, why don't we exchange numbers and you can text me a reminder." This CTA would have given Carly a direct action that would further Mary's sales process.

Pitch Script Templates are useful to begin your elevator pitch. However, do not rely on them to create a coherent, engaging pitch by simply plugging in words and phrases from your Productization lists into the template's rigid format.

Script. Rewrite. Edit. Revise. And continue to revise over time, is the process required for creating, and continually delivering, brilliant elevator pitches throughout the life cycle of your business.

Initial pitch drafts, like the one required at this juncture, are created to excite, initiate buzz, but also, pitching our offering in progress is meant as a guide to keep all stakeholders on the path to achieving the pitches' specified outcome. The working pitch for *PHP Advocates* specifies my software will be a *peer-to-peer network of advocates that can help users online or in-person in minutes*. The more I chat up this outcome, get people excited about my upcoming application, and keep everyone working on developing and marketing my offering on the same train, the more likely I will achieve startup success.

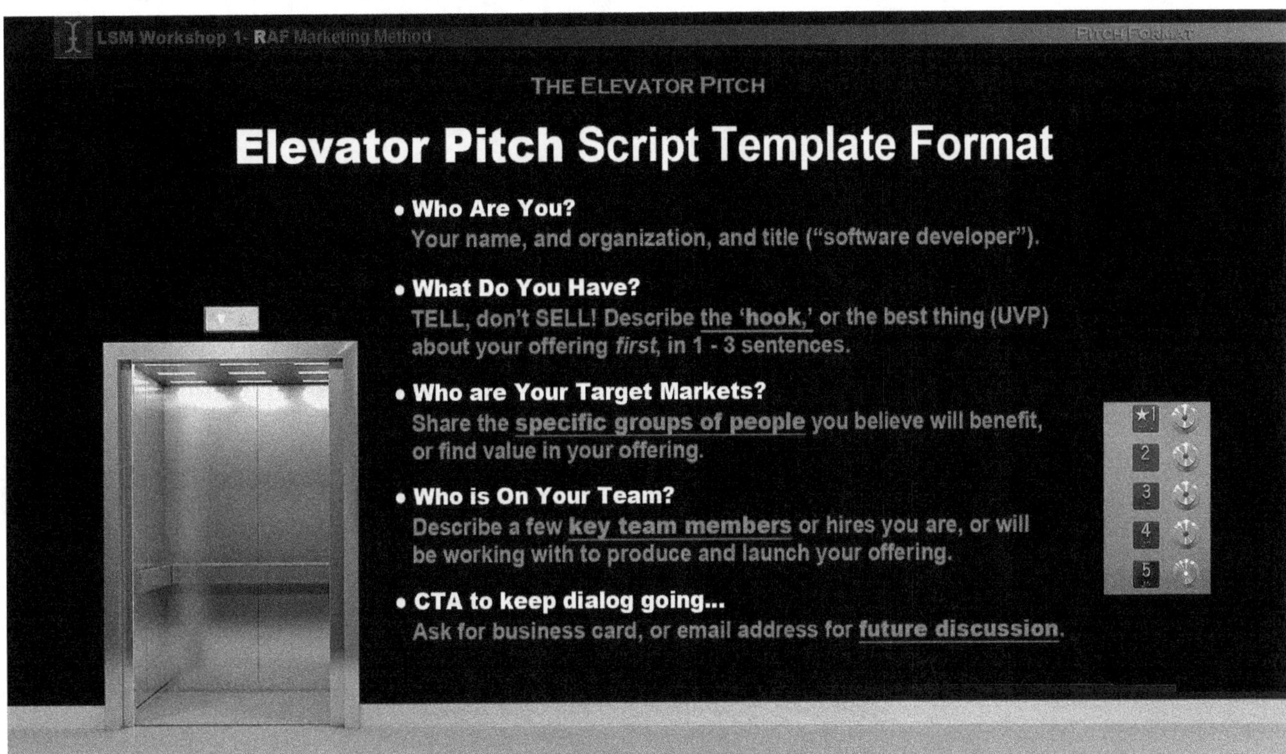

MODULE 7: THE ELEVATOR PITCH REVIEW

- Your #1 job as CEO of your **productized** offering is to market/*sell it*.

- An **Elevator Pitch** is a 5 – 30 second **engaging speech** to spark interest in your potential offering, and company.

- At networking events, parties, gatherings, freely **pitch** to whoever will listen, as it will help you:
  —Create buzz about your upcoming product or service.
  —Give you input to make your initial idea into a better offering.
  —Define your idea better as you're pitching it.
  —Show you what features excite your audience as you **pitch** your offering.

- **Stealth mode**, or fear of revealing your idea before launching it, because it may get stolen, is unwarranted paranoia. Ideas are intrinsically valueless. Most everyone has ideas. Hardly anyone puts in the time and energy to actualize them into useful offerings.

- Your **Elevator Pitch** should not give away the algorithms to your new SaaS offering, or the recipe for your great cupcakes. But, passionately talking about your offering, even in broad strokes, will attract USERS, partners, employees, and keep all stakeholders on the path to actualizing your startup's success.

Find What You're Looking For Faster than Before

When I was a kid, I loved reading encyclopedias. I often used them to research school projects, and while they were great to have available in my parents home when I was growing up, I'd often get distracted by the many full color pictures on each spread on the way to looking up my subject. The images would draw my attention, and then, of course, I had to read the caption, and if that was cool, well, then there was an entire section to read on the subject! Only problem with all this—it was 10:00 at night and my mom was telling me to go to bed, lights out at 10:00 p.m., and I didn't complete my report for class the next morning.

The access to information, and the speed in which it's obtainable, is faster than ever before. But in today's wired world, it's easy to get lost in the mire of content out there. In the business world, time is money. It isn't just a colloquialism, it is a fact. Searching for what we want to know, we often get distracted by the sheer amount of content we get back with each query. Finding what we want or need to know often seems so overwhelming, so daunting, we neglect to look at all. But this is bad marketing. It's important to keep abreast of the latest trends in social media, technology, business. And it's critical to identify and monitor your competition throughout the life-cycle of your company!

The **iterative search process** makes it easier and faster to get exactly what you are looking for. And even better, it keeps you on track to finding what you want, as effectively as possible, while avoiding distractions of unrelated link returns, that may seem interesting, but have nothing to do with the answers you originally went searching for. Iterative search is next.

◆◆◆◆◆

MODULE 8: ITERATIVE SEARCH

Discovering What You Don't Want to Know

You're starting to get excited. The more you productize your idea—initiate the Productization process—the more sure you are than ever that you've got a great offering, that more than one market the 'size of Texas,' will just love! Fantastic! If you've identified some substantive features, benefit, solution and targets for your offering, you're on a good trajectory for startup success.

Thing about good ideas that a lot of people will likely find value in, it's equally as likely that someone else, besides you, has already thought of it. They've already figured out how to solve the same issue, or added the same benefit to our lives that your offering does, and have been selling their product for a couple of years now. They have the target users you were planning on targeting with your marketing efforts. They are garnering more and more 'market share'—percent of the target markets *you* want—by the day.

Our inventor friend, Tom Edison, introduced at the beginning of this workbook as an example of an effective innovator, was not the only inventor of the light bulb. He was just the first one to commercialize it—market it—for mass use.

Being a smart innovator, Tom Edison was aware of who else was working on the same thing he was. In horse and buggy days, 120 years before the advent of today's internet, Tom was aware of English chemist, Joseph Swan, and Canadian inventors Henry Woodward and Matthew Evans. In 1879, Edison bought their patents for the light bulb he would later commercialize.

Believe it or not, someone, somewhere, has likely thought of your idea, or something closely related to your potential offering. And maybe even produced it as well. But how do we find our competition when, well, truth be told, we don't even want to look, fearing we may find some? Even if we suck it up, and initialize competitive analysis, we literally don't know *who* we are looking for. We can't type a company name into *Google's* search bar because we have no idea what companies may be our competitors. Yet. So, let's review how to apply **iterative search** techniques to discover competition for your offering.

Find What You Want Fast

Want to learn how to work a program or application you've never used before? You can take a class, ask a friend or colleague, or hire someone to do the work for you. Or, you can look it up on the internet, and get hundreds of returns for *YouTube* videos that will show you how to use that software.

Want to find out who your competitors are, even when you don't know who you're looking for?

Iterative searching allows each of us to become our own greatest resource! The true beauty of the internet, is it gives everyone who has access to it a gateway to virtually an endless source of information. Like a public library on steroids, the internet can help us find information, or people we seek, or teach us almost anything we want to learn, frequently at no cost.

Find a job, a date, a house, a mate. Look up how to spell a word, or what it means, or the latest news, or a good dentist, doggy daycare, or near-by diner, most of us use the internet daily to access information. We usually find what we need quickly because *Google* understands *simple*, very specific requests like, "Italian Restaurants in San Francisco." The search engine will instantly return hundreds of Italian restaurants, with their mapped locations and ratings.

Not sure exactly what you're looking for, like searching for unknown competitors, and unsure of the phrasing to query in the search bar? This is generally where search engines, even *Google's*, fall down. We all waste enormous amounts of time, trying to articulate what we need into search engines from *Google*, to *Facebook*, to *LinkedIn*. The iterative search process lets us mitigate this time sink, by getting us to the specific information we are looking for faster.

Get Relevant Returns to Your Queries

To understand how to get the most relevant returns from your search efforts, first you must understand how search engines work.

Whether typing into the search bar, or speaking directly to *Google* or *Bing*, using language the search engines understand is one of the hardest nuts to crack in computing.

Natural Language Process (**NLP**) is evolving. We now have Voice Command software that allows us to make direct requests in somewhat the way we normally speak. However, these requests are simple, and repeated often: "Call *Primo's Pizza*." We still can't say, "Order the usual from our usual pizza place," even though we usually get the same thing from *Primo's Pizza* every time.

Whether using voice command, or typing directly into a search box, it is the function of search engines like *Google*, or even on-site engines for high-traffic sites like *Amazon*, to return the most *relevant* links in response to a search query. We will closely examine **search engine optimization** (**SEO**) in LSB Workbook 2, Branding, and learn how to write SEO-friendly copy for your marketing efforts as well. For now, let's review a few basics on what **relevant content** (according to

Google) means.

- **The most current information available.** It can be real or fake information, but the site must have a continual stream of new content. From *Twitter* to the *Huffington Post*, social media platforms, even streaming video services, are constantly adding new content. You, too, should be continually changing images and copy content on your corporate website, blogs, vlogs and social media marketing (SMM) profile pages, to realize the utility of SEO marketing.

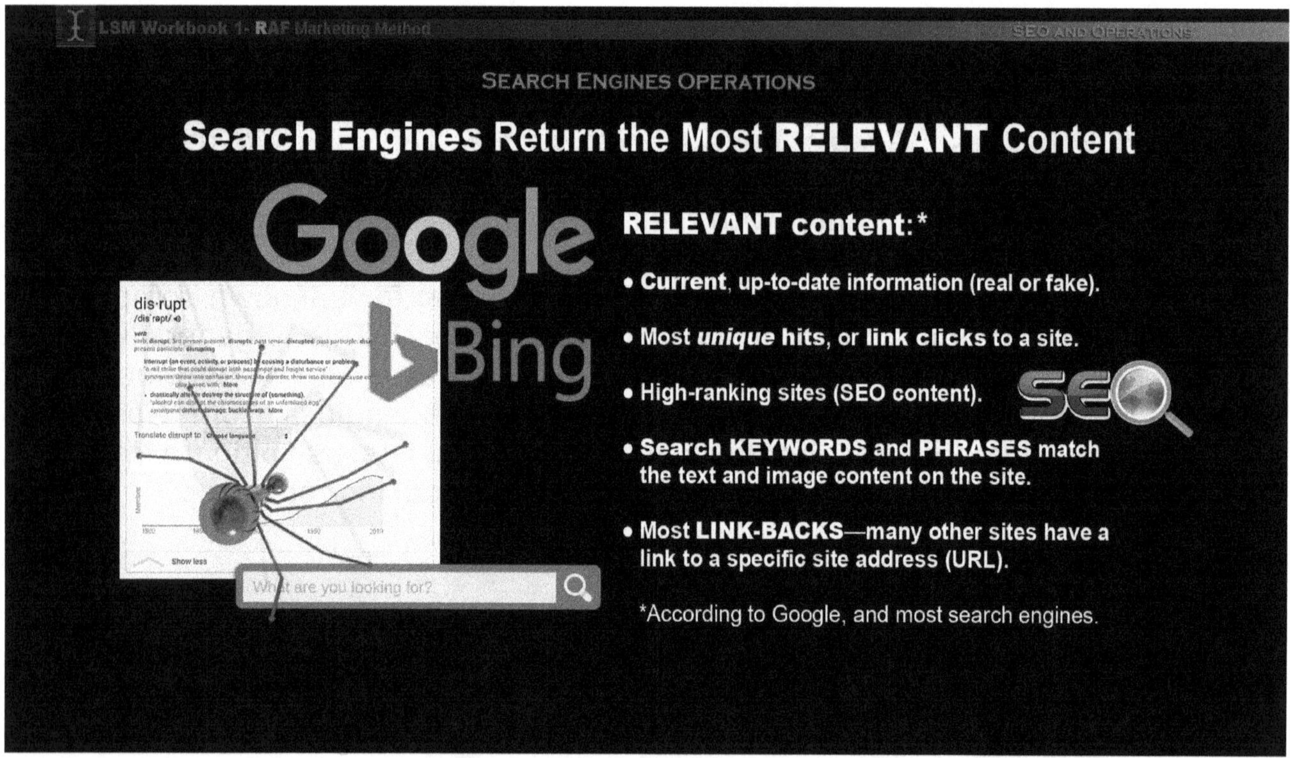

- **Search terms that match the text and image content on a site.** If I'm searching for a *Bird Vets in San Francisco*, Google will return websites and links of veterinarians in S.F. *only* after its algorithms have crawled the site to make sure it really *is* a vet, that takes care of animals, instead of the Veteran's Administration that takes care of military vet[eran]s.

- **Search Engine Optimization (SEO)** techniques use keywords in the metadata and content of any web page for discovery and identification, such as title (company name), description (what it does), author (About), and other keywords related to the subject of the website. When the keywords of the search term match similar terms in the content on the web page, the site link will appear closer to the top—#1, of page 1—of *Google's* search returns.

  An evil marketing practice to drive traffic to a web page [under false pretense], is to use trending keywords and phrases in the site's metadata or digital campaigns, that have no relationship to the offering being promoted. The popular vampire series *Twilight* sparked many authors to use the keywords '*twilight*' or '*vampire*' in their metadata and/or advertising, even though their novels had nothing to do with twilight, and there weren't any vampires. *Google* does not look kindly on this practice. **Avoid SEO tricks** like this, and keep your content focused on how your offering's features and benefits fulfills a desire of a particular group of people.

- **Most unique hits, or link clicks to the site**, meaning a lot of different people clicked on a link to your site, from your advertising campaigns, or even *organic* clicks from search returns.

- **Most Link-backs**, where your URL, or site address, appears on another 'safe' site. This could be from interviews, or reviews you've done that included your name and site address. **Link-backs** may include *Tweets* or updates you've posted that have been shared by others, or blogs, vlogs, or news about you or your company that has a link to one or more of your business site addresses.

Don't forget, search engines, like *Google*, return the most frequently updated content their spiders/crawlers find on the internet. Businesses that add, and change the content on their sites frequently, with blogs, vlogs or other marketing tools, will generally be among the first links returned from your search query.

As stated, we'll drill deep into SEO content, and how to create advertising and marketing that increases your search engine ranking, in LSB Workbook 2. For now, let's examine how to effectively navigate the limitations of most search engines, by utilizing what *they* consider relevant, and how to make it work for us in searches for offerings similar to what our company produces, i.e. find our competition.

Depth-First Search

Iterative search is defined as *the process of calculating a desired result by repeating the cycle of operations,* meaning doing the same process over and over, but iterating each new search based on the previous search results. Each iteration of our query is refined by the latest search returns, to get us closer to the information we seek. Iterative search can turn us on to information we didn't start out looking for.

When we are *not* sure of the search terms to use, or only have a vague idea of what we want to find, the iterative search method will help us identify what we want, efficiently. We *begin* by keyword searching—typing words and phrases related to what we're searching for into any given search bar. You already have several bullet lists of key phrases directly related to your offering in your Productization lists! Input any one of these terms, and the search engine 'spiders,' or 'crawls' the internet's collection of web pages, i.e. websites, documents, media feeds, videos...etc, to find a close 'match.'

Known in computing as **Depth-First Search** (**DFS**), we start at the root, in this case **keywords of our concept**, and explore as far as possible along each branch before trying a different search term.

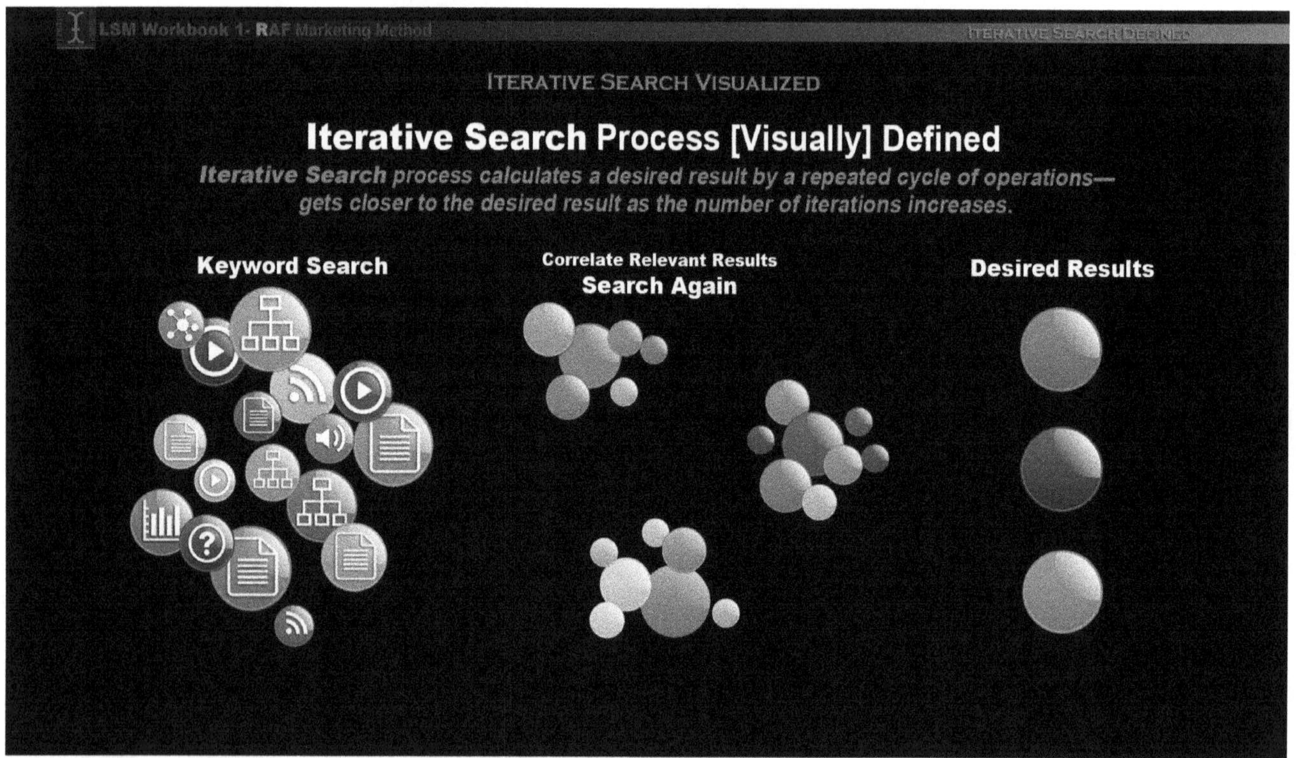

Google returns pages of links to websites with information the search engine *thinks* is relevant to our search term. We then correlate these websites, documents, videos and so forth into *loose* categories. Some groups we discard as irrelevant to our needs. If I'm still searching for a veterinarian close by, and use the keyword search term, "animal doctor," I don't need to click on link returns for *human doctors*, also among my initial list of search results.

I gather all the search returns relevant to my needs together in usable groupings. I find several websites with promotional videos, as well as ratings on local veterinarians, though none specialize in tropical birds. I have other groupings of vets that do handle birds, but they are further away.

Each grouping represents sites, documents, videos, with information relevant to my initial keyword search term, "animal doctor." I pull keywords and phrases directly from the most relevant initial search returns, to construct my next search term, and repeat this process again and again until I find exactly what I want.

The Iterative Search Process

Iterative search begins with identifying the **key concept**, or constructing the question you want an answer to. We'll drill down on iterative searching to find competitors in the next module. For now, we're focusing on the steps of the iterative search process itself.

1. **First, identify the key concepts of what you're searching for**, to find the words that will form your first search term.

   As an example of effective iterative search, let's suppose I'm looking for vacation ideas for my family this summer. I'm not sure to where, yet, but I am restricted by time, budget, kids, as well as health and safety concerns. I begin my search using the words most closely aligned with my key concept.

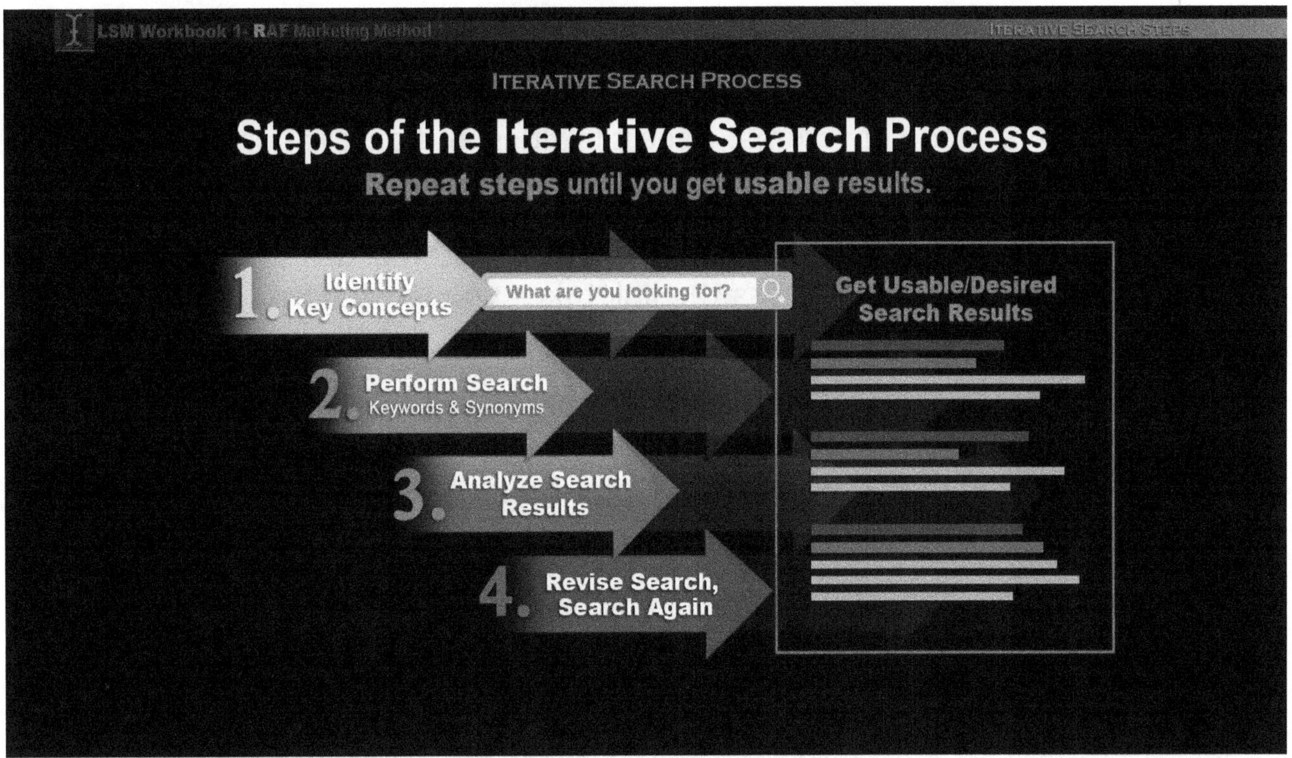

2. **Perform your first key phrase search.** I type, *'Family Vacation Ideas,'* into *Google's* search bar. It doesn't matter to *Google* whether my search term is in all caps, upper and lower case, or all lowercase. *Google* will return the same results regardless of the letter case. Below the search box, as I type in my string of keywords, *Google* recommends some things I'm not interested in, so

I use my broad key phrase search term first.

Google returns over nine million links, that, according to *Google*, have some relevance to *'Family Vacation Ideas.'* The problem is, *Google* isn't only returning relevant links to the keyword '*Vacation.'* It's also returning links to the keywords "Family" and "Ideas," which may or may not have any relationship to vacations.

To get link returns relevant to the *specific* term you type in, put quotes ("") around the search term, especially with proper names.

Simply putting quotes around "*Family Vacation*," I've lowered the number of returns down to 800,000. And though this is still too large a number to look at each of them, these links will be directly related to "*Family Vacations*."

I've perform my initial keyword search, with the most relevant words and phrases to my concept, in this case, my desire to create a summer vacation for my family. *Google* has returned the 800,000 links they considers the most relevant websites, documents, news, videos and information on the internet regarding "*Family Vacations*."

On the very first page of returns, I see site titles and descriptions that interest me. I look at their URL's next. It is very important to note where the link takes you—to what website or landing page. Titles are often misleading, a trick evil marketers and hackers use to 'fool' *Google's* algorithms into serving up crap. Check the URL—the web address the link takes you to—before clicking on it! If you've never heard of the site, or the dot extension is not familiar, DO NOT CLICK ON THE LINK!

Always have a FIREWALL and security software on your network and computers *at all times*. It is worth the investment, to have the security, rather than lose everything on your device, or networked devices, with one bad click.

3. **Analyze your search results.** I scan my search results, noting the titles and descriptions to see if *Google* has returned anything I'm interested in. I know from my security software that most of *Google's* list of links are likely safe for me to click on. Numbers attract attention quickly, and the titles with numbers, like "*40 Great Family Vacations*," attracts mine, but reading their quick descriptions under the link, I'm not interested in U.S. vacation destinations, so I continue scrolling.

   We'd already taken our kids to most *Disney* theme parks, and National parks across the nation. I'm not sure *where* I want to take our family, but I know it's not what I'm seeing on my first page of search returns. I continue to scroll through the **first 3 pages of returns** before moving on with another search term. What *you* think is relevant, *Google* may not. They may have buried the information you seek several pages down.

As I scroll the pages of links, I see other places on the planet our kid's haven't seen. Europe would be interesting, with our kids now in their teens.

4. **Revise your search term, and search again.** I revise my search term. I input "*European Family Vacations*," into Google's search bar, and search again. By naming a specific destination, I've narrow the returns down to 22,500 online sites with information relating to family vacations in Europe.

   I scroll through the list of link returns, and for one reason or another, don't find any links I want to click on, but certain words pop out at me, like London, and Rome. I go to the next page, and the next, without seeing anything of interest. But I'm enticed by countries like England, and Italy. Again, I stay on this search term for 3 full pages, scanning quickly to see if any more link titles or descriptions pop out at me with intriguing suggestions.

   I revise my search term, and search again.

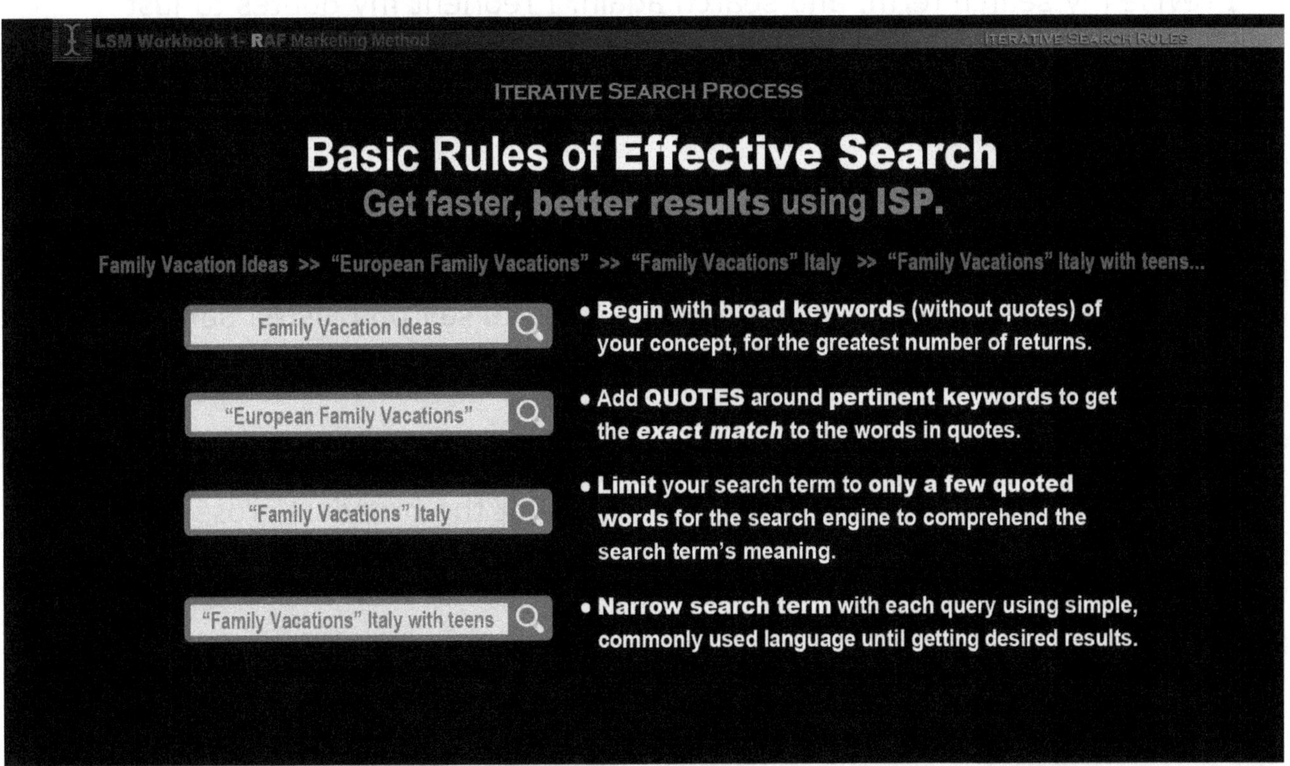

I type "*Family Vacation Italy with Teens*," putting the entire phrase in quotes to limit the returns to my exact search term. I get over 3 million returns. As with most search engines, *Google* can not handle more than a few exact, and common word matches. In fact, they offers no recommendations, at all. Unfortunately, the search engine could not handle the exact request of five quoted words strung together in an unfamiliar pattern, and has only returned a list of results with my quotes taken off.

In 1.13 second Google's spiders crawled the internet and returned over 3 million results of sites related to *family* and/or *vacation* and/or *Italy*, and/or *teens*. And this long list of returns may or may not have anything to do with family vacations in Italy with teens. *Google's* inability to understand our natural language process—the way we normally speak and write—likely buried many sites I would have found of interest, and still may be found with a different search term.

I have no desire to waste my time sifting through 3 million links. I revise my search term, and search again. I narrow my quotes to just a few keywords. The search term, *"family vacations italy" with teens,* yields fewer results, but on the first pass of the first three pages of returns, none seem related to families with *teens*.

I revise my search term, and search again. I reorient my quotes to just *"family vacations" italy with teens,* and finally get my desired results of websites, documents, videos, news, and reviews all directly related to family vacations in Italy, and many are for, or from, families with teens.

With each search term iteration, I get closer and closer to the information I want, enabling me to make an informed decision about planning our summer vacation for Italy this year. I'll use the same iterative search process to plan, and pay for the trip by researching what parents say on trusted parenting sites, then look for special airfare deals and family packages at recommended, and highly rated hotels.

I'll begin by identifying what it is I want to know, my *key concept*, then perform my initial search without quotes, to get the broadest cross-section of returns. If I don't find what I need within 3 pages of results, I'll refine my search term, again and again, until I narrow down the return results to exactly the information I desire.

Instead of wasting thousands of dollars hiring a travel agent, who may or may not create the vacation I envision, using the iterative search process, I am empowered to securely plan and execute a summer vacation to Italy for my family, all from my office in San Francisco.

You can use the iterative search process to find virtually *any* desired information.

Follow the four simple steps of effective search, *in order*, and find answers to your queries on almost any subject more efficiently.

MODULE 8: ITERATIVE SEARCH REVIEW

- Perform the **Iterative Search process** (**ISP**) utilizing **keywords** and simple, common **phrases** related to your what you're looking for, to get the most relevant returns to your search queries.

- Find **search terms** of **keywords** and simple **phrases** related to *your* product or service on your **Productization lists** to get relevant returns associated with your company's industry and offerings.

- *Google* ranks URL's (website and landing page addresses) by **relevance**. The more **relevant** your site, the closer your site link (URL) will appear to #1, or the first URL on the first page *Google* returns. Key factors *Google* uses to determine **relevance** are:

    —Most current, up-to-date information (real or fake).

    —Sites that get the most *unique* hits (different people visiting the web page).

    —Sites with the most **link-backs** from '*safe sites*.'

    —Sites or web pages that get the most clicks, from unique or repeat visitors.

    —**Search terms that match the site content.**

- Put **quotes** ("") around the term you enter in the search bar to narrow *Google's* search returns to exactly what you're looking for.

- To protect your computer and networks against viruses and infections from malware on the internet, use a **firewall** *and* **security software**.

Think You've Got the Next Big Thing? PROVE IT!

Most of us think our ideas are great, and unique to us, as if we are the first to conceive the notion. But as discussed, this is fiction. The gas powered automobile was developed by Karl Benz, years before Henry Ford commercialized it. *Apple's* first personal computer was developed by *Xerox Parc* engineers. Steve Jobs saw it on a tour there, went to 'Woz,' Steve Wozniak, and told him, "build this," as

Jobs didn't know how to code.

Learn how to find direct, and indirect competition for your offering, then identify, and even create differentiators, that make your idea unique, great, and *better* than your competitors.

◆◆◆◆◆

MODULE 9: COMPETITIVE ANALYSIS

Get to Know Your Competition

We're now three quarters of the way through Step 1: Get Ready, of the RAF Marketing Method to actualizing your product, and/or startup, into an offering of value, that other people, besides you, want. Before we begin the branding process of producing your corporate identity, and a breadth of advertising and marketing material to sell with, you must have a productized offering, with features/functions that will benefit a specific group of target users.

After we've established the first four pillars of Productization, List 1A – 2B, we're now ready to discover our competition, and identify what makes our offering different, *better*, than theirs.

Competitive Analysis is the third phase of the Productization process.

Be Brave, and Startup in Reality

I want to find competitors for my fictitious *PHP Advocates* application. Well, let me be clear. I *don't* want to find competitors already producing my brilliant offering, but I know it's smart to look for them before investing a lot of time (and time is money, in business), in developing and marketing an idea that's already available.

I am unsure of who my competition may be. As stated, I really don't want to find any, so my brain probably isn't accessing the possibilities of who these companies could be if my heart isn't into the competitive analysis process. I need a *plan*, a method, some steps to follow and perform, to find out what I don't want to know, and locate my competitors.

To quickly locate direct and indirect competition for my app, I use the **iterative search process**. I choose keywords and phrases to create search terms closely related to my offering. How do I choose the most efficient words to begin my initial search? I have bullet lists of keywords and phrases directly related to my offering on my Productization lists for *PHP Advocates*.

My FEATURES and BENEFITS lists—1A and 1B, and my TARGET MARKETS and TARGET USERS lists—2A and 2B, respectively, are rich with keywords and phrases about my upcoming peer-to-peer (P2P) service, and groups of people who will likely be interested in my **software-as-a-service** (**SaaS**) application.

I utilize these Productization lists by lifting words and phrases to use as search terms to find competitors producing an offering directly or indirectly like mine, meaning, not only very close to my offering, but similar offerings to mine as well.

Like iterative searching for a vacation for my family, I begin on *Google*, as it is, by far, still the broadest reaching public search engine on the internet.

My **key concept**—I'm looking for competitors for my *PHP Advocates* application—so I start with a key phrase repeated multiple times in my features and benefits lists: *Live Chat with Industry Pros.* I start without any quotes around this search term, to get the broadest cross-section of possible competition, since I'm not sure who they are, or what they have that's like my offering.

I scroll down the list of *Google's* returns, and read the titles and their brief descriptions, as well as note the URL location of each result. I go through [at least] the first 3 pages of returns, check out a few links that sound similar, but don't really find any significant competitors for my offering. I start to feel happy I'm on to something of unique value.

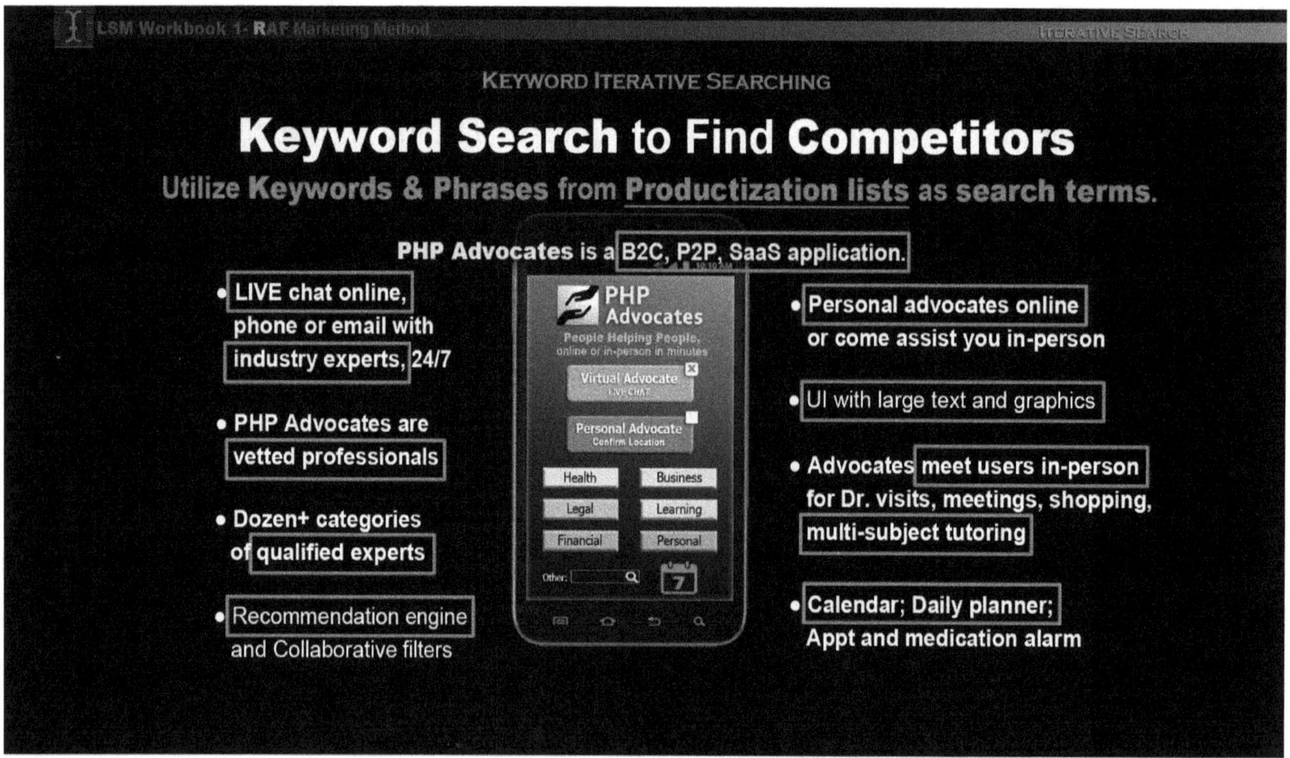

I try making my search term more specific with quotes. There are *always* competitors, even indirectly, that *are* doing, or *will be* doing, what each of us can conceive.

Quotes around the entire phrase, *"Live Chat with Industry Pros,"* produces very few results, and none that are usable. Quotes around only *"Live Chat"* produce more results, but analyzing my search returns reveals using the search term *"Live chat"* gets me companies that sell chat-bots (pop-up windows for live customer service) for websites, which has little to do with what *PHP Advocates* offers.

I'm feeling downright giddy now, that my on-call advocates mobile app idea is an out-of-the-box stroke of brilliance.

If I'm brilliant enough to create a great piece of software, then I'm smart enough to continue searching for competition for my application, until I find some producing even similar offerings to mine.

I iterate my next search term by lifting another key phrase from my features and benefits lists. I type in the term, *Personal Advocates,* and only get applications for health and medical advocates. And while my application has medical advocates, I have so much more. I iterate my search again, and try *Personal Experts Online*.

Google yields immediate recommendations, and I try their suggestion in their pop-up menu under the search bar: *Online Expert Services,* as a close match.

First page of returns, first result on the page, I find one of my direct competitors. *Presto Experts* has many of the same functions I want to put in *PHP Advocates*, such as round-the-clock industry experts, and academic tutors in a variety of categories, offering their professional services online.

I get that sinking feeling that my idea isn't all that unique, or great, after all.

I continue searching, knowing it's smart to do so, even though I don't want to. I'm going to investigate *PHP Advocates* competition, and bravely face the results of this research.

It is likely I'll find many other competitors. As mentioned, more often than not, our great idea is already being produced, either in part, or completely, by someone else. This does *not* mean it's time to abandon my idea. It's time to **iterate** my original idea, and turn it into a unique offering of value. Performing the competitive analysis process will give me clues how to make my idea even *better* than my competition.

Many startups, likely most, iterate their first offering multiple times before launch. It is common that the products and services we purchase, had little to do with their original ideas.

Part of our job as entrepreneurs is to find solutions to roadblocks we'll come across again and again in the startup process. Competitive Analysis is usually the first of these roadblocks.

Research, using the iterative search process, helps us become aware of our competition, which allows us to continually produce *better* offerings than theirs. You must monitor known competitors, and continually search for others with the same or similar offerings to yours throughout the lifespan of your business. Knowing who, and what your competition is doing, will help you to continually create offerings of *unique* value, and win the race for similar target users, commonly called, '**market share.**'

List 3A: Identify Competition for Your Offering

Productization List 3A, is a list of companies found in your ongoing research that have exact, or similar features, and therefore benefits, to your offering. These competitors likely have the same target audiences as well.

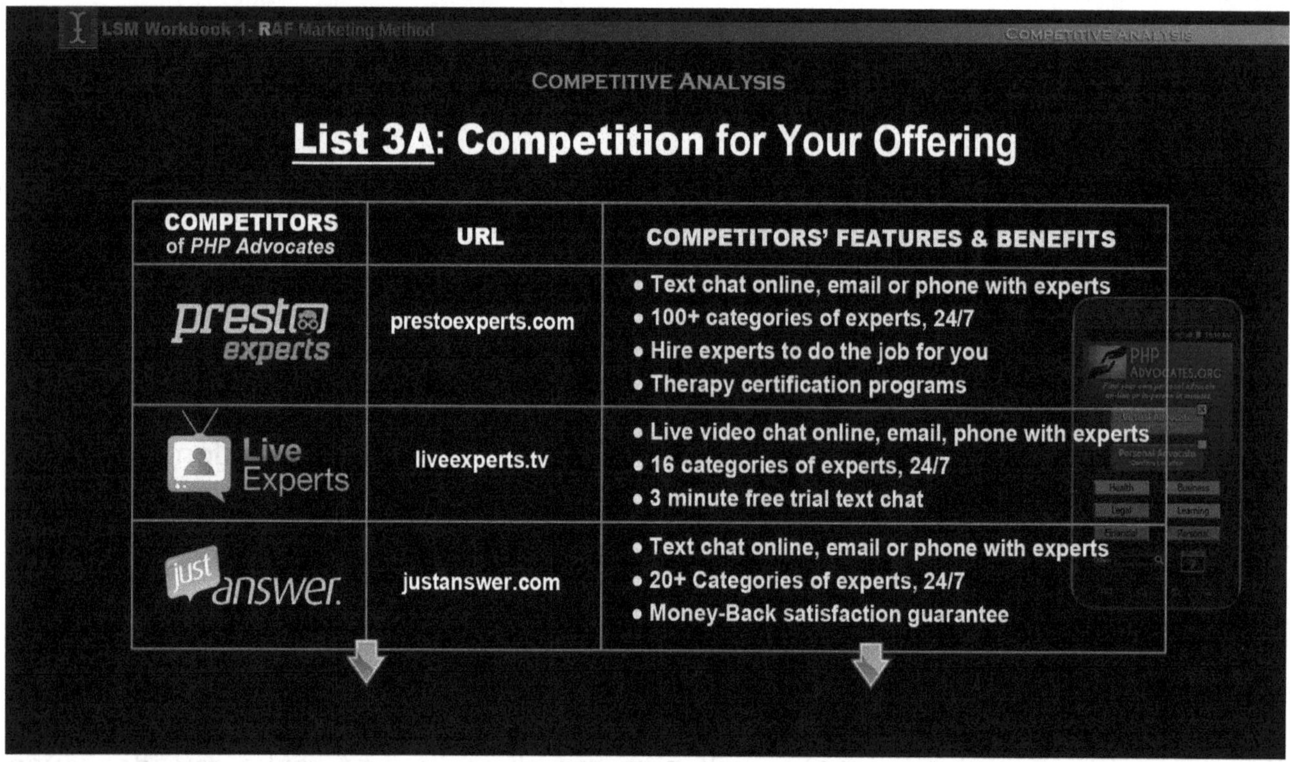

I created List 3A, for my fictious app, *PHP Advocates*, and populated it with competitors, along with their URLs (website address), and a bullet list of the characteristics of their offering/s that are similar to mine. It is important to list the features, benefits, solutions, and even target markets of your competitor's offering, to quickly identify what your competition has, and then compare their offering to what you envision for yours.

Through my iterative research, I found *Presto Experts, Live Experts* and *Just Answer* as three companies producing offerings most similar to mine. I'll use these three examples to illustrate the competitive analysis process. However, *your* competition list should be *far more exhaustive*, with whoever is producing competing or similar offerings to yours. Your list of your competitor's features, benefits and target markets should be far more extensive as well.

Productization List 3A: COMPETITORS for *PHP Advocates:*

- **Presto Experts**: www.prestoexperts.com
  - Text chat online, email or phone with experts.
  - 100+ categories of experts, available 24/7.
  - Hire experts to do the job for you.
  - Therapy certification programs available.
  - Etc...

- **Live Experts**: www.liveexperts.tv
  - Live video chat online, or email or phone with pros.
  - 16 categories of experts, available 24/7.
  - First 3 minutes free trial chat online.
  - Etc...

- **Just Answer**: www.justanswer.com
  - Text chat online, email or phone with experts.
  - 20+ categories of pros, available 24/7.
  - Money-back satisfaction guarantee.
  - Etc...

- **Etc**...

Prioritize List 3A with the closest competitors to your offering *first*. Indirect competitors should fall to the bottom of your list.

It is critical to the success of your business, *any* business, to keep a dynamic list of your competition. Carve time out of each week to do a quick *Google* search. Fridays, with your morning coffee, iterative search the internet, and identify any new competitors that have popped up, or discover a known competitor's product upgrade or new release. Do *not* delete competitors that go out of business, but indicate the date they folded or liquidated. By continually searching for your competition, you'll find out about them quickly, and be able match, or *surpass* their new offerings with great new offerings of your own.

We also use Productization List 3A: COMPETITION, to discover new features, benefits, and solutions our competitors have implemented, that we've yet to consider. In fact, I'll add many of my competitor's functions and benefits to my

PHP Advocates offering before launch, to assure my target users they'll only *gain* functionality using my great new application over my competitors.

As I populate List 3A with competing companies, I'm beginning to think it would be brain dead to spend time developing and launching my idea, since it's already being done by others, currently building the market share I want. Most every innovator runs up against this issue when they perform competitive analysis. But remember, it doesn't mean your idea is dead, just because you've got competitors. A part of your job as the CEO of your idea, is working around roadblocks. THINK about what you must add to your original product idea to make it unique. Consider what your target users are not getting from your competitor's offerings, and carve a new space with your improved offering. Disrupt an industry, or the status-quo, with your brilliant, unique new offering.

-Unique Value Proposition-

Find Your Offering's Uniqueness

Once you've identified who your competitors are, and what they have, (List 3A) you must differentiate your offering from theirs. To stay ahead of your competition you must continually develop unique and valuable **differentiators** for your offerings.

The construction of **Productization List 3B** *begins* with a **competitive analysis chart**. It visually illuminates our offering's **Unique Value Propositions** (**UVP**), or what makes *our* product or service different—features, benefits, and solution that make our offering *better* than our competitors. We'll drill down on promoting your offering's UVPs in your marketing campaigns, in LSB Workbook 2: Branding. For now, let's just examine how to perform the competitive analysis process, to discover UVPs for any offering during the Productization process.

Step 1. Construct the Chart. I've constructed my competitive analysis chart, to compare the features and benefits of my *PHP Advocates* application with similar offerings of my three greatest competitors. It is likely you will have many more than three competitors, but to simplify this process, I'll use just the three I've already identified.

In List 3A, I identified *Presto Experts, Live Experts,* and *Just Answer* with products and services that are closely aligned with my application. I've carefully reviewed their websites, and listed the features and benefits of their offerings, as well as their projected target markets. I have Productization lists 1A: FEATURES and 1B: BENEFITS for *PHP Advocates* as well. Along the top of my chart I give each of my primary competitors their own vertical columns. I give *PHP Advocates* the very last column on the right side of my chart.

The far left vertical column of my chart, I fill with a combined list of the features and benefits from *my* offering, *and* features and benefits of my competitor's offerings. Many of these features and benefits will overlap, i.e. be the same. That's the point. I'm trying to see what my application has that is the same as my competition, but also find differences in what they have in their offering, from what I have in my application.

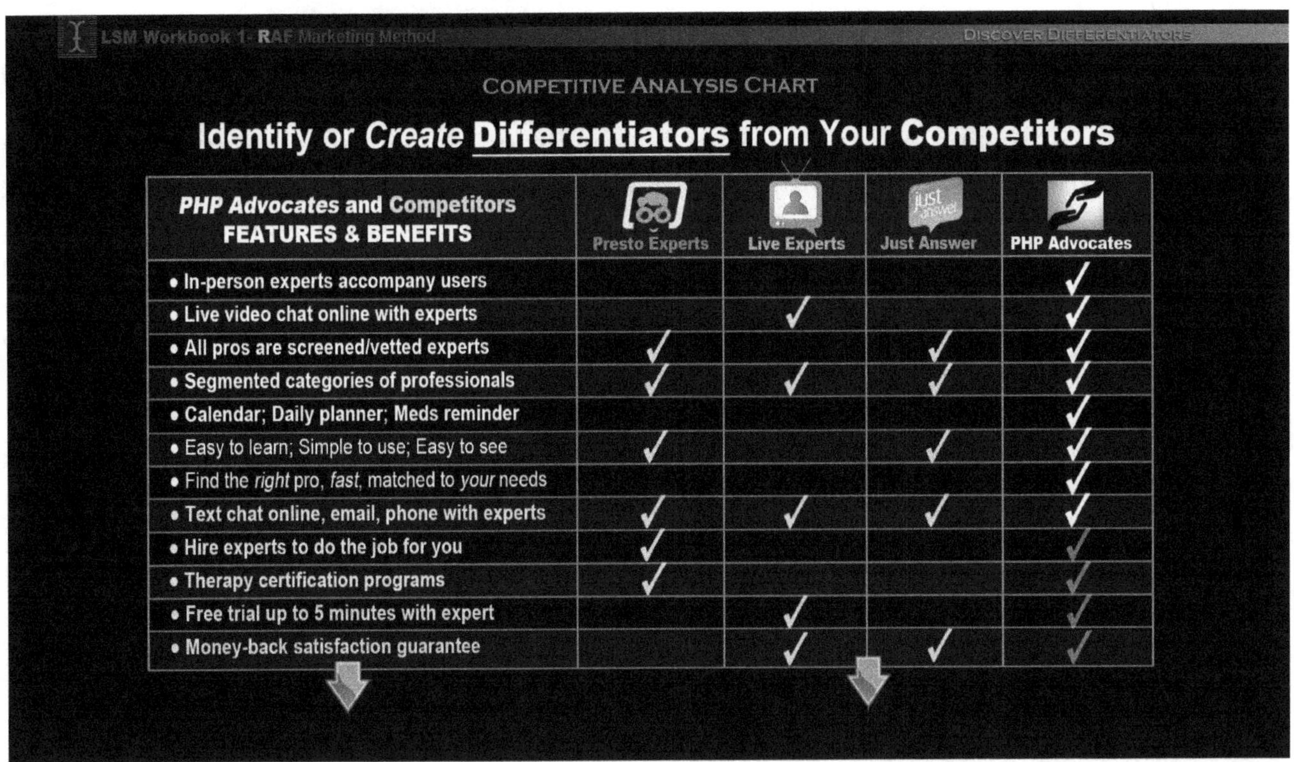

PHP Advocates and Competitors FEATURES & BENEFITS	Presto Experts	Live Experts	Just Answer	PHP Advocates
• In-person experts accompany users				✓
• Live video chat online with experts		✓		✓
• All pros are screened/vetted experts	✓		✓	✓
• Segmented categories of professionals	✓	✓	✓	✓
• Calendar; Daily planner; Meds reminder				✓
• Easy to learn; Simple to use; Easy to see	✓		✓	✓
• Find the *right* pro, *fast*, matched to *your* needs				✓
• Text chat online, email, phone with experts	✓	✓	✓	✓
• Hire experts to do the job for you	✓			✓
• Therapy certification programs	✓			✓
• Free trial up to 5 minutes with expert		✓		✓
• Money-back satisfaction guarantee		✓	✓	✓

I begin with my *PHP Advocates* features and benefits list first, and add my competitors lists below mine:

- **In-person experts accompany users at meetings and appts.**
- **Live video chat online with professionals.**
- **All experts are thoroughly screened and vetted.**
- **Many segmented categories of experts.**
- **Calendar; Daily planner; Medications and appt reminders.**
- **Easy to learn; Simple to use; Large text and graphics.**
- **Recommendations to find the right pro for you, fast.**
- Chat with experts via text, email, phone, 24/7.
- Hire experts to do the job for you.
- Therapy certification programs available.
- 5 minute free trial meeting with expert.
- Money-back satisfaction guarantee.

- Etc...

Constructing this visual **competitive analysis chart** allows you to see which features and benefits are unique to *your* offering. It also shows you what your competition has that perhaps you should consider implementing into your offering to compete with theirs, if necessary. Most of your advertising and marketing efforts should focus on the *best bits*—the UVPs that define your offering's *unique* value.

Step 2. Perform competitive analysis. I go down the vertical list of each feature/function and each benefit (on the left side of my chart) to execute a side-by-side, apples-to-apples, comparison of our products. Along the top of my chart is a column for each of my competitors, as well as *PHP Advocates*. I put a check mark in the column of any competitor that has each particular function or benefit on my combined list, including *PHP Advocates'* column. As I fill this chart with check marks, I can visually see what features and benefits I have in common with my top three competitors—what they have that my app does not, *and* what my app has that they do not.

'Live chat with experts,' *'Online live video chat with pros,'* are common features and benefits in *PHP Advocates* and all three of my competitors. But none of my competition offers live, *in-person* advocates for in-home care, meetings and appointments like *PHP* does. And though *Live Experts* offers on-site education and business coaching, customers have to come to them. *PHP Advocates* goes to the customer, so I've identified two unique solutions of value to my potential target users, over my competitor's approach.

I continue scrolling through the combined features and benefits list of both *PHP Advocates*, and my competitors. None of the features and benefits I've found in my competitor's offerings tout a recommendation or personalized matching system, so I've just identified another unique differentiator of *PHP Advocates*. I'll use this function to market my application to investors, and to attract data scientists to hire, but it's hard to understand the value of a recommendation system for most people, so I need a better differentiator for launch, to get the greatest response on my roll-out marketing efforts.

Presto Experts and *Live Experts* have a calendar function, similar to *PHP Advocates,* that let users input appointments and get notifications. Only *Just Answer* doesn't have this function. So, I have a differentiator with my calendar function from *Just Answer*, but not from my other competitors. Because two of my three primary competitors already have a calendar function, I will *not* market the calendar component of my app as its greatest differentiator, or best UVP.

I continue to check mark common features and benefits of both my application and my competitors. And while I find many in common, the one that stands out as my *most* unique function and benefit is '*Expert advocates, actual people come to help you*.' This is easily my greatest UVP.

Beyond identifying unique differentiators of our offering, a competitive analysis chart is used to help us identify features and benefits our competition is offering that we've yet to conceive. *Presto Experts* gives customers the ability to record and archive engagements on their site. This is a valuable function, that I, too, can implement in *PHP Advocates* to compete with them when I launch, or as an additional function to add in my next product release. Two of my competitors also offer the first appointment, or a part of it, free. This is a great sales gimmick. I'll use that too, at launch, and beyond, to entice new target users.

It is likely my competitor's offerings will attract the same target markets and users I've projected for *PHP Advocates*. Closely examine your competition's target audiences. Examine what benefits are derived from the features of your competitor's offering, to determine who their target users may be. Get to know your competitor's customers and market to them, and perhaps adopt their users as yours down the line.

List 3B: Your Offering's UVPs

Differentiating your product or service from its competition is essential to creating a memorable brand, selling your offering, and ultimately creating a sustainable company. Your product must have some *unique* value, or, at least, the perception of unique value, to be noticed at all among similar offerings of competitors, especially if their product is released, and already establishing market share.

Productization List 3B is an ongoing, *dynamic* list of the the *best bits*, or UVPs of your offering. This list should be added to all the time, every time a new feature and/or benefit is conceived, or created. While this list will include some of the same features and benefits your competitors have, you'll *begin* List 3B with *the differentiators* that make your offering unique.

From my competitive analysis chart, I've identified the *most* unique function of *PHP Advocates,* is that *actual people come to help you*. The first entries on my list will be my *most unique* features and benefits, or the *best things*, the **unique value propositions** (**UVPs**)—*the* differentiators—that make my application *better* than my competition. I'll expand on these differentiators to include a wide variety of UVPs my application offers, as shown in the bullet points below.

Productization List 3B: UVPs (unique value propositions) for *PHP Advocates:*

- In-person advocates meet users for doctor visits, help with shopping,

in-home care, physical therapy.
- Expert childcare advocates, local, vetted professionals pick up kids from school *and* tutor, babysit, shop and prepare meals.
- Personal advocates can walk your dog, or meet you for workouts, be your party chef, and/or individual or couples therapist.
- Professional business advocates can meet you for sales meetings, salary and/or software licensing negotiations.
- All advocates are vetted professionals you can trust, with qualifications and references online.
- Live video chat with experts for tutoring, advice, or knowledge.
- Appointment and medication reminders prevent deadly mistakes.
- Application tracks prescription refills, dosages and interactions.
- Find the right expert for your specific needs, fast.
- First 5 minute free trial meeting with expert.
- Money-back satisfaction guarantee.
- User Interface (UI) that's responsive, secure, is easy to read and simple to navigate, with one-click access.
- Etc...

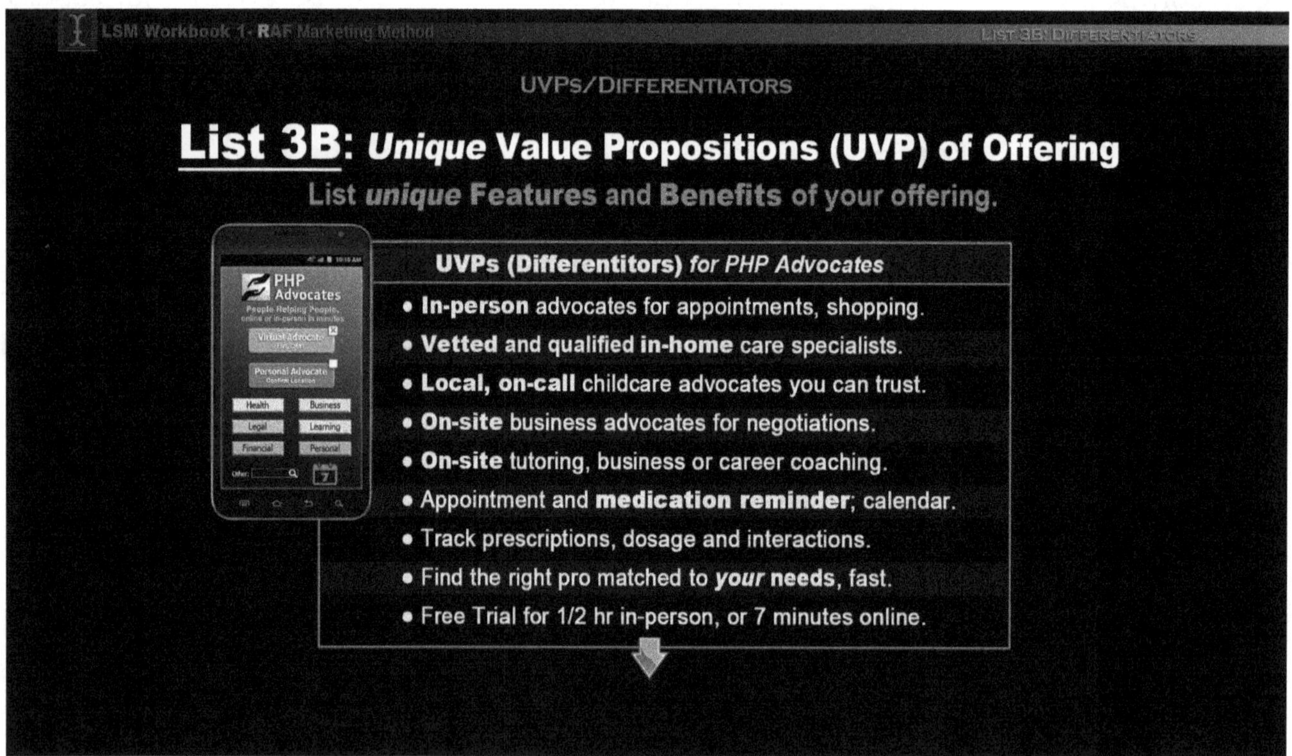

If you find you do not have enough differentiators that separate your offering from your competition, it's time to iterate your projected product or service. Competitive analysis is the process we use to identify, and, if necessary, to *create* differentiator—UVPs—unique features and benefits that separate *your* offering from your competition, out of the gate at launch, and beyond.

Productization List 3B is perhaps the most valuable piece of marketing you create, and update regularly. This list makes it easy for all stakeholders in your new venture to quickly find the ongoing and current UVPs, the *best bits* about your product or service. You, and your marketing team, will lift words, phrases, and messaging from List 3B to use in your campaigns, because your marketing efforts should consistently promote the *best things*—the features, benefits and solutions that make your offering valuable, as well as distinguish your offering as unique from your competitors.

All Productization lists, including List 3A: COMPETITORS, and 3B: UVPs, should be ongoing throughout the life-cycle of your offering. Even with no direct competition at launch, competitors will ride on your success. It is imperative *someone* in your organization continually search and monitor your competition. The third place startups fail is selling their initial release too long. Also known as "*one hit wonders*," these companies lose their market share to competitors continually releasing similar, or better offerings. Before implementing any new features/functions, include them to your weekly competitive analysis, to see how that feature compares with similar features in your competitor's current offerings.

Remember to put List 3A and 3B in their proper folders in your Startup Hierarchy!

MODULE 9: COMPETITIVE ANALYSIS REVIEW

- **Competitive Analysis** is the process of identifying our competitors, and *specific* characteristics—the features, benefits and target markets and users—of their offerings.

- We find *unknown* competitors of our offering using the **iterative search** process of lifting **keywords** and **phrases** from our **Productization lists** to use as search terms.

- Once we've identified competitors, we **research their social media pages** and profiles to find additional marketing efforts that will give us insights about them. We study the images and language they use (as well as the social platforms they post on) to create **user profiles** of their most likely target audiences, to perhaps adopt as ours down the line.

- We **list our competitors**, their URL's, and shortlist the features and benefits of *their* offering that are similar to ours. We list additional features and benefits of their offerings we've yet to conceive or implement.

- We create a **Competitive Analysis chart** to determine what makes the features and benefits of our offering *different* from our **competition**.

- The acronym **UVP** means **Unique Value Proposition**, or, what makes our potential offering different, unique, *better* than competitors.

- If we find competitors producing an offering with no discernible difference to ours, we **iterate** our original idea, to include some *unique* features and benefits that will **differentiate** our offering **from our competition**.

Marketing for Launch and Beyond

Beyond the initial groups of projected target markets and users who will likely find benefits in the features of our offering, any business needs a continual stream of customers to survive, and thrive. But how, and where, do we find more people likely interested in what we have to offer?

Remember, the third place most startups fail is they neglect to implement new offerings, or even new features and updates to their original release. They bask in their initial success too long. Continually developing upgrades and new products, as well as researching new markets, are essential to creating a sustainable business.

Horizontal and Vertical marketing helps us develop new products and updates that will keep our offering valuable, and relevant, a year after launch, as well as three years, and five years down the line. H & V models also help us find additional target markets and users in various market segments to sell to. This keeps our offerings, and company, ahead of competitors looking to cash-in on our growing market share.

We examine Horizontal and Vertical marketing next.

MODULE 10: HORIZONTAL & VERTICAL MARKETING

Plan B, C, D...Etc.

Remember the three primary reasons startups fail?

1. **No one productizes the offering they plan to sell.**
2. **Startup launches without brand, and/or infrastructure** to support fulfillment.
3. **No one invests the time and/or money into research and development** of new or improved offerings, after their first release.

Smart businesses continually perform Competitive Analysis, and will quickly find what is selling, and even just getting attention in our connected world. It is imperative you produce new features/functions *and* related offerings to your original release every 6 - 9 months or so, to keep the first adopters of your product, as well as to stay ahead of competitors, who will exploit your success as soon as you have any. Additionally, each new upgrade, feature, or offering you implement will lead to more markets and users who will find benefits in what you are selling.

LSM Workbook 1- RAF Marketing Method PLAN B, C, D...ETC.

HORIZONTAL & VERTICAL MARKETING

Horizontal & Vertical Marketing

HORIZONTAL Markets

- Defined by offering's features' applicability for business and personal use.
- Broad markets across many industries, job functions, and consumer uses.
- Can be cooperative, often seeking joint marketing partnerships to expand 'reach.'

VERTICAL Markets

- Business is defined by the industry the offering serves.
- Specific 'niche' markets that [generally] do not cross industries.
- Marketing to specific target users within a specific industry.

Horizontal and Vertical marketing (H & V) models are guidelines to help us continually identify potential new targets to market our offerings—ones we'd not considered during the initial target marketing process. We utilize H & V modeling during the Productization process, to broaden our reach to as many as possible who may be interested in our product, service or message *before* we begin the branding and advertising of our offering and company.

Similar to market segmentation, H & V modeling is a technique for focusing on just two *qualitatively* different industry segments to determine where our offering fits, and then identify the *people*, through their job functions, who will likely benefit from our product or service within these targeted industries.

As mentioned, research and development are essential to creating a sustainable company. The Productization process helps us actualize ideas, or offerings into products or services of *value*, but it also helps us identify and overcome road blocks that we will likely encounter throughout the startup process. Competition is one of these roadblocks. If your original idea has been developed and released by competitors before you launch yours, creating lists of potential horizontal and vertical products during Productization, can help you iterate your original idea into a *marketable* product or service with unique features and benefits. If your launch offering is not gaining traction—building brand awareness, and/or selling, your H & V Productization lists will help identify potential new markets to sell to.

Horizontal Marketing

Horizontal marketing helps us focus on finding new target markets and potential **users across a wide range of businesses and industries** that will benefit from our offering.

Consumer goods, like food, fashion, electronics, are considered business-to-consumer markets (B2C), because these offerings will benefit a large variety of people in many types of jobs. Horizontal marketing helps us figure out what people, in which job functions, *regardless* of the industry they work, would benefit from the particular features of our offering.

Most everyone, in any job function, needs office furniture. But we can *not* market effectively to *most everyone*. To get the greatest response to our marketing efforts, we must drill down as closely as possible to an individual's particular tastes, interests, and desires. Since *'most everyone'* is too broad to target effectively, I want to market to my *lowest hanging fruit*—the most likely groups of target users that will find interest in what I'm selling. From purchasing managers for large corporations, considered a business-to-business (B2B) market, to entrepreneurs working out of their home (a B2C market)—anyone purchasing furniture for their business environment would be a good candidate to market my office furniture. Remember, the tighter we target our marketing efforts, the better our conversion rates (buy, try, subscribe), even in broad, horizontal markets.

Most *Apple* devices can be used by everyone, across most any market segment. *Iphones* to *iPads*, *Apple* devices are user-friendly technology that crosses all industries. *Apple* target markets their products both horizontally and vertically, meaning they have both broad markets and niche markets they sell to. However, *Apple* grew to the enormous corporation it is today, by targeting one group of potential users per campaign.

The *Macintosh* computer is now marketed to graphic designers, video editors, photographers, developers...etc. It's a complex machine used by professionals for business (B2B). The *Mac* is marketed horizontally—to many groups of users across many industries. Publishing, to movie production, to software development, the *Mac* is a versatile computer that can be utilized by many types of business professionals.

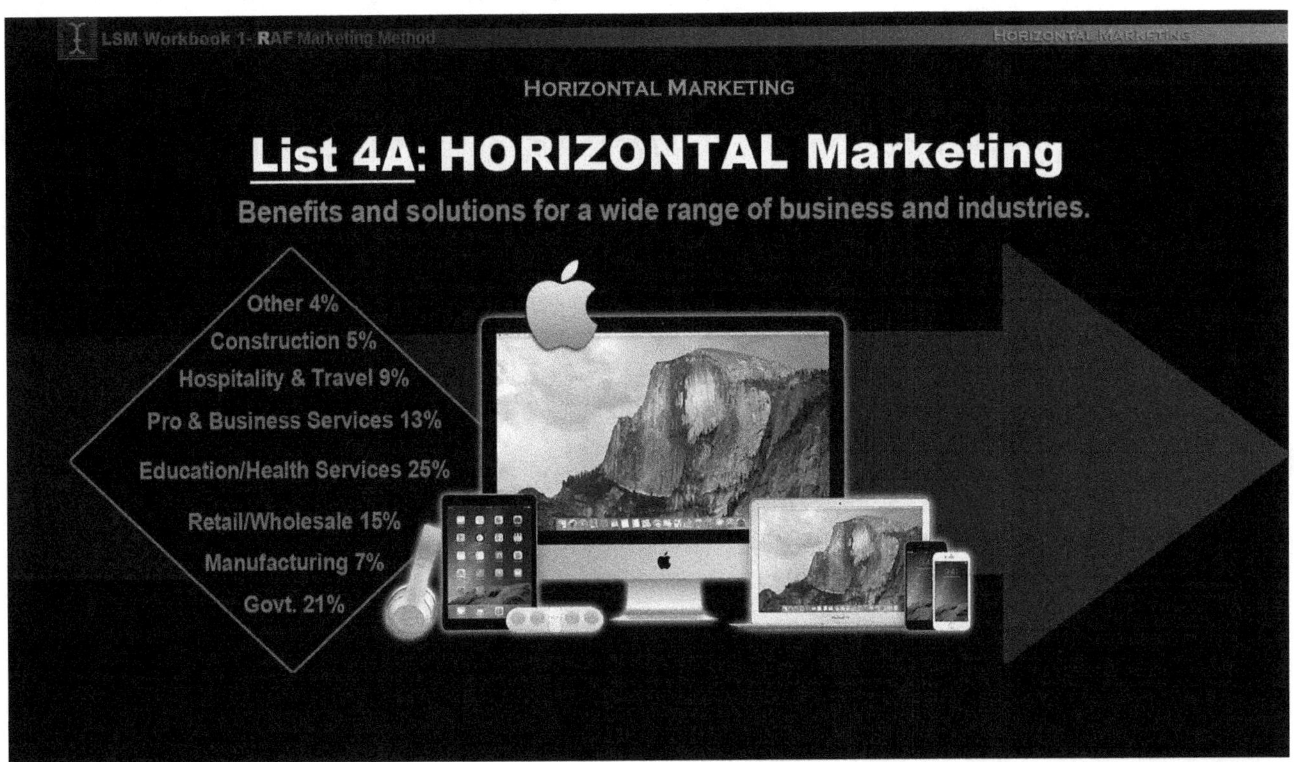

Most *Apple's* laptops, however, are marketed to consumers (B2C), from students, to parents, to business pros. While *Apple* sells to these B2C and B2B markets, each are considered horizontal markets because their laptops will benefit many people across multiple fields and industries.

Beyond their electronic devices, *Apple* has many software products, such as *iTunes*, *iBooks*, *Apple Pay* (a mobile credit card-type payment method), and the

App Store, which functions as a reseller for online applications and video games.

Let's say I choose to use *Apple's App Store* as a reseller for my new video game. There are only a select group of people who will be interested in "Brain Games," my MMOG (massive multiplayer online game) of dynamic games and puzzles for *smart* people. Software developers, maybe lawyers, accountants, C-level executives, will want to play, and revel in feeling smart when they level-up. These target users are *not* industry specific—most can be found across a wide range of industries—which is why these groups are considered horizontal markets for my video game.

Horizontal marketing blends particularly well with **cooperative marketing**. Companies with related offerings that compliment each other often develop alliances, and produce advertising strategies and campaigns merging the two businesses. The firms combine their resources, such as production and distribution capabilities, in order to maximize their reach, and subsequently, sales. A natural fruit drink company may partner with an organic chips maker, and the two products are marketed, and sometimes even distributed together.

We'll examine my fictitious app, *PHP Advocates*, potential horizontal and vertical markets in a minute. To project horizontal targets for *your* offering, for launch and beyond, consider how the features of your product or service can solve a problem, or add value to someone's life or job tasks across a broad range of industries. How does your offering serve specific people (target users) across multiple industry sectors?

Vertical Marketing

Vertical Marketing is specialized for a specific industry. Most consumers don't need a $30,000 baking oven, but a baker does. In fact, the oven she has was built specifically for commercial bakeries.

Vertical marketing is generally business to business (B2B) markets—referring to people within a specific trade or industry who will benefit from our product or service, which was usually designed as a solution to meet a specific need.

Intel sells computer chips for computers, refrigerators, cellphones, etc., for the electronic device manufacturing industry. Of course, when *Intel* markets to this very broad target industry, they'll segment these groups into target users, such as appliance manufacturers, and computer makers...etc.

Vertical markets, helps us find customers within **specific industries and businesses**.

Generally, products and services that solve a need for a specific industry or job task, were conceived and developed for that purpose. When we consider vertical markets for our offering, we have to identify how our product or service benefits a specific job function, or industry trade.

Voxx International Corp. produces peripheral products for vehicles, exclusively for the automotive industry. *Voxx* markets their offerings to car manufacturers from *Ford* to *Tesla*. Additional vertical *products* to their existing product line could be rear-view, or side-mirror cameras, or a magnetic charging mount for cellphones. Additional vertical *markets* for these new products could be aftermarket auto parts and accessory stores, instead of just the car manufacturers *Voxx* has been targeting with their marketing efforts.

If *Voxx* wanted to expand into horizontal markets, they could develop a personal entertainment platform, like a music or video streaming service, that many individuals across many industries may want, and sell it directly to consumers. Right now, however, *Voxx* is producing vertical products, and vertically marketing their offerings exclusively to the automotive industry.

Vertical markets for my "Brain Games" video game would be to sell my game to gaming companies like *EA* (*Electronic Arts*), or *Sony's Playstation*, as one of many games in their library.

When projecting vertical markets for *your* offering/s, consider if there are features/functions and benefits of your product or service that can be marketed to serve a *specific job task within a specific industry*. If so, for what industry sector, or job function, would the features of your offering serve?

Productization List 4A: Horizontal Modeling

To identify additional target markets and users for my factitious application, *PHP Advocates*, I create my final two of the eight required Productization lists—List 4A: HORIZONTAL MARKETS, and 4B: VERTICAL MARKETS.

I begin with List 4A, and identify horizontal markets for my application. While horizontal marketing can give us broad groups to target with our marketing efforts, we still must drill down to *who* these people actually *are*, what they like and don't, where to find them, and how to reach them. It is important to focus your campaign messaging on solving an issue or fulfilling a desire of specific **target users** within any given broad horizontal market, as *Apple* does, in the example above. Remember, targeting individual fulfillment with your marketing efforts will garner the greatest response.

During the Target Marketing process, I've already identified *millennial students, entrepreneurs* and *business professionals* as potential target users for *PHP Advocates.* I'd like to expand on these groups of horizontal markets, to identify more potential users for my application.

We derive our target markets and users from the features and benefits our offering/s provide. So, to find additional markets, I need to examine my application, and identify, or *create* additional features and benefits I did not previously consider. I can use H & V modeling to do this, to help me segment ideas into two qualitative categories. I'll begin with horizontal functions that I can implement in *PHP Advocates* at launch, or down the line. These additional functions will identify more potential target markets who can utilize them.

Legal experts for online and in-person consulting can be another function, benefit, and solution of *PHP Advocates.* Lawyers can be available to chat 24/7 with *mid-life women* considering divorce, live online. Attorneys are also available to *join* users at business meetings as a legal advocate, to assist *entrepreneurs* with contract negotiations. The *legal consultant* category of *PHP Advocates* will likely serve many horizontal markets, across a wide range of industries, but I must consider each market separately, to identify *individuals* within these broad horizontals to target my marketing efforts.

Nutrition experts can help *single millennials* to *parents*, to *mid-life women and men* adopt healthy lifestyles. Live, online, they can counsel users on meal preparation, or join them shopping to demonstrate how to read labels and find healthy food choices for themselves and their kids. This new category for *PHP Advocates* is horizontal because nutrition experts can benefit many groups of target markets across many industries or job functions.

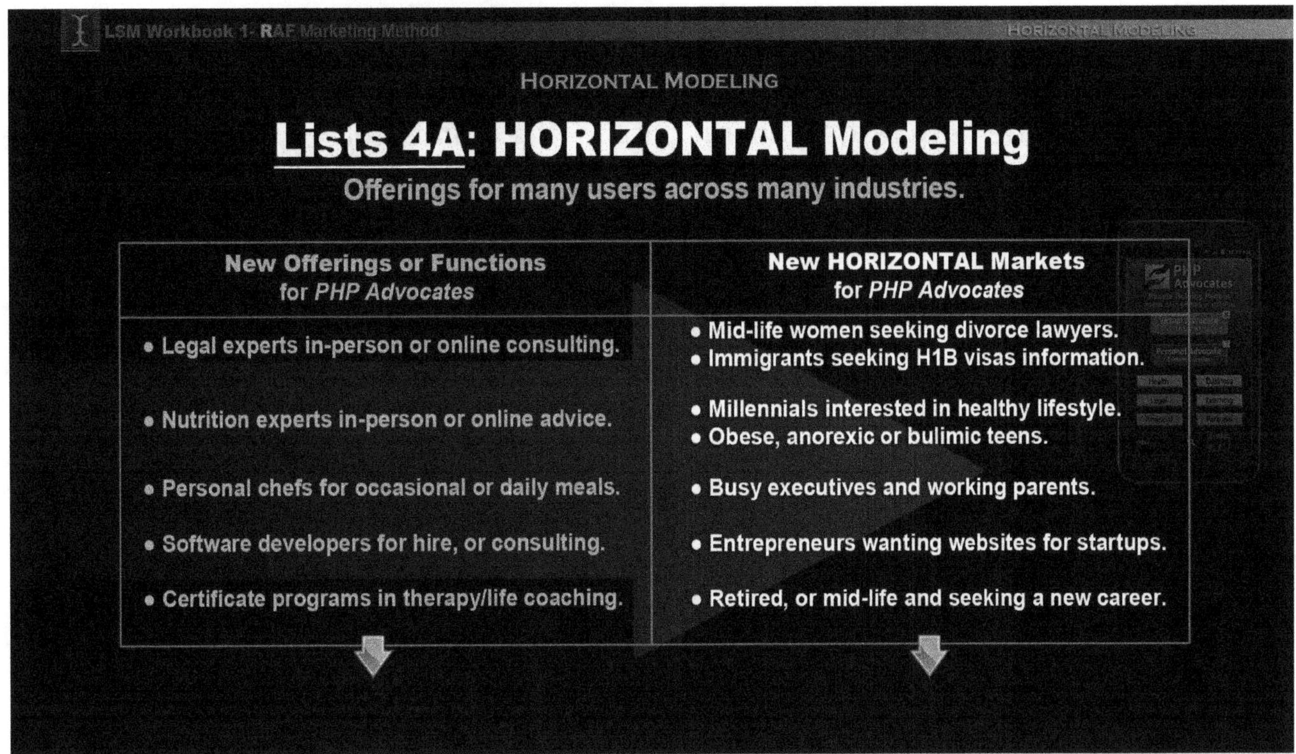

Have you ever been working in a program or application and have no clue how to make it do what you want it to do? Software developers are an additional category I can implement in *PHP Advocates*. They can act as consultants, live online, or I can hire them directly to produce my websites or a recommendation engine for my new application.

I derive List 4A: HORIZONTAL MARKETS for *PHP Advocates* by transposing these new categories and offerings into groups of potential new target markets.

Productization List 4A: HORIZONTAL MARKETS for *PHP Advocates:*

- Mid-life women looking for legal advice about divorce.
- Immigrants looking for legal advice on employment with H1B visas.
- Single millennials interested in a healthy lifestyle.
- Working parents wanting to prepare quick, healthy meals for family.
- Parents of obese, anorexic, or bulimic teens.
- Busy executives throwing work-related, or networking parties.
- Entrepreneurs wanting websites for startups.
- Business pros seeking help working a program or application.

Constructing this list of potential horizontal markets not only gives me additional people to market my application to, it also gives me **product ideas** to implement for launch, or in the future.

Once I've identified some potential horizontal markets for my application, I'll drill down into these broad targets, narrow them down to potential users, just as we did with Productization lists 2A and 2B—detailing characteristics of target markets into tightly segmented target users. I'll do the same for my list of potential vertical markets as well.

Productization List 4B: Vertical Modeling

Just like your horizontal markets, VERTICAL MARKETS, List 4B, like all target markets, are derived from the features and benefits your offering/s provide.

Students are a broad horizontal market for my *PHP Advocates* app. To serve more markets, I project that *PHP Advocates* will [eventually] have online courses, tests and projects that meet federal academic guidelines and standards for K-12 public education. A vertical market for this particular function of my application would be *public school educators*. But I'll start with my 'lowest hanging vertical fruit,' and market this function directly to *public school district administrators*, as they can supply all the teachers in their district with the benefits of courses that meet the federal standards that *PHP Advocates* will provide.

The *legal consultant* function of *PHP Advocates* may also be vertically marketed to *lawyers*. I can promote the wide variety of legal researchers, or expert trial witnesses, such as crime pathologists and psychologists for hire, that my application offers *lawyers* and *law firms*.

Ill, injured, or chronic pain suffers are broad horizontal markets. I wish someone would implement a private, secure platform exclusively for *doctors* worldwide to exchange cases, treatments and outcomes to accelerate healing, and the curing of disease. I'll add this as an additional [projected] vertical function in *PHP Advocates,* to target some of my vertical marketing efforts at *doctors*, *hospitals* and *health care institutions*.

Entertainers, athletes and *public figures* need agents to help them get gigs and negotiate contracts. I can add entertainment agents and agencies as an additional category for my application.

Complex hardware and software, like *Oracle's* offerings, often need a specialist on staff to troubleshoot issues that continually arise, with everything from connectivity to networking. *PHP Advocates* can offer accredited programs to train employees as Oracle experts.

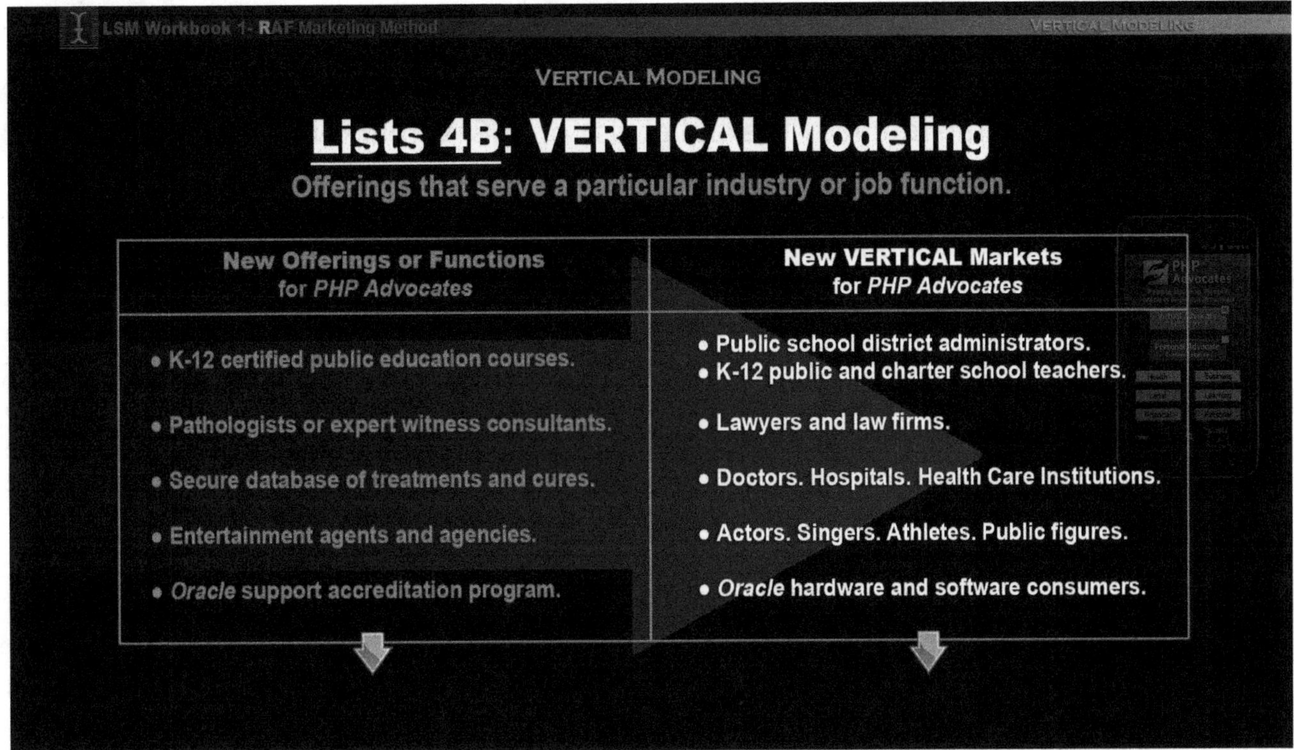

These, and other Vertical functions can be implemented for launch, and down the line, to have a continual stream of upgrades and new offerings to release for my application. With each additional function, a benefit is derived. With each additional benefit, a target market is discovered.

Productization List 4B: VERTICAL MARKETS for *PHP Advocates:*

- Public school educators offering online courses.
- Public school district administrators adding online courses to their curriculum.
- Lawyers and law firms looking for legal consultants and experts.
- Doctors interested in curing disease and accelerating healing.
- Hospitals and HMOs interested in lowering costs by accelerating healing through informed, effective treatments.
- Actors, singers, athletes, public figures looking for representation.
- *Oracle* hardware and software consumers.

Effective H & V Modeling

While some of these functions and markets, whether horizontal or vertical, will be implemented far into the future, when there will likely be more demand for the technology I am envisioning, I add it to my H & V lists anyway. The objective of

Horizontal and Vertical modeling during the Productization process, is to come up with as many additional features/functions for your offering as you can conceive that will benefit additional markets you'd not considered during the Target Marketing process.

Regardless of how far-fetched, the bullet list of H & V markets in List 4A and 4B are about noting possibilities. Performing H & V modeling will help guide your product development with potential iterations of your offering, *and* identify additional marketing opportunities. You're going to need Plan B, C, D...etc., options, when, during competitive analysis, you discover the original offering you've conceived is already being done by someone else. You're also going to need dynamic lists of potential new features/functions, benefits and solutions for your offering, as well a constant stream of target markets and users to sell to create a sustainable company. Horizontal and Vertical modeling keeps you on the research and development track to creating a successful startup at launch and beyond.

Put Theory into Practice

Still not sure what the difference is between horizontal and vertical products and/or markets? To help you identify which type of market you are selling to, remember the two simplified equations below to discern horizontal from vertical marketing.

- **H= B2C and B2B markets**
  HORIZONTAL targets can be both business to business, and business to consumer markets. **Horizontal products** are used by many people across a wide range of industries and job functions.

- **V= B2B markets**
  VERTICAL targets are [usually] business to business, and/or wholesale markets. **Vertical products** are specialize for a specific industry or job function.

While there are exceptions to these rules, use them as guidelines to understand how horizontal and vertical modeling can be applied in real world marketing. Don't ignore the fact that your business will require a continual stream of potential users in which to market your offerings, even if you garnered many actual customers at launch. Utilize horizontal and vertical marketing to help you discover who these target markets and users may be, what they like, and don't, where to find them and how to reach them.

The horizontal and vertical marketing process provides a framework to help us discover additional target markets and users for each particular feature/function of our offering. H & V modeling also helps us conceive and create unique features and solutions, that will benefit potential new markets. It really doesn't matter how we label these new markets, so don't get hung up on trying to figure out if a potential target audience is horizontal or vertical. Use these models to help you streamline the process of targeting new markets and users, for the life-cycle of your offering.

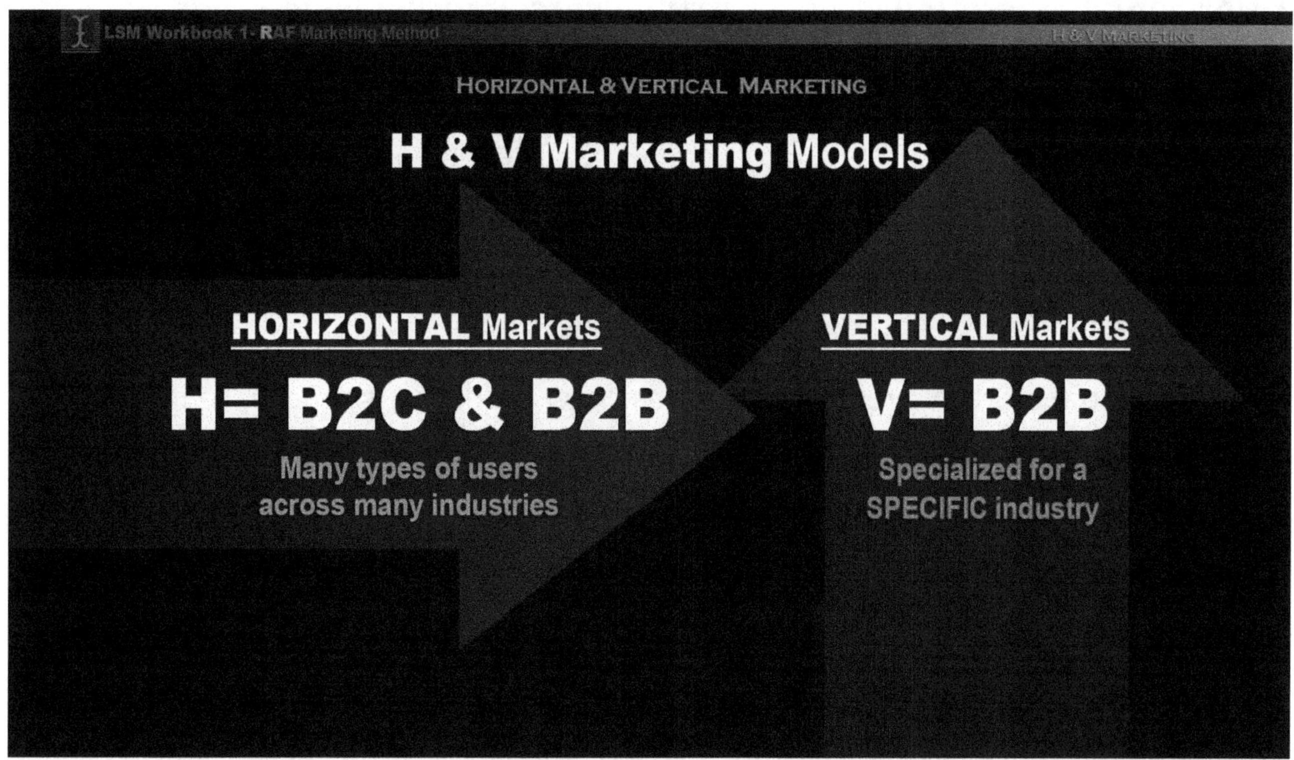

Like *all* Productization lists, H & V lists, 4A and 4B, should be filed in their proper folders in your Startup Hierarchy, and available to all stakeholders in the development and marketing of your offering/s.

MODULE 10: H & V MARKETING REVIEW

- The third reason why startup fail is the company rides on the success of their first offering for too long. It is mandatory to invest in **research and development** of new products, upgrades, and even profit models, to serve your current customers, but also to attract new users.

- We utilize **H & V modeling** during the **Productization process** to broaden our reach, to as many as possible who may be interested in our offering at launch, and beyond.

- Identifying additional **Horizontal and Vertical markets** in the **Productization process** provides a continual stream of potential target markets and target users to sell to.

- **Horizontal marketing** identifies **many users across a wide range of industries,** that will find value in your offering. To find **Horizontal markets** for your offering, consider how your product or service benefits users across many industries.

- **Vertical marketing** identifies a **specific industry or job function** that may benefit from purchasing or utilizing your offering. To find **vertical markets** for your offering, consider how your product or service benefits a particular industry's needs.

- It is essential startup's release upgrades, new products, services, features and benefits, every 6 - 9 months or so, to keep your offering relevant to first adopters, and to garner additional H & V markets with each new release. If *you* don't, your competitors will. Welcome to the internet age.

Creating Offerings of Value, for PROFIT

We've productized our idea into an offering, by listing some of its **features** and **benefits—List 1A and 1B**. We've listed potential **target markets** and **users** who will likely find value in our product or service—**List 2A and 2B**. We've documented **competitors** producing similar offerings to ours, and identified **differentiators** and unique value propositions (**UVPs**) that make our offering great—**List 3A and 3B**. And we've conceived new features and benefits that will keep it relevant to both **horizontal** and **vertical markets** down the line—**List 4A and 4B**. And we've developed an **elevator pitch** to chat up our great new product or service everywhere we go, to everyone we meet.

Step 1 of the RAF Marketing Method— Get Ready, and productize your idea into an offering of value is well underway. But LSM is more than just actualizing ideas into products or services of value. It's also marketing them, for profit. Examining profit models for your new venture is next.

◆◆◆◆◆

MODULE 11: PROFIT MODELS

How Will Your Startup Make Money?

Facebook, Twitter, SnapChat, all IPOed—became public companies—with billion-dollar valuations, without being profitable. In other words, these companies made less money than they were spending at the time they went public, became publicly traded companies.

So, why do you need to project a **Profit Model** at this early stage of development? As of this writing, *Facebook* is very profitable.

LinkedIn, the business/jobs platform, was profitable with a **Premium profit model** *before* going public. Their public offering price-per-share opened at $45, and *doubled* before the session closed on May 19, 2011.

Facebook's per share stock price was *lower* than it opened ($38 a share) for well over a year, until they devised an **affiliate marketing** revenue profit model that brought in more than they were spending. *Twitter, Snapchat* and others without profit models that projected a path to a healthy net profit after launch, to date of this writing, have yet to find their footing, and their stock continues to decline, or has stayed flat in value.

There is a viral sickness around Silicon Valley these days, with startups thinking all they have to get is users on their site, which, somehow, down the line, will translate into profits. But this is not true. Online traction does *not* mean sales, or even profits. Impressions, Shares, Likes, even clicks on your landing pages or folks pursuing your website does not necessarily translate into sales. You need a *plan*, a profit model that illustrates how you will make money on each sale of your offering, or each visitor to your business or your website.

Revenue models generally change over time as a business grows, but establishing a realistic revenue stream before launch, insures all stakeholders in your new venture are working towards the same goal of actualizing an offering of value, for *profit*.

Devising a profit model is the last component you must initialize in the Productization process, to get your offering **Ready** to brand and market. Only *after* we've figured out *what* our offering is, who will find value in it, and defined what makes it *better* than our competitors, now, and down the line, can we assess what our product or service is likely worth.

Your profit model at launch should encourage user engagement. **UX** (**user experience**) takes on many forms. Get people to come in to a new local yogurt shop with **Freemium** incentives, like taste-trials of any of their 20 flavors. Get users to sign-up and engage on your social platform with initial low or no cost options, such as a Premium profit model, like *LinkedIn* offers. The launch profit model is generally to collect market share, not *necessarily* make a profit. However, as your company grows, hopefully gains a loyal following, even a modest one, a year down the line, it may be time to reconsider your initial profit model, and implement another, with a higher monetary return.

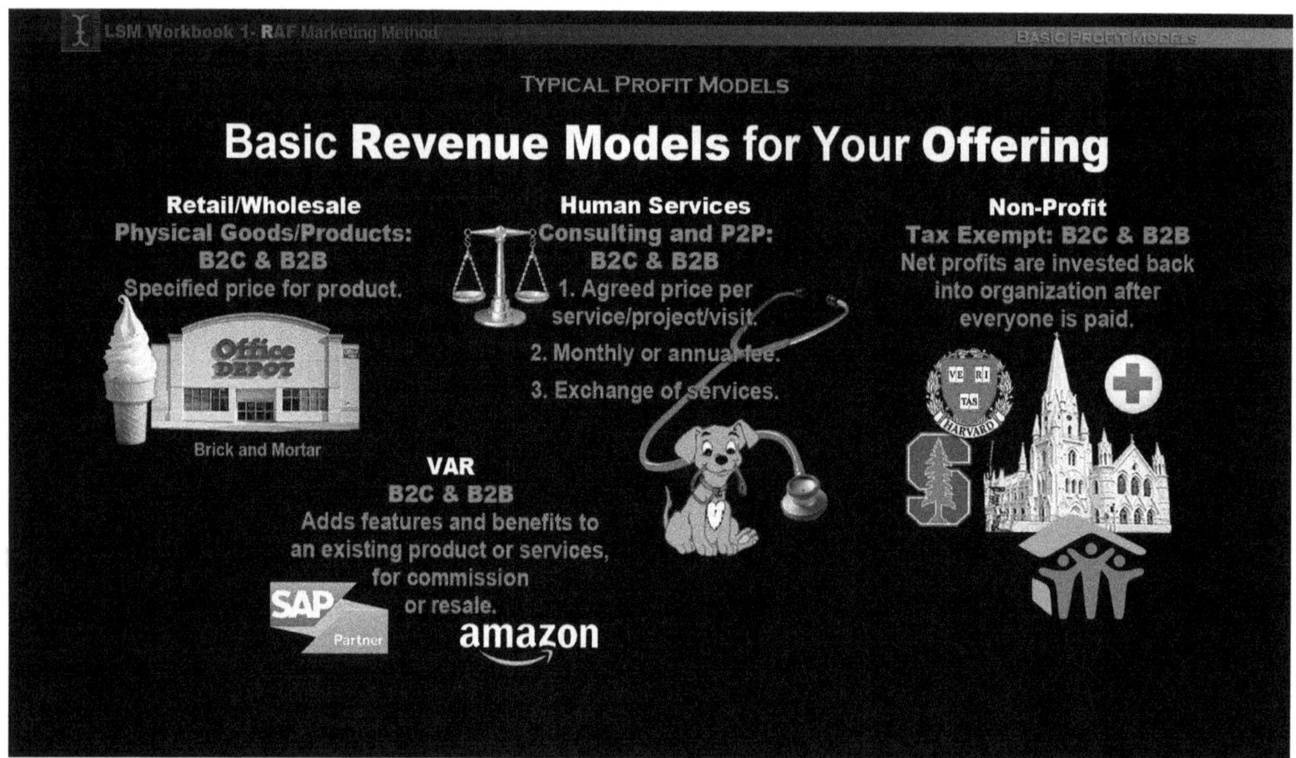

Let's examine some typical ways businesses make a profit before we take on software profit models. We'll begin with traditional profit models that we're all familiar with.

- **Retail and Wholesale**
- **Value Added Resellers (VAR)**
- **Human Services**
- **Non-Profit Organizations**

Retail vs. Wholesale

We start with one of the oldest revenue models—**Retail** and **Wholesale**. Whether selling products and services directly from a store, known as a 'brick and mortar' location, or online through the internet, **retail is considered business-to-consumer (B2C) sales**. Consumers, clients, users, whatever we call them, retail sells to individuals, like you and me.

The **wholesale profit model sells to businesses**, corporations, and government entities at a reduced rate, who then turn around and resell the offering for a profit via wholesale to another distributor, or retail—directly to the consumer. Wholesale generally sells large quantities of a product, or specialized services that can be repackaged and sold by others.

Retail and wholesale profit models generally set a specified price for their offerings. Online purchases are *severely* hurting brick and mortar [physical location] sales. We'd rather buy our consumer goods online these days, than wait in line at a store we have to drive to, and likely pay for parking. Online sales are projected to cut deeper and deeper into brick and mortar sales, so think twice about only selling your offering from a specific location. If at all possible, sell through online venues as well, even if it's simply to pre-order for pick-up.

Value Added Resellers

Value Added Resellers (VAR), for wholesale or retail products, like *Google Plus*, or *Amazon,* are storefronts that provide services like secure transactions on their high-traffic platforms, for a percent of the money from each purchase or use of your offering. If you price your widget at $100, and sold one through a typical VAR, like *Etsy*, you'd only receive, in some cases, less than half that amount for the sale. The VAR keeps the other half of the money for supplying the platform to complete the sale's transaction.

VARs are also found in professional services. Technology consultants that set-up integrated systems, to B2C services like the *Geek Squad*, that install software, troubleshoot, and customize your personal computer, are considered VAR profit models. If you have no interest in starting a startup at this time, and only want to produce your original idea and sell it directly to consumers, a VAR will help you achieve this goal. We'll examine how to utilize VARs to sell *your* offering directly, through platforms like *Amazon, Google Plus*, and *Etsy* in the Online Marketing module in LSB Workbook 2.

Peer-to-Peer (P2P) and Other Human Services

Human Services may be delivered live, and/or online, and include consultants, from real estate brokers to dentists, accountants, psychologists...etc. They can be P2P services like *AirBnB*, or my fictitious app, *PHP Advocates*. A Human Services profit model is usually a specified or agreed upon price for the service, visit, or project, or a monthly or annual fee.

Exchange of Services (EOS) means you trade your skills, time and expertise, even money to complete the job if necessary, for the skill set of a professional that you need, with no monetary compensation paid by either party. Historically, EOS was utilized often, however, trading services is rare these days. It doesn't hurt to ask, though. Need help with a professional service you can't afford? Put a free ad on *Craigslist* to look for pros willing to do an EOS.

The Beauty of Nonprofit

Nonprofit is a **tax-free profit model**. Non-profit organizations issue no stock, and they can not be publicly traded. They have no private owners, and show no profits. This does *not* mean no one is making money. In fact, some of the highest salaries are awarded to executives of nonprofit's. University professors, priests to U.S. senators enjoy excellent salaries and exceptional benefits packages, all under the nonprofit umbrella. Nonprofit simply means all the profits, through donations or direct payments, as with college tuition, are invested back into the operation of the organization, so at the end of each fiscal year they show no profit.

Nonprofits exist as both brick and mortar locations, such as *Goodwill* stores, and accredited universities across the country, as well as online, with companies such as *Khan Academy*, a global education technology platform.

It is a sly marketing practice to launch a startup as a nonprofit, then a few years down the line, when they've garnered enough of a user-base, switch to a profit-based model. *Change.org*, the petition site, began as a nonprofit organization. They got users to sign petitions, even donate money, with the notion that they were supporting causes out of philanthropy, and no one was making a profit with their signatures. *Change.org* is making money with every signature they gather on their 'supported' petitions, put up by organizations that paid *Change* to showcase their marketing efforts. To date, *Change* still carries the *.org* extension, even though they and no longer a nonprofit business.

Your startup must fall under select guidelines to qualify for nonprofit status. If you think your new venture may be better suited as a nonprofit business, look up what these guidelines are, as they vary per industry sector and region. If you're looking to create a tax-free business from the ground up, start a charity, or a religion, or a school, or perhaps a new political party...; }

Typical Software Profit Models

A good percentage of today's innovators are developing software products, or **software-as-a-service** (**SaaS**) applications. What this means is, there are no physical materials needed to produce the software, because software programs, applications and platforms have no physical properties. With software, you're not selling anything corporeal. You're basically marketing a service through a space, or *portal* on the internet.

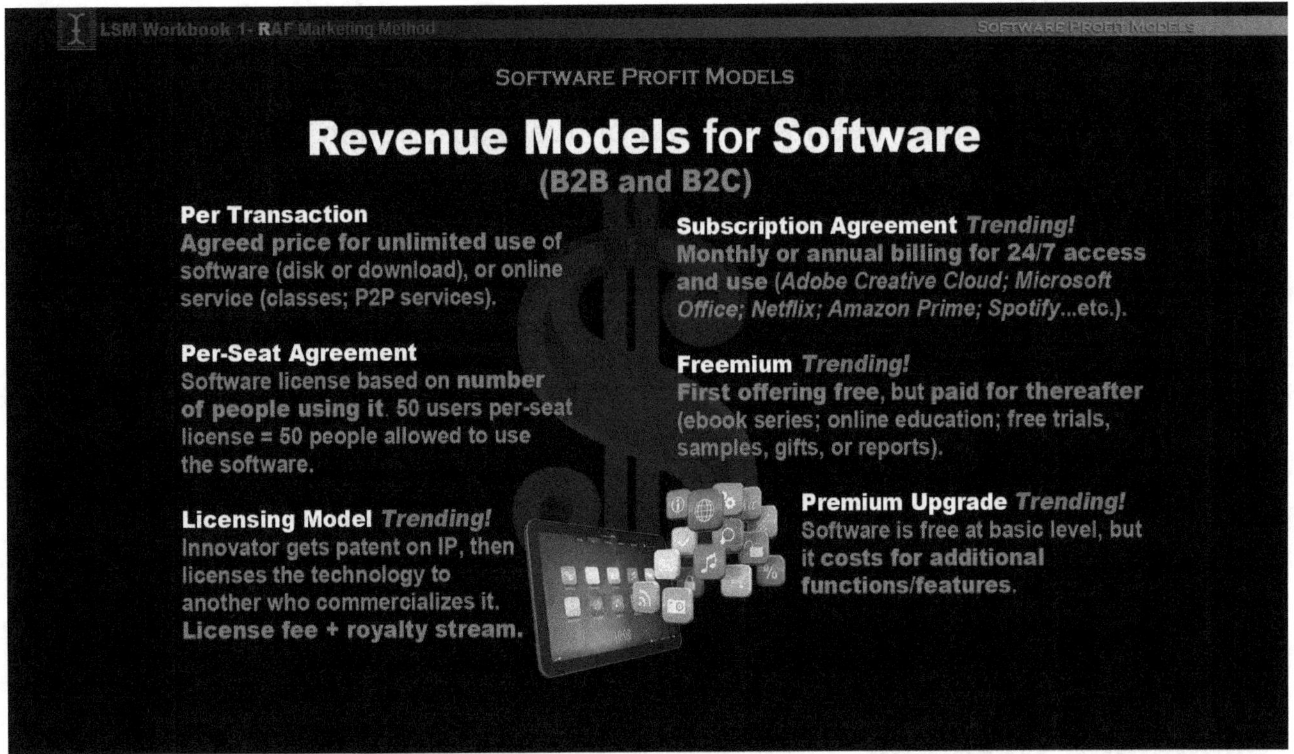

Developing a SaaS application and selling it directly, as with online gaming, or building a startup around gaming, like *SteamPowered*, is smart business. Software is cheap to reproduce and distribute across platforms, from your cellphone to your laptop (cloud computing). It's quickly scalable (or should be), since nothing needs to be physically produced, so it's easier to fulfill increased demand by users, by adding more servers, and tighter compression algorithms for load-time delivery. It can be licensed, instead of sold directly, and therefore individual developers can reap continual profits from the sale of offerings in which their software is embedded.

Using our loose definition of SaaS—software sold and accessed through the cloud (on the internet)—we'll include peer-to-peer (P2P) applications like *Lyft*, or *Airbnb*, to data management and analysis programs like *Salesforce*, to web hosts and customer management systems (CMS) like *WordPress*, to sales platforms like *Amazon*, and drill down on some of the profit models these companies employ.

- **Per Transaction profit models** are generally an **agreed upon price for the software**. Every time one of my books, in print or ebook, is purchased, I get an agreed upon amount of money from the sale. The book can be read, or even shared as many times as the buyer desires, but I only get paid from the initial purchase. Though prices may fluctuate, most ride sharing apps like *Uber* and *Lyft* charge per ride. E-learning (EdTech) platforms like *Udemy* charge per course. Individuals, like me, and companies like the above, use Per Transaction agreements. *Wordpress* (*WP*) also utilizes a Per Transaction profit model, when you purchase one of their premium website themes, or trending software plugins that adds functionality to your site. (You can also purchase URL's through *WP*, and other webhosts on an annual subscription basis. All URL's are purchased on subscription, regardless of where they are purchased, and must be renewed through a domain name registrar, generally annually.)

- **Per-seat licenses** are B2B profit models, and **limits the number of users to a specified amount** at purchase. Per-seat agreements are trending profit models, since we generally access software from the cloud today, usually on subscription basis, and it's easy for a SaaS business to charge *per computer* that the software is accessed from. While this profit model is easily abused by people claiming they need to access the software through multiple computers, only an *agreed upon number of people* in your organization may *legally* use per-seat license software. *Adobe Systems* employs a per-seat license subscription profit model that allow businesses with multiple users to access their *Creative Cloud* software.

Developing IP to Sell

Licensing models are contractual agreements between an inventor and [usually] a business. The inventor, or owner of the **intellectual property** (**IP**)—may be an algorithm, or a formula for a new medication—protects their IP with a patent, a copyright, or a trademark. The owner of the IP then sells a license of the innovation to a second party. This other party is usually a larger company, a corporation with the production, business and marketing knowledge and/or resources to turn the IP software into a feature/function of a larger application.

There are many types of licensing profit models, such as an exclusive license, where the buyer of the software or formula get to be the only company that repackages and distributes it. The original inventors of the image editing software, *Photoshop*, licensed it to *Adobe Systems*, who then sold it to *Apple*, through an exclusive license agreement until the late 1990s.

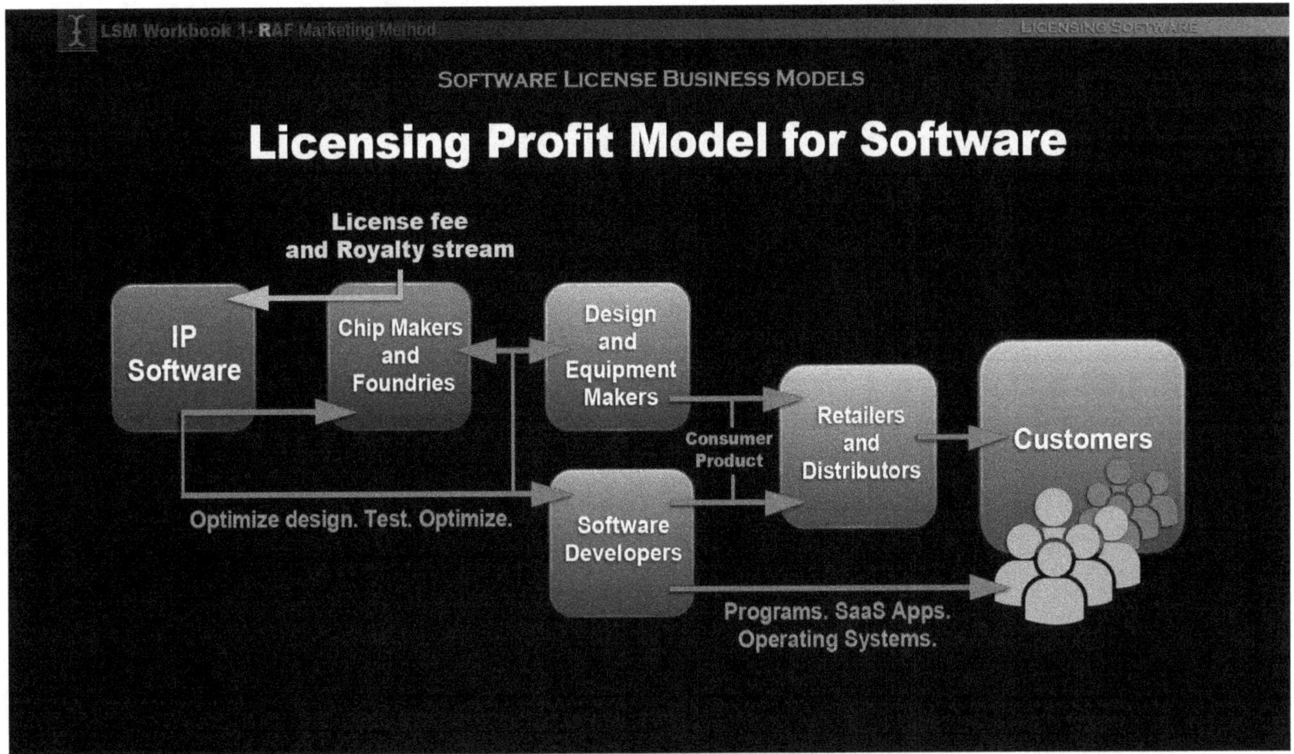

The profits to the IP holder (usually the software inventor) utilizing licensing agreements, generally come from two sources—an initial fee from the corporation for being allowed to use the software at all, and then a royalty stream, meaning every time the commercial version of the software, or with the software in it, is sold, the IP holder gets a percentage of the profit from its sale or use (similar to the VAR model). The rights to use the IP is usually an agreed upon fee, plus royalty, and usually the basis for the licensing business model.

Licensing profit models are often complicated, and should be reviewed by a lawyer working for *you*, not the attorney of the corporation to which you're licensing your software. If you are considering a licensing agreement for your software offering, consult an IP/contract attorney.

While licensing models sound tempting, there are risks having someone else handle the production, distribution and sales of your invention. It's important to evaluate your potential licensees carefully. Make sure the company has a track record of successfully launching products with software like yours. And be aware, a patent, copyright, or trademark is valueless unless you can afford to defend it. The high cost of litigation, suing someone for patent infringement—using your software without permission—is only doable if you can afford to hire legal counsel.

If you are a software developer, or inventor, with no interest in starting a company, but want to work for yourself, be your own CEO, then consider a Licensing profit model. Design and develop underlying technology that serves a function in another application.

Subscription Profit Models

Subscription Agreements are hip, slick and trending right now. Until recently, *Adobe Creative Suite (CS)* was available on disk. You paid for it once, loaded the applications onto your laptop or PC, and used them for years. Same with *Microsoft Office*. Today, both companies have gone to a subscription profit model, which requires users to pay them on a monthly or annual basis, whether we use the software or not. Movie and book streaming services like *Netflix* and *Amazon Prime* also use the popular subscription profit model.

Subscription agreements serve companies adopting this trending profit model in a variety of ways. It stops people from ripping off their software, as the latest versions are only accessible through the corporation's cloud. (We'll review cloud computing in the Online Technology module in LSB Workbook 2.) Additionally, the subscription profit model supplies a continual stream of income to the seller, as long as they can retain the user. Beyond this, subscription software often runs on the seller's servers. In other words, you are using the software on the seller's cloud, which gives them access to everything you produce with their software.

Google's algorithms can see and read everything you produce in *Google Docs*. When you checked "I Agree," to access *Google Docs*, you agreed to let *Google's* algorithms read the documents that you create in, or upload to, their application. *Google* can then use anything they want from your documents, for any purpose they want, at any time, without your consent. They 'mine' this data from billions of users, and analyze it to find patterns in language usage, and purchase behavior. Even the emojis you choose are used to match your words to how you're feeling, to help them 'get inside your head,' and more effectively market to you. *Google* then matches your psychographic and behavioral data using **collaborative filters**, to find others like you to sell to, then they sell this information to **Affiliate Marketing Networks**, which we'll examine next.

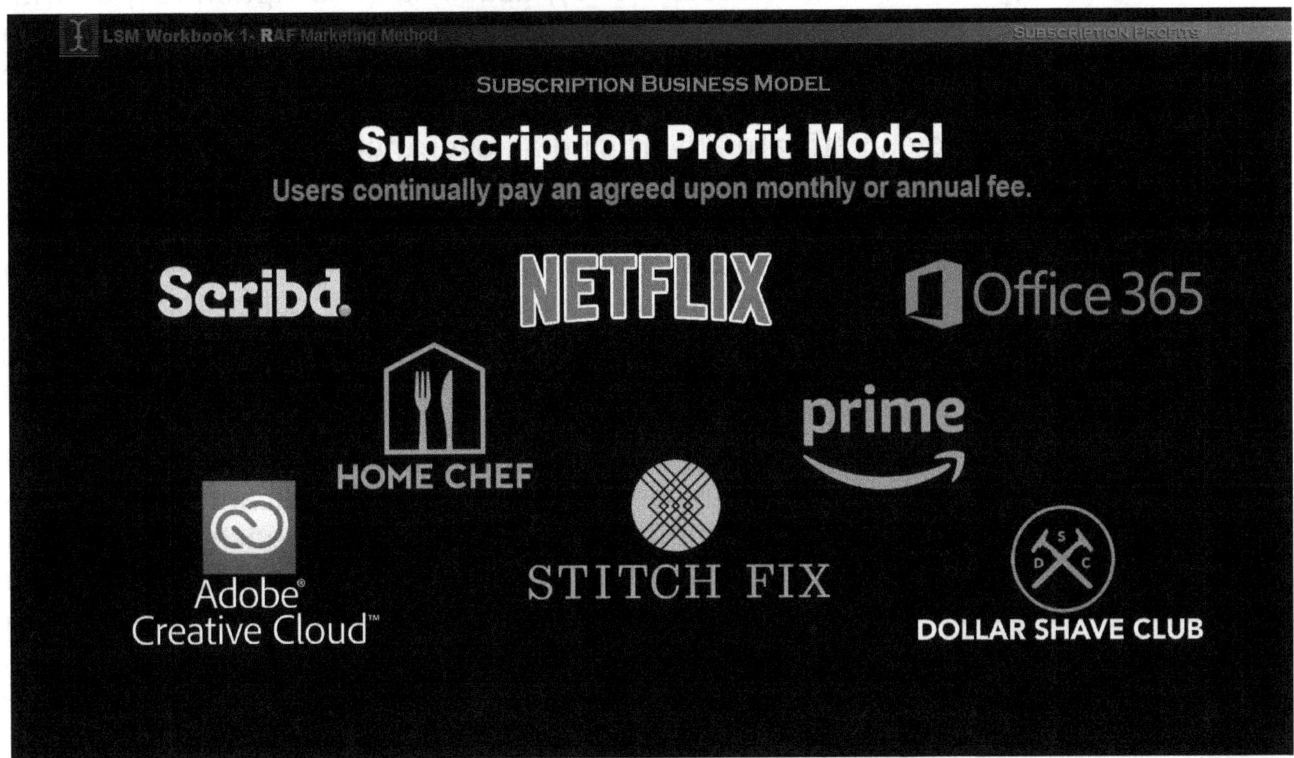

About the only advantage of a subscription agreement to the user, is that bug fixes can be automatically implemented every time the software is accessed. The obvious disadvantage to the user when we purchase a subscription agreement, is we are now forced to continually pay, whether we are regularly using the software or platform, or only use it intermittently.

Freemium and Premium Profit Models

- **<u>Freemium</u> profit models** are widely used in generating conversion through free trial offers. Most all of us love free stuff, which is why this profit model entices new users. Freemium works well for SaaS as a launch profit model, if the software has a user-friendly interface, and is intuitive and easy to use. Offering a trial use of your software for a week, or month, will show your potential target users just how great your new SaaS product is!

  The freemium profit model works well for many types of offerings. Giving away the first novel in a series motivates sales of the sequels. Special promotions, like getting a free pastry at a local bakery, are meant to entice recipients to purchase a coffee with their 'gift,' or come back and buy more another time.

- **Premium Upgrade profit models**, similar to the Freemium model, but offers *part* of the application's features for free. While free access is continual, to get full functionality of the software costs money, usually a subscription fee, as with the job site, *LinkedIn*. *Wordpress* offers their content management system (CMS) free, but there is a per-transaction cost with each product or service purchased. *Outlook*, *Microsoft's* email application, requires a premium upgrade to get rid of the annoying affiliate advertising all over their platform.

Freemium and Premium Upgrade profit models are meant to pique interest, and therefore effective for launching new products and startups that have yet to garner market share. These models are a 'no-risk' insurance policy for users get acquainted with your offering, hopefully fall in-love, and look forward to more, even if it means they have to pay for it.

The models discussed above are typical SaaS profit models for licensing and purchasing software. If you are planning to launch a SaaS application during the LSE Workbook series, be sure to implement a profit model for launch, as well as a year, three, and then five years down the line, as part of the Productization process, to insure all stakeholders in your new venture are on the path to creating and marketing an offering of value, for *profit*.

MODULE 11: TYPICAL & SAAS PROFIT MODELS REVIEW

- **Brick & Mortar** locations should have some type of online component—feature or service—to encourage in-store sales, even if it's only pre-order for pick-up.

- The acronym **VAR** means **Value Added Reseller**. **VARs** typically add features or functionality to the original offering. *Amazon* offers retailers a platform to sell their products, and also offers software companies, servers on their cloud platform (*Amazon Web Services*). **VARs** make a profit from an agreed price per transaction, or subscription for service, and/or commission fees.

- The typical **profit model** for **Human Services** is an agreed upon price, or fee for each service.

- A **nonprofit** organization shows no profit, and pays no taxes. Net earnings (including donations) are invested back into the company at the end of each fiscal year. Government entities, religious, charitable, or political organizations are **nonprofit**, **tax-free** businesses.

- Your **profit model** should change over time as your business grows. A LAUNCH **profit model** should encourage user engagement with **incentives**, such as a **Freemium** profit model.

- A **Subscription profit model** should be implemented *after* a company has an established, and loyal customer base.

- A software **License Agreement** means the original developer permits the use of their software as a function within another company's product or service, for a fee, as well as a royalty stream.

- Utilize new **profit models**, such as a **Premium Upgrade**, by adding horizontal and/or vertical features to your first release.

- Determining a **profit model** for LAUNCH during the **Productization process** helps keep all stakeholders on the path to actualizing an offering of value, for *profit*.

Success Breeds Affiliate Advertisers

Once your company or software offering has launched, and is gaining traction, additional profit models may be implemented. 'Selling air,' or a 'space' on the internet, like space on your website, blog or vlog (video blog), can be very profitable indeed, *if* you have enough unique visitors daily.

-

-

-AFFILIATE MARKETING-

Affiliate Marketing for Profit

Facebook, LinkedIn, Twitter, most any social network you can think of, uses the **Affiliate Marketing profit model** to sustain and grow their businesses. The *Huffington Post* to the *New York Times* also use affiliate marketing as their primary income generator. Affiliate marketing is becoming so popular that practically any site with traction is opting for this trending profit model.

Affiliate marketing isn't new. Embedding advertising, such as product placement in movies and TV shows, where the show's star drinks a *Diet Coke*, slowly savoring each gulp, is still a massively popular form of marketing. Viral affiliate marketing has been going on for years. *Sony,* and other video game makers find the most popular kids in school, and gives them the latest games and the consoles to play them on, so they'll show it to all their friends. The #1 way to get someone to take an action is through recommendations from trusted sources, like friends and family.

Facebook made almost $40 *billion* dollars on affiliate marketing in 2017, and that figure is projected to grow substantially in the next five years. That means advertisers—companies looking to market their products and services—are buying virtual space on *Facebook's* platform, so their ads will appear on the pages, and even in the feeds of popular, and not so popular *Facebook* users.

The idea with *digital* affiliate marketing is to get advertiser's ads in front of the people most likely to find interest in them. According to *Google*, and *Facebook*, they know who these people are because they track our behavior, and analyze the content of the posts of each and every one of their users, so they claim to know what we like and don't, where we hang out, what attracts us, and what we'll pass on. However, even with all this data crunching, *quantitative* data doesn't really tell us *qualitative* reasons why anyone really does most anything. This is a fatal flaw with machine learning, often called AI (artificial intelligence), and why, even with all this data, response rates are still between .05 - 5% with most digital marketing efforts.

There are many problems with the affiliate marketing profit model.

People lie. We *all* do, as previously stated. Like it or not, every one of you reading this book lies. A lot! We lie to ourselves—to feel smart, to appear kind, politically correct. We tell ourselves all kinds of crap to excuse unhealthy behavior, and rationalize our position with even more crap that we tell others, usually because we've convinced ourselves of falsehoods. Everyone does. Lying is a human condition, like self-interest.

When *Facebook* tells you *they know* who will find interest in your offering, well, they are lying to you. When people post on their *FB* feed, they often post falsehoods, either because they've convinced themselves they believe it, or because they are trying to convince others they are a certain type of person.

Additionally, advertisers, and advertising lies. Marketing sells real benefits, as well as *perceived* benefits. *Apple* sells the perception their devotees will be 'more creative' if they use *Apple* devices, but this is a lie. Creativity comes from inside of us, not from the technology we use to create it.

Affiliate networks don't have a clue who is lying and who isn't in their marketing campaigns, so when they try and match the content in an ad to the content on an affiliate marketer's site, their algorithm is basing this 'match' on keywords and phrases in the ad content, *not* whether the advert is true—really selling what it says it is, is tongue-in-cheek, or selling perception.

Affiliate networks (like *Google* and *Facebook)* **don't really care if YOU make money** on your marketing efforts with them. *They make money*, whether you do or not. In fact, every time someone clicks on an ad, the affiliate publisher makes money. *Google* might place your ads on a neo-nazi *YouTube* web page with messaging that you abhor. And you have no say, and won't even know your ads appeared there. Why do they do this? Their algorithms are too stupid to know that the neo-nazi group, using key phrases like *'first-amendment rights,'* and *'right to life,'* are really selling racism and hate.

Social networks allow this publishing of hate, and fake news through their affiliate marketing programs because they don't know, and don't really *care* what the ad is about, as long as they are getting paid to publish it. In the 2016 U.S. Presidential election, it has been proven that Russia, and likely other countries, spent millions in affiliate marketing with **pay-per-click** (**PPC**) ads that promoted fake news to get Donald Trump elected.

So, why do affiliate marketing at all as a fledgling startup with little cash, if it is so corrupt, and you'll likely make no money?

You *can* build your brand awareness, even get sales, and not spend a lot of money either, doing your *own* affiliate marketing! We'll go deep into how to get response with SMM (social media marketing), in LSB Workbook 2: Branding.

Additionally, LSM is Lean Startup *Marketing*, not Lean Startup *Morality*. The LSE series is designed to teach you a step-by-step *real-world* process for marketing an idea into an offering of value that generates a profit. The LSE series doesn't know *what* you are planning to produce and market. This course is meant to help you create effective marketing to sell your offering, whatever it is, inexpensively and effectively. And affiliate marketing can be a cost-effective venue to publish your digital marketing efforts.

Become an Affiliate Marketer for Cash

Affiliate Marketing is a trending way to not only market your offering to sell, but also to make money selling space on your internet properties, such as your websites, profile pages, and other digital platforms. Create a popular blog, *YouTube* vlog, or social media platform like a job, or peer-to-peer site, that gets a lot of hits—unique visitors—and then sell advertising *space* on your virtual property.

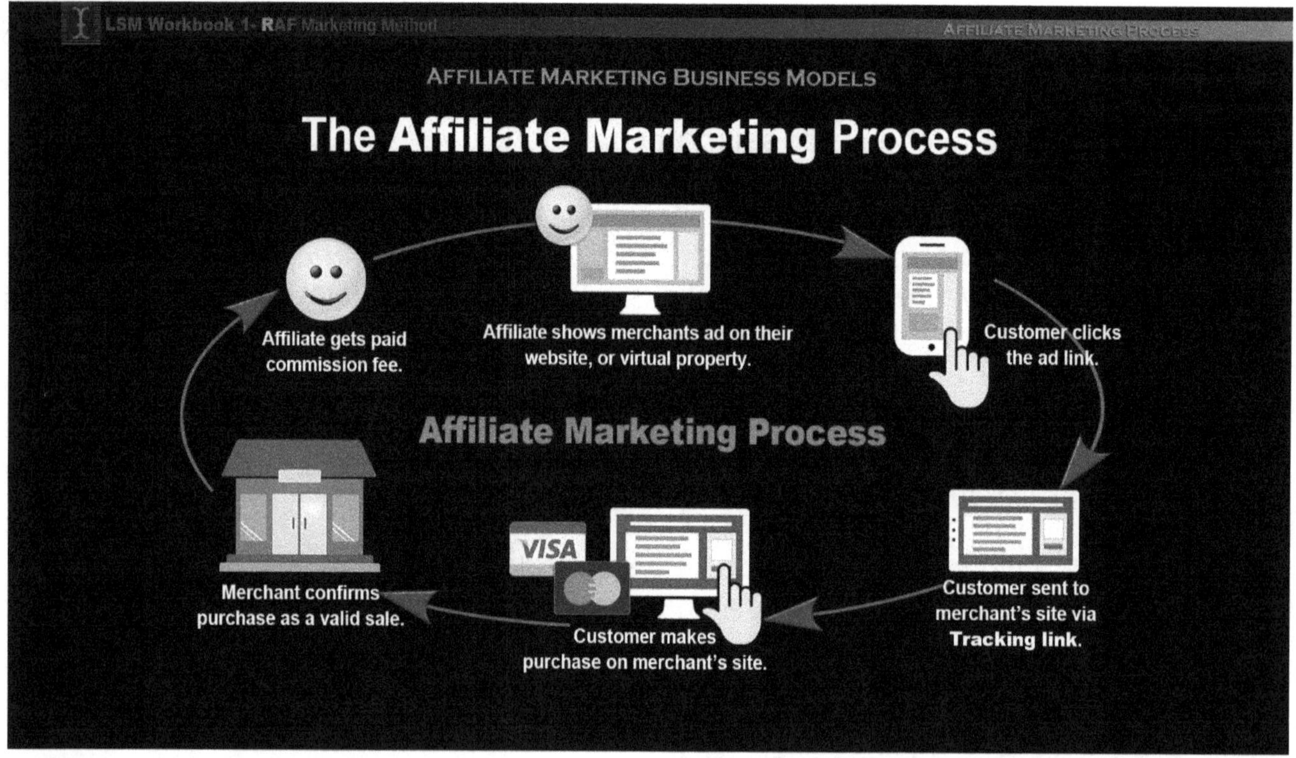

To become an **affiliate marketer**, also known as an **affiliate publisher**, you must first create an internet property of value. Once you have a website, or a popular *YouTube* vlog, with a lot of traffic, you sign up with a marketing firm, or an **affiliate network**—a third party company that houses many affiliate publishers—offering businesses virtual property to advertise their offerings.

When a visitor, i.e. user clicks on an advertisement on your web page, it generally takes them to the advertiser's landing page, or directly to their website, via a tracking code. This code follows the customer's behavior on the landing page or website—how long they stay, on which pages, when they leave the site, and if they purchase anything or ask for more information. If the agreed upon **cost-per-action (CPA)** is performed by the user, usually that they click on the link in the ad, the affiliate publisher confirms the transaction, and pays to you, the website owner, for the ad appearing on your site.

You typically get a commission fee every time someone makes a purchase, fills out a form, or takes the desired action the advertiser's campaign directs. *Action* is loosely defined. **CPM** campaigns—**cost-per-thousand impressions**—pays the affiliate marketer when an ad on their site gets a thousand *impressions* or more. (CPM is an absolute waste of money for advertisers. Don't do it!)

There are many affiliate networks available that you can sign up with, to start making affiliate dollars on your internet property. *Google AdSense* is likely the most popular. And though this seems like an easy way to make some bucks, not so much. The commercial site you create better have a *lot* of hits, with both unique and repeat views, as well as a growing audience you can *prove* (through *Alexa*, and other traffic ranking sites), to make any real money as an affiliate marketer.

Become an Affiliate <u>Advertiser</u> for Sales

Affiliate <u>advertisers</u> pay the **affiliate <u>marketer</u>**, or the **affiliate <u>network</u>** to positioned their ads on sites that are [ostensibly] *relevant* to the advertiser's campaign, and/or offering. We've already reviewed a few reasons why, more often than not, affiliate publishers *don't* tightly target our ads to affiliate sites with visitors likely interested in what we are selling.

Amid the half-truths we all tell, in our lives and in our marketing, affiliate marketer's algorithms can only *guess* who will find value in your offering. Just like you guess, when identifying potential target markets and users during the Target Marketing process. Except you know your product way better than *Facebook* or *Google,* or any affiliate network. And, by now, you should have a long list of target users to sell to. *So, do!* Don't let *FB*, or any other affiliate publisher target your advertising. Whenever applicable, *you* choose the websites and types of affiliate sites you want to target with your marketing efforts.

We'll examine how to create effective **PPC (pay-per-click)** ads to use in your affiliate marketing campaigns in the Digital Marketing module of LSB Workbook 2. For now, let's examine how to achieve optimal page placement of your **PPC** ads, save money on your keyword pricing, and increase your advertisements ranking with your affiliate marketing campaigns.

There are a variety of affiliate marketing campaign types. With *Google's Search Network* you can do just text ads, that appear on top of *Google's* search results, as well as above your email user interface (UI), and also embedded in user's feeds on their affiliate social platforms.

Google Display Network allows you to create full display ads with imagery, or even videos, in variable size campaigns that present the ad on the affiliate marketer's website dynamically, to fit in a space allotted for ads. The most optimal placement of your ad on an affiliate's website is determined by *Google's* **Quality Score**.

You can choose just *Search*, or *Search* and *Display Networks,* that simultaneously publish your ad on *Google's* affiliate sites. Combining their affiliate networks to publish your campaign, extends your reach substantially, but the best bit is it allows you to choose your own targeting, and, again, this is highly recommended when utilizing affiliate networks.

Once you create the type of campaign you want, you 'bid' on keywords and key phrases that are typical search terms, or popular social media terms. A low-quality keyword will costs you .03 - .10 cents or so, every time someone clicks on the CTA (call-to-action) on your advert. But some trending, or high-quality keywords can be as high as $10.00 with each click! *Google* then 'matches' the keywords you pick, and the content of your advert, to keywords and phrases on millions of their affiliate's websites to determine 'best fit.' Sort of. At least, this is what they tell you.

The point of affiliate marketing, is to get our advertising on sites that reflect *something* about our offering. When *Google* matches your $5 key phrase, "unwanted pregnancy," to an anti-abortion, right-wing conservative website or *YouTube* page, it has failed to match your *Planned Parenthood* ad to an appropriate affiliate website. And this type of bad placement is a regular occurrence with affiliate networks and publishers, regardless that most are working to prevent this mismatch with quality scores.

Google, and other affiliate networks, use some form of quality score to determine where to place ads—on what particular websites, and in what space on their affiliate marketers' sites—and also to determine your cost on keyword bidding. The cost per keyword bid is actually lower, the higher your quality score.

Basically, a quality score determines how relevant an ad, keyword, and landing page or website is. Remember what *Google* finds relevant:

- Current, up-to-date information (real or fake), so high-quality affiliate sites (where you want your advert to appear) will have updated content daily.

- High **Click-through rates (CTR)**. If the link you are marketing *in your advert* gets a lot of *unique hits*, like the athletic shoe maker *Nike*, or the campaigns you've produced in the past have gotten a lot of clicks—*historic* CTRs—this also leads to a higher ranking quality score.

- Sites with a lot of **link-backs**, in which the URL you are marketing in your ad is mentioned on many other legitimate websites and blogs. (Example: On one of their website pages, *Bubba's* micro-brewery website may have: "For some great food and brew combos check out *Betty's BBQ Wings* at www.BettyBakes.com." *Betty Bakes* website link on *Bubba's* beer site is considered a link-back.)

- Keywords and phrases in your advert must match the content on the web page (landing page or website) the link sends visitors to. This is extremely important, and one of the main ways affiliate networks are trying to control poor placement of misleading ads and websites. Be sure that the content in your ad campaign matches the content on the landing page or website you send visitors to when they click on the link in your ad.

- Load time—how long it takes for your ad to load, i.e. *appear* onto the webpage, *and* how long it takes for your landing page or website to load (appear on your screen) once someone clicks on the link in your ad.

Google (and most search engines) uses these relevant factors, and more, when determining quality scores. Remember, this metric determines your ad position, but also determines how much you pay-per-click with any given *AdWords* campaign. This quality score also illustrates the effectiveness of your affiliate marketing campaigns, programs and strategies.

An effective affiliate marketing strategy is complicated, and commission fees are often negotiable, if your site has enough clout (traffic/hits/visitors). Simply *Google*, "Best Affiliate Networks (current year)," to find a highly rated affiliate publisher that will serve your company's marketing needs. Find the right affiliate network specializing in the type of affiliate marketing program you need to effectively reach your target audience.

CPC and PPC Advertising

Affiliate Marketing has become so popular, an entirely new industry is emerging around this profit model. First, some basics. Interestingly, **cost-per-click** (**CPC**) advertising was *not* invented by *Google*. The CPC model began with a "pay-per visit" model, developed by *Packard Bell* in the mid-1990s, and has expanded since to include the long list of popular acronyms used to identify the types of CPC campaigns available. Affiliate networks create and sell new advertising packages and plans all the time. To find the newest CPC model, simply *Google,* "CPC Ad Models," to find an affiliate marketing campaign type that aligns with your company's digital advertising strategies.

The process of CPC, aka **PPC** (**pay-per-click**) advertising has been refined over the years, to more effectively, but not yet *exactly*, reach our target audiences. As discussed, affiliate networks correlate the keywords and common phrases you 'bid' on, with similar content on their affiliate's web pages (text and image content on affiliate's site) that show your ad. The idea, of course, is to correctly match visitors to a popular site with advertising that may interest them, so they'll click on your ad. With each click, the affiliate network makes more money.

Google assumes if you have an interest in the site where your ad appears, you'll likely have an interest in the ads shown on that site. If your keywords, phrases, even sentiments expressed in your advert content match the affiliate's keyword content, *Google* predicts it's a 'match,' and your ad will appear on that internet property. This is how *AdWords* works, as do most affiliate networks.

We'll drill down on creating effective CPC campaigns in LSB Workbook 2. For now, let's examine the process of creating PPC campaigns (or any marketing efforts) that get the greatest response.

We *begin* with Productization. Go back to all your Productization lists, to find keywords and short phrases you've listed in bullet points about your offering. Take words from your FEATURES and BENEFITS lists, 1A and 1B. Again, at this point, you should have a good idea of *who* will likely benefit the most from your offering, so consider what target markets and users you are trying to reach with each CPC campaign, and note which types of websites they are likely to visit, or virtual locations they hang out at. Also, to identify and possibly attract additional target users, reference List 4A—your COMPETITION, to perhaps market to a target audience of your competitors. Be sure to focus your PPC campaigns on touting the *best bit*, your UVP's, or greatest differentiator, from your competition. Your campaigns should provide a benefit that can not be found elsewhere, or getting it is harder and/or more expensive, than obtaining *your* new offering.

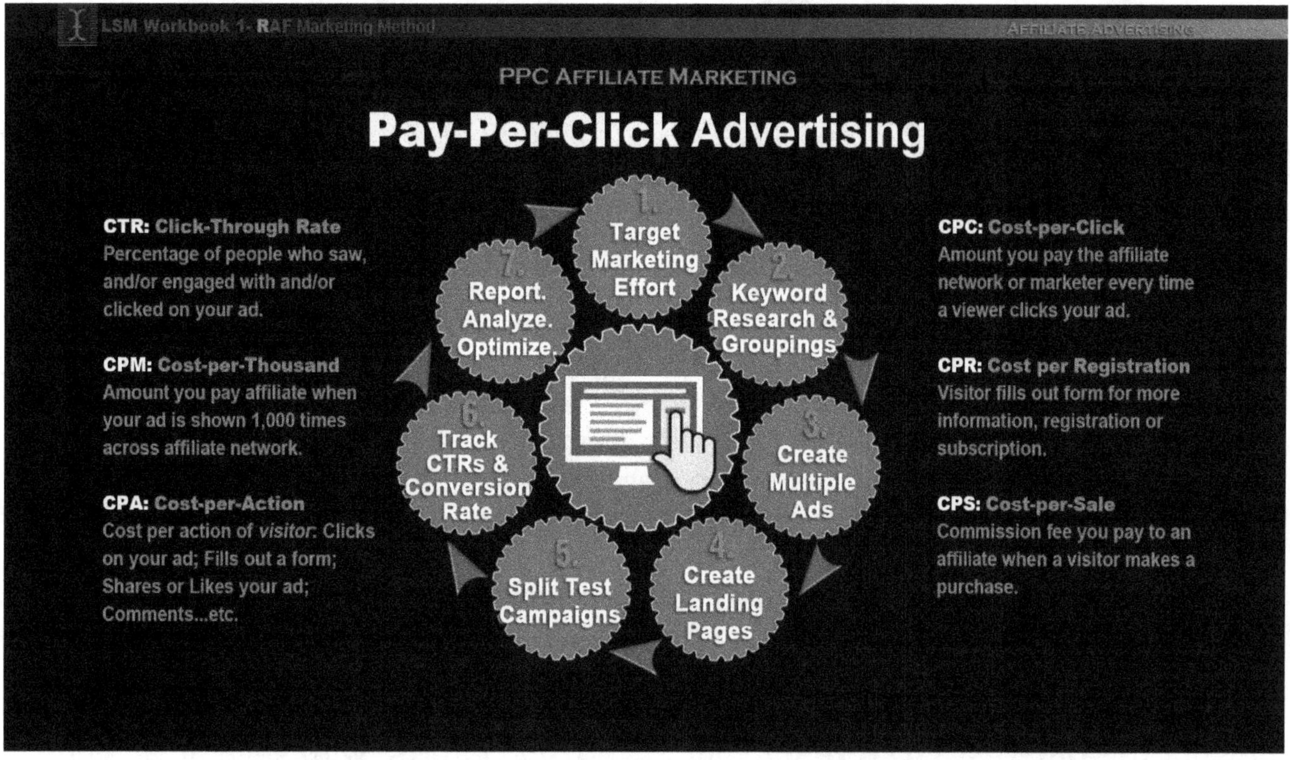

Your Productization lists also provide the bullet points of keywords and phrases you'll 'bid' on, for optimal placement of your PPC campaigns. For the greatest response on any given PPC campaign, compile a comprehensive list of your offering's keywords, directly related to what you are selling, that will likely interest your potential target users. Research the cost of using these keywords and phrases, through your affiliate network provider. Make sure you understand how much you will be charged, each time someone takes an action (CPA), or even passively sees your ad on a web page (CPM), before signing on with any affiliate publisher.

Once you know who you are selling to, and have some keywords and phrases likely to get your advertisement on sites [ostensibly] related to your offering, create *several* ads with different headlines and incentives, to motivate viewers to act.

Be absolutely sure that the link on any digital advertising you create, takes potential target users, who clicked on your CTA, to a landing page or website that pays off your advert's messaging. Doing an incentive campaign? Pay off the incentive—give the 'free' gift, points, or discount on sign-ups—within one click on the ad's link.

Let's assume I'm using an affiliate network, to publish a CPC campaign for my fictitious app, *PHP Advocates*. To populate my new platform with users, I create an incentive campaign, "Try *PHP* Free Today." Of course, restrictions will apply, like only one live online meeting with an expert of your choice, for five minutes. I target my 'lowest-hanging fruit,' and go after *White or Asian, child of an aging parent, mid-life Baby Boomer, upper-income, living in the suburbs*...etc., with this CPC campaign. I also choose an *AdWords* package that lets me target, as tightly as possible, the affiliate sites I'd like my multiple ads (for 'split' testing) in this campaign to appear.

Google launches my CPC campaign across their affiliate sites, that I've loosely targeted with their minimal selection of target markets. Someone sees my advert on a senior care counseling website. *Google* actually got it right, and matched my offering with a potential target user who found interest in my ad enough to click on the CTA. Yea! That click takes the person to my latest landing page that lets them log directly into *PHP Advocates* to experience a free trial of my platform. Of course, login requires filling in a form that captures their name and email, which I'll use later in targeted email marketing campaigns, whether they use the free trial, or not. Regardless of the fill-in form, I am paying off my campaign promise of getting access to my application for a free trial in *one click*.

Be sure to **split-test (A/B test)** your advertising efforts, with several versions of the *same offer per campaign,* to find the keywords that get the best response. You can split-test offers and incentives down the line, but initial PPC campaigns should focus on finding keywords and phrases that align your company's offerings with the affiliate sites in which your adverts will appear.

A strategic PPC campaign will have 3 to 5 versions, typically each with a different headline of keywords. Test market each advert to only a few sites where your target users hang out, before rolling out the campaign to your wider affiliate network sites with the headline that got the greatest response.

It is important to note, when creating campaigns for split-testing, change only one element in each ad at a time. Do *not* change the headline *and* offer when split-testing any given campaign. The only way to tell *what* element evoked the change in response rate is to change just one element per ad.

The *free trial incentive offer* is one of my launch PPC campaigns for *PHP Advocates*. I do *not* change the offer to run an A/B test campaign. I change the headline *only*. No other element, not the image, or the CTA button, or the descriptive text changes. Just the headline. I write three different headlines, and test these ads to a limited pool of potential target users. The ad with the headline that gets the best response 'wins.' This winning ad, with the specific winning headline, I then 'roll-out' as a full affiliate network campaign to extend my successful advert's reach, for the best possible conversion rates on that particular campaign.

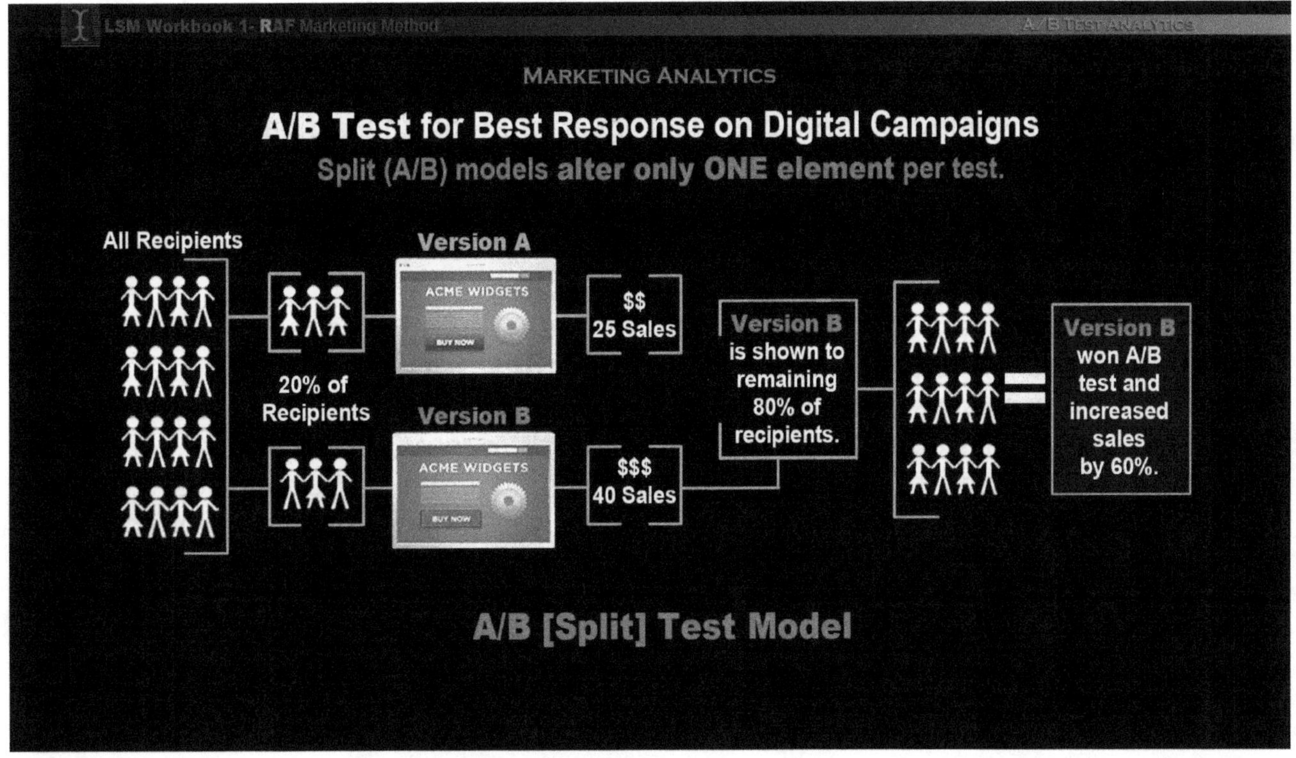

Once you've collected some data on response, or even lack of response, to your PPC affiliate campaign—track the click-through-rates (CTR), but also a range of other data that may possess valuable insights. How long did click-through visitors stay on your landing page or website? What pages did they visit on your site? For how long? How long after arriving, did they leave your site? Did they complete a registration form? How far did they get through the purchase or download process?

You can track and find insights on the data collected from your affiliate PPC campaigns with *Google Analytics, SalesForce*, and many other Data Analysis firms, or through your affiliate network provider. Study the results of each campaign. Analyze what keywords, which headline, link button color, and other various tests got the best response. Finally, optimize your next campaign using the data collected from your previous marketing efforts, to increase your conversion rates with each marketing effort.

The PPC advertising process, performed *in order,* with a reputable affiliate network provider, is starting to show acceptable to good conversion rates. But beware of the sales pitch from affiliate networks promising CPM (cost-per-1000-impressions) campaigns will build your brand or sell your offering. And try not to let yourself feel heady by a lot of clicks on your CTAs, assuming you get a lot. Link clicks on your PPC ads do *not* [necessarily] translate into sales, or even conversion. In fact, the response rates to most CPC/PPC ad campaigns is rather low, between .01 and 3%, as previously mentioned. And for the most part, they are getting lower, not higher, because new and disturbing issues with the affiliate marketing profit model keep arising. The persistent problem since its widespread inception, is the value to the advertiser over that of the affiliate network with each click on your PPC ad's CTA.

Ongoing Issues with Affiliate Marketing

Another problem, among the issues already mentioned with the affiliate marketing model, is **click fraud**. There are **click farms**, employing a form of click fraud, where large groups of low-paid workers in developing countries are hired to click on paid advertising links for a *click master*. Competitors sometimes hire these click farms to deplete your advertising dollars. Sometimes, the *click master* owns one or more high-traffic affiliate marketing websites or web pages, where your ads are placed (unknowingly by reputable affiliate publishers, who don't really care whether you get sales with your campaigns or not). The more clicks on your PPC ads, the more money the *click master* (owner of the fake affiliate sites) makes, while depleting your marketing budget with fake clicks you are paying for whether they are fraudulent or not.

Ad (aka Banner or Content) Blindness is another problem with PPC advertising. We are bombarded by advertising on every web page we visit, and every *YouTube* video we watch. We are becoming blind, quite literally, to the extraneous information, such as ads, we encounter when we visit a site. Our eyes focus only on what we went to the site to find, and *not* on all the motion ads screaming for our attention on the headers and along the sidebars of a web page. Even pop-up ads that block our view of the web page we came to visit, our eyes simply search for the 'X' that let's us delete the pop-up, or we stare at the little banner that shows the countdown to bypass the ad in 5 seconds.

Remember, your PPC advertising is generally placed on affiliate sites, that are too broad to effectively reach your audience (unless a location-based, brick and mortar store, and you target zip codes with your PPC campaigns). Before blowing a lot of cash on affiliate marketing campaigns with the PPC model, create **click-campaigns** with video or images, great headlines, and effective incentive CTAs. Post these click-campaigns on your company's social media profile pages, free, as well as in groups and on chats where your target users hang out. First, *you* know who your potential audience is, and how to target them better than any algorithm to date. Second, even if you get a lot of fraudulent clicks, at least you don't have to pay for them.

We'll walk the process of creating effective CPC affiliate marketing campaigns, which can and should be utilized as click-campaigns, in LSB Workbook 2: Branding. For now, don't forget, the more tightly we target our marketing efforts to the people who will likely benefit from our offering, the greater our response rates will be. The more we are able to reach our target users directly, and make them aware of how our product will serve them, the more likely we are to *sell* them on our offering, and brand our new venture as a company of value that yields a profit sooner than later.

Profit Models Over Time

The final phase of **Step 1: Get Ready**, in the **RAF Marketing Method**, is picking a profit model for launch, and also projecting additional revenue streams for a year, three, and five years down the line. It is imperative we forecast future profits, not only to keep all stakeholders on the road to growing company revenue, but also to show venture capital, or potential investors, that we plan to pay them back for their investment in our company, and continue to make them money throughout the life-cycle of our business.

During the development phase of any offering, it generally *costs* the fledgling company money, if not in real dollars, then in time to develop and market the new product or service.

At launch, implementing a Freemium profit model won't bring in immediate revenue, but free trials entice people to try an offering. Once they do, and find out how great your product is, and then tell all their friends, your business begins to grow.

Your marketing efforts help build your brand awareness. The viral messaging of users chatting up your offering, garners more users. Sales of your offering increase, and continue to do so over time, *if* your company continually produces offerings of value, especially in the first few years. After a sustained period of growth, when your company's offerings have gained enough market share, and users of your product are satisfied enough to feel a need to continue using your brand, it may be time to switch to a subscription profit model, for greater revenue with each sale.

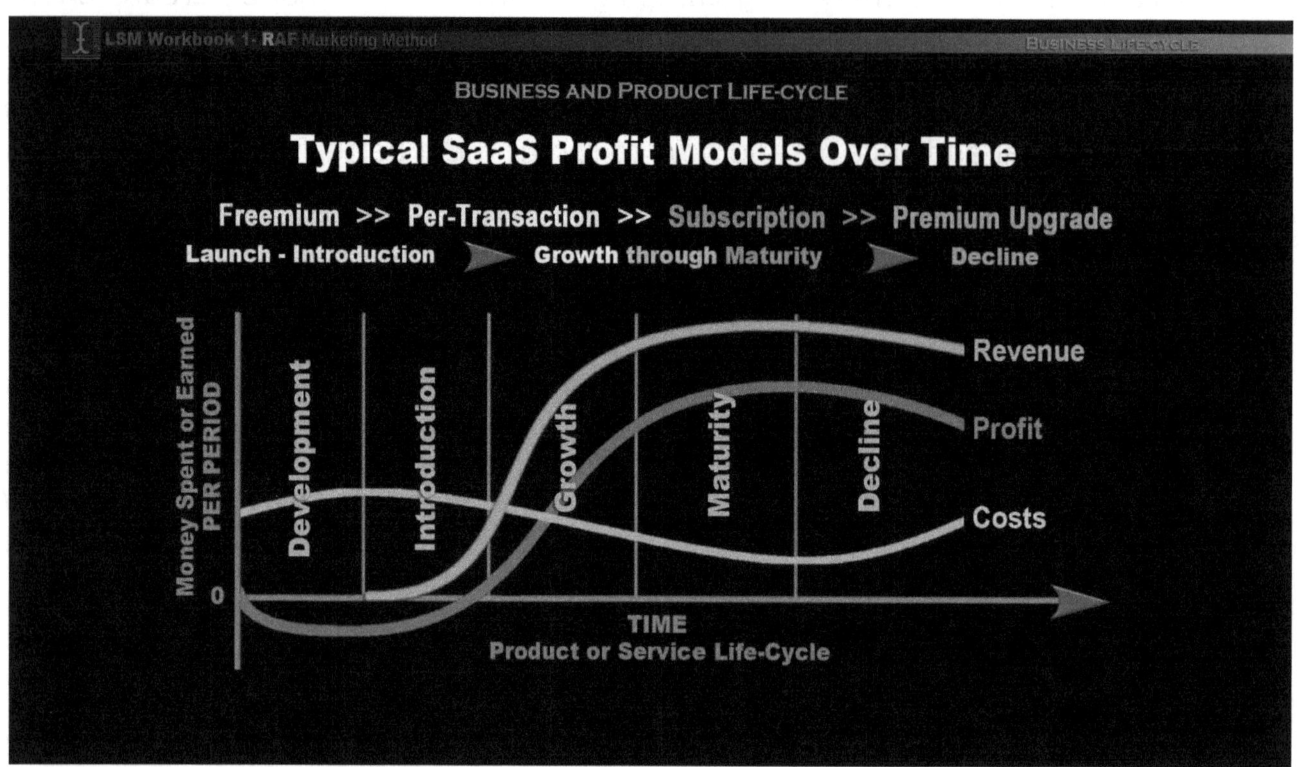

As stated, a product or service without continual upgrades or new product releases, will fail in short order, especially in the internet age where product advancement, and competition is faster than ever before. When an offering shows decline in sales, from competitors with a similar product release, or a new paradigm that's better than your original offering, it's time to upgrade your product, and perhaps add a premium rate profit model to your subscription agreement. Not only does the user pay monthly for your application, but to get all the features/functions of your offering, there are tiered upgrade plans, with several price points to choose from.

New software profit models continually emerge. Others fall out of favor. Research the most current and trending models, to making money with your startup offering. Use your Productization bullet point lists throughout the LSE series as checklists, to assure you stay on track to creating a *marketable* offering of value, to specific groups of people, for profit.

◆◆◆

MODULE 11: AFFLIATE MARKETING REVIEW

- To make money with **AFFLIATE MARKETING**, become a *popular* online internet property. Create a trending blog, vlog, website, podcast, or social media platform, that gets a *lot* of unique visitors, and sell advertising space *and* time on your site.

- **Affiliate ADVERTISERS** are the businesses that market their offering on the **affiliate MARKETER'S** website, or popular internet property.

- The acronym **CPC** stands for **Cost-Per-Click**. In **CPC** campaigns, the **advertisers** pays an **affiliate PUBLISHER** or **affiliate NETWORK** every time a viewer clicks, or sometimes even passively 'views' their ad online.

- **Affiliate networks** [ostensibly] perform extensive analysis to place your ads on sites relevant to your target audience, for greater response to your marketing efforts. However, begin with caution, and don't spend money you don't have for '*impressions*' of your adverts. Post your **PPC** (pay-per-click) **display ads** as **click-campaigns** on your startup's profile pages, and other social media groups and forums, for free!

- **SPLIT (A/B) TEST** PPC campaigns to a limited number of affiliate sites, to identify which keywords in your headlines garner greater response, *before* rolling out a full affiliate network campaign. Always post your click-campaigns on your startup's social feeds for free, to see if the campaign garners equal or better response than your paid **PPC Affiliate Marketing** plan.

- **Click-farms** are a form of **click fraud**. Large groups of low-income workers fraudulently click on your **PPC ads** to pocket your advertising dollars that they are depleting with each click.

- *Effective* **PPC campaigns**, as with *all* marketing efforts, should be highly targeted for the greatest possible response. **Affiliate networks** can *not* target your campaigns near as well as *you* can! By initiating the **Productization process**, and populating the eight required **Productization lists**, you now possess an *intimate* knowledge of your upcoming product or service, as well as **target markets** and **users** who will find value in your offering.

(or developed product, service, or message) into an offering of *value*, is well underway. Remember, **Productization is an ongoing process!** Effective Productization lists, pitches, and profit models, are dynamic. They should be continually refined, added to consistently, and they change over time.

Actualizing an IDEA into a sustainable offering and/or a company, or making an existing offering valuable, *begins* with Productization—the process of getting intimate with your offering. Most startups fail out of the gate because they neglected to perform this very first step in the Lean Startup Marketing process.

It is imperative that you implement the Productization process *before* creating branding and advertising your offering. You can not effectively create marketing campaigns for your product, service, or message, or build your *brand,* until you know WHAT you have, what it DOES, and WHO will find value in it.

The process of Productization isn't rocket science, but it has many components that must be implemented *in order* to create marketable offerings of value. The **RAF Marketing Method** *begins* with getting your offering **READY** to brand and sell. Creating and populating Productization lists with specific details about your product or service will give you direction, guidance, keywords and phrases to chat it up, live, in-person, and in all your digital and print marketing efforts.

It is essential that you understand and execute the major components of the Productization process *before* moving on to **LSB Workbook 2: Take Aim and BRAND** your productized offering. To test your knowledge of Productization, before beginning the PROJECTS for this Workbook, take one last CHALLENGE, for fun!

-

-

STOP! Do CHALLENGE #12 before moving on.

◆◆◆

CHALLENGE #12: Engage in Productizing YOU!

Regardless if you are married, engaged, or seriously dating someone, **imagine you are single, and looking to date**. Now, **create a PERSONAL AD**, to a potential date on *Match.com*, *eHarmony*, or other dating platform.

BEFORE you write the ad:

1. **LIST [at least] 5 FEATURES of YOU.** Start with basic demographics and geographics—your gender, how old you are, where you live (the general location, not your street address). What is your career, and job title if you

have one? Do you have kids, a pet? Next, move on to psychographics, such as *who* you are—what you're passionate about—then on to what you value or find important, as in family, or a cause, or religious affiliation, or lack thereof.

2. **LIST [at least] 5 BENEFITS of YOU.** List what you enjoy doing. Add other benefits, such as if you are fit, live a healthy lifestyle, cook or bake particularly well. List some details about your personality. Are you playful, practical, physical—enjoy touching, back-rubs, holding hands? List some of your accomplishments, like advanced education, maybe fun classes you've taken, or meetups you go to regularly, or philanthropy you've engaged in.

3. **LIST characteristics of your projected Target MARKETS** using all four data sources in the **Target Marketing process**: DEMOGRAPHIC, GEOGRAPHIC, PSYCHOGRAPHIC, BEHAVIORAL. Remember, you must know WHO you are marketing to, for the best conversion rates on your ad—getting response from candidates that *you'll* likely find interest in dating.

4. **LIST characteristics of your projected Target USERS** using the typical data sources for Targeting USERS: PSYCHOGRAPHIC and BEHAVIORAL. Describe the date you want *in detail*, what they like, and don't; where they'd likely hang out, and with who typically, such as friends, or family. Drill down on what they are likely to buy, and own, from the type of dwelling in which they live, to the car they drive, to the type of clothes they might wear. Will they have a pet? If so, dog, cat, other? List what you'd like to have responding to your personal ad.

5. **RESEARCH your COMPETITION—other personal ads by people like you** —the same sex, basic age, sexual orientation, interests...etc, and **LIST [at least] 5 of the most common features and benefits of people like you**, competing for, or getting the attention you'd like from the same USERS your personal ad will target.

6. **Identify and LIST features and benefits of YOU that are DIFFERENT**, *better* than your competitors. Do you have a parrot or other exotic pet? Is your job something most other's don't do for a living? Do you have a hobby that is unique, like ceramics or building furniture? A sport most don't engage in, like bungee jumping, or spelunking. Maybe you like ethnic cooking, and have a ton of family recipes you'd love to share. Through researching other ads by people similar to you, find what makes you different from them—a **unique value** (**UVP**), and put these things, these *best bits* about you in your personal ad *first*.

7. **WRITE the personal ad. Title it with your UVP—the best thing about YOU** (*not* what you are looking for!). Next, describe, in story form—**tell, don't**

sell—what makes you unique, then add your BENEFITS to concretize the messaging in your description, *before* you go on to what you are looking for in a date. Most personal sites have areas for your age, and general location, so you don't need to include these FEATURES in your description.

Productizing yourself, teaches you how to **productize**...anything! Do not publish your personal ad, (unless you want to...; }), but do show it to friends and family as market research, to see how effective they think your ad is.

◆◆◆

◆◆◆◆◆

MODULE 12: PROJECTS

There are **three multi-dimensional projects** to complete in **LSM Workbook 1: PRODUCTIZATION**. If each is completed, *in order*, you will have the **marketing content to create branding and advertising campaigns in LSB Workbook 2**, which guides you step-by-step through creating professional marketing material that generate greater response.

A quick review of the project's subject will follow the project itself. Use the bullet lists of key points in each review as checklists when you are creating, *and* after completing the projects, to be sure you've met the requirements of each. Establishing **Productization lists**—documents with bullet points of *intimate details* about your product, service, or message—will give you a text library of keywords and phrases directly related to your offering, to utilize in creating effective marketing campaigns you'll produce in **LSB Workbook 2: BRANDING**.

It is extremely important to complete each of the PROJECTS, whether or not you plan to launch an offering, and/or startup, by the end of **LSL Workbook 3: LAUNCH**. To really understand how something works, you must *work the process*. One-third of the step-by-step **RAF Marketing Method** is provided in each of the three Lean Startup Workbooks. Working each step *in order*, enables you to actualize an IDEA, most *any* idea, (or even fully-developed product or service) into a marketable offering of *value*, for profit. Engage in the process of **RAF Marketing Method** with the following PROJECTS, and you'll gain the most from the **Lean Startup Entrepreneurial Series**, guaranteed!

PROJECTS (► = Project)

PROJECT #1: Productization Lists

1. Implement PRODUCTIZATION LISTS 1A – 4B.

Produce and populate **eight PRODUCTIZATION LISTS:**

1. **FEATURES**,
2. **BENEFITS/SOLUTIONS**
3. **TARGET MARKETS**
4. **TARGET USERS**
5. **COMPETITORS**
6. **DIFFERENTIATORS/UVPs**,
7. **HORIZONTAL MARKETS**
8. **VERTICAL MARKETS**

List 1A: FEATURES LIST

► **List** [at least] **10 bullet points** describing, in a few *specific* words each, the features of your IDEA, or fully-development offering.

List 1B: BENEFITS LIST

► **List** [at least] **10 bullet points** describing, in a one *specific* sentence each, the benefits (focused on SOLUTIONS, and/or satisfying a desire) the features of your projected offering provides. Derive your offering's **BENEFITS** from List 1A—the FEATURES of your product, service, or message.

MODULE 4: PRODUCTIZATION 101 REVIEW

- To **productize** an idea, or developed offering, we begin by giving clear, concise, and *specific* answers to the following three (3) questions:
    1. **What IS it?**
    2. **What does it DO?**
    3. **For WHO?**

- **Productization** begins with identifying our offering's '**Product/Market Fit**', defining our idea by where it 'fits' in the marketplace of sellable items. Is our offering a **Product**, a **Service**, or **Message**?

- Once we've defined our offering's 'fit' in the marketplace, we must describe what it IS—its characteristics, or FEATURES, in software known as FUNCTIONS.

- When we have a lengthy list of the FEATURES of our potential offering, we align them to BENEFITS or solutions that the FEATURES of our offering will provide.

- And finally, we project WHO—the potential MARKETS and PEOPLE, in software also known as USERS, that will benefit from the FEATURES/FUNCTIONS of our upcoming offering.

The **Productization process** lets us actualize our ideas with a simple step-by-step method, that helps guide us to create products and services that serve a purpose, and will likely have value for specific groups of people. Actualizing a product, service, or message—**Getting Ready to market your potential offering—always begins with Productization**.

List 2A: TARGET MARKETS LIST

▶ **List** [at least] **5 bullet points** describing, in one sentence each, the **projected target MARKETS** for your offering. Derive these *broad groupings of people* for your product, service, or message, from List 1B—the BENEFITS of your offering. Use **demographic**, **geographic**, **psychographic**, and **behavioral** data, to assess common characteristics of the type of people you project may benefit, or find value in your projected or fully-developed offering. List the most obvious **target markets** ('lowest hanging fruit') for your offering *first*.

MODULE 6: TARGET MARKETING REVIEW

- **TARGET MARKETING** is the second phase of the Productization process, because we use the features and benefits (phase one) of our product, service, or message, and align them to *groups* of potential users likely to find value in our offering.

- **Target markets** are broad groupings of people with similar characteristics and desires, that will likely find benefits or solutions in the features of our offering.

- To identify potential **target markets** for our offering, we segment people using **four main data sources**:
  - ◆ **Demographic** data—age, sex, race, education level, income level, marital status, occupation, religion.
  - ◆ **Geographic** data—location, ethnicity, climate, and environmental conditions of potential customers.
  - ◆ **Psychographic** data—psychological data, such as personality traits, values, attitudes, political orientation, interests, religion, beliefs, and lifestyles.
  - ◆ **Behavioral** data—purchase data, customer loyalty, web-surfing habits, clicks on links, social media posts and updates, search keywords and phrases, etc., virtually anything you do, or post on the internet cloud. Even live purchases, like restaurant meals, are tracked, correlated and sold to affiliate networks.

- To find **target markets**, begin with the "lowest hanging fruit"—the most obvious broad group of people likely to benefit from the features in your offering. Briefly describe each **market** in **List 2A** (even if it's just you, as *you* are a *type of person*), using the **four main data sources** marketing uses to broadly segment people.

- We derive **target markets** from the benefits and features our offering provides to particular broad groupings of people.

- Creating a **visual Target Marketing graphic** is an effective way to communicate the target markets you have in mind that will benefit from the features of your offering.

- The **Target Marketing process** must be implemented during Productization for startup success, because it identifies likely *groups of people* who will find value in our offering, to focus our marketing efforts.

List 2B: TARGET USERS LIST

► **List** [at least] **5 bullet points** describing, in one to two paragraphs each, the **projected Target USERS** for your product, service, or message. Derive your **target users** from List 2A—the TARGET MARKETS for your offering, by examining details about the *individuals* within your projected *broad* target markets. THINK about WHO these people are, their concerns and issues, what they desire, what motivates them, what matters to them. Consider what these people like, and don't, their politics, religious affiliation, if any, their education level, income, job title, hobbies, where they hang out, both in-person an online, who their friends may be, what they watch on TV. Profile each user *intimately!*

MODULE 6: TARGETING USERS REVIEW

- We are never selling to **target markets**. We are always selling to *people*. **Targeting USERS** means directing our advertising and marketing efforts at an *individual's* particular interests, issues, and/or desires.

- We derive potential **target USERS** by identifying common characteristics of individual members in each of our broadly segmented **target markets**.

- One of the most effective ways to find **target USERS** is to use **psychographic** and **behavioral data** of your **target markets,** to find patterns of behavior within groups of individual **USERS**. Observe, and note what people *really* do, NOT what we *say* we'll do, to learn what truly motivates each of us.

- **Identifying characteristics of individuals—targeting USERS**—helps us discover what they want, what they like, and don't, where to find them, and how to reach them with our marketing efforts.

- **Big data** collection provides *some* framework for analyzing **USER** behavior, but still does NOT tell us *why* people took an action. Analytic systems simply record that they did, then correlate individual **USER** data, and the behavior of similar people, to *predict* future behavior of potential **target USERS**.

- Marketing our offering to potential **target USERS,** tightly focuses our **marketing content** to address *individual* desires and issues.

- You will dramatically increase the response to your marketing efforts, by **tightly targeting your marketing and advertising to your most likely target USERS**.

List 3A: COMPETITIVE ANALYSIS LIST

▶ **Iterative search for competition**—companies producing products or services that are similar to yours. Examine competitor's offerings through their website/s. *Google* each competitor for more information about them, as well as search for additional marketing efforts on their social media profile pages on most major platforms, such as *Facebook, Twitter, Instagram, LinkedIn*.

▶ **List** [at least] **5 companies** (along with their URLs) **competing directly or indirectly with your offering**.

▶ **List the features and benefits of their product or service** that are closely aligned with yours. List additional features and benefits that your competition has that you have yet to conceive or implement.

▶ **List the likely target markets and users** your competitors are trying to reach with their marketing efforts. Study the images and language they use (as well as the social platforms they post on) to create **user profiles** of their most likely target audiences.

-

-

COMPETITIVE ANALYSIS CHART

▶ **Create a COMPETITIVE ANALYSIS CHART.** Along the top of the chart, give each of your greatest competitors a vertical column. Give *your* offering the last vertical column along the top of your chart to the right.

On the left side of your chart, list the FEATURES and BENEFITS of your offering, followed by those of your competitors, giving each its own row. Put a check mark for each **feature and benefit** that your offering, as well as your competitors' offering, possesses. Be sure to fill out this chart with check marks in each column of your competitors, as well as your offering, for a visual representation of the **features and benefits** you have in common, as well as **features and benefits** they have that you do not, and visa versa.

This **COMPETITIVE ANALYSIS CHART** will help you identify your offering's **differentiators** from your competitors.

-

-

List 3B: DIFFERENTIATORS (UVPs) LIST

▶ **List** [at least] **5 differentiators—features**, **benefits and solutions** of your offering, that are *different* from similar offerings available from your list of competitors. **List 3B** is the *best things*, the **unique value propositions** (**UVP's**) that make your offering *better* than your competition.

Utilizing your **competitive analysis chart, begin List 3B** with *the UVP's* that make your offering *unique*. The first entries on your list will be the **features, benefits and solutions** your offering has, that your competition does *not*.

Next, add to **List 3B** to include additional UVP's of your offering. Include UVP's your competitors have in their offering, that are not in yours, *yet*. If you find you do not have enough **differentiators** that separate your offering from your competition, go back to the drawing table and **iterate** your projected product or service—**create diffferentiator**—*unique* features and benefits that separate *your* offering from your competition.

List 3B must be extensive, because your marketing efforts should consistently promote the *best things*—the **features, benefits and solutions** that make your offering *valuable*, as well as distinguishes it as unique from your competitors.

◊◊◊

MODULE 9: COMPETITIVE ANALYSIS REVIEW

- **COMPETITIVE ANALYSIS** is the process of identifying our competitors, and *specific* characteristics—the features and benefits—of their offerings.

- We find *unknown* competitors of our offering using the **iterative search** method of lifting **keywords** and **phrases** from our **Productization lists** to use as search terms.

- Once we've identified competitors, we **research their social media pages** and profiles to find additional marketing efforts, that will give us insights about them. We study the images and language they use (as well as the social platforms they post on), to create **user profiles** of their most likely **target audiences**, to perhaps adopt as ours down the line.

- We **list our competitors**, their URL, and a short list of the features and benefits of *their* offering, that are similar to ours. We list additional features and benefits of their offering we've yet to conceive or implement.

- We create a **COMPETITIVE ANALYSIS chart,** to determine what makes the features and benefits of our offering *different* than our **competition**.

- The acronym **UVP** means **Unique Value Proposition**, or, what makes our potential offering different, unique, *better* than competitors.

- If we find **competitors** producing an offering with no discernible difference to ours, we **iterate** our original idea to include some *unique* features and benefits that will **differentiate** our offering from our **competition**.

List 4A: HORIZONTAL MARKETS LIST

► **List** [at least] **5 HORIZONTAL MARKETS** (in *addition* to List 2A—TARGET MARKETS), for your projected offering, or fully-developed product. Consider WHO—what broad groupings of people—will likely find interest or value in your offering's **features, benefits and solutions** *across many industries and job functions, as well as for personal use* (even if just for entertainment purposes).

List 4B: VERTICAL MARKETS LIST

► **List** [at least] **5 VERTICAL MARKETS** (in *addition* to List 2A—TARGET MARKETS), for your projected offering, or fully-developed product. Consider WHO will likely find interest or value in your offering's **features**, **benefits and solutions** *within a specific industry, or for a particular job function*.

BONUS LIST: Horizontal and Vertical PRODUCT Ideas

► **List** [at least] **5 new products, services, or upgrade IDEAS** for your new venture. Stay ahead of competitors with a dynamic list of projected new offerings! Startups must release **new products and/or upgrades every**

nine months or so, to stay relevant to current users, and pique the interest of new adopters.

MODULE 10: H & V MARKETING REVIEW

- The third reason why startup fail, is the company rides on the success of their first offering for too long. It is mandatory to invest in **research and development** of new products, upgrades, and even **profit models**, to serve your current customers, but also to attract new users.

- We utilize **H & V modeling** during the **Productization process,** to broaden our reach, to as many as possible who may be interested in our offering at launch, and beyond.

- Identifying additional **HORIZONTAL and VERTICAL markets** in the **Productization process,** provides a continual stream of potential **target markets** and **target users** to sell to.

- **HORIZONTAL marketing** identifies **many users across a wide range of industries,** that will likely find value in your offering. To find **HORIZONTAL markets** for your offering, consider how your product or services benefits *users across many industries*.

- **VERTICAL marketing** identifies a **specific industry or job function,** that may benefit from purchasing or utilizing particular features of your offering. To find **VERTICAL markets** for your offering, consider how your product or service benefits a particular industry's needs.

- It is essential that startups release upgrades, new products, services, features and benefits, **every 6 – 9 months** or so, to keep your offering relevant to first adopters, and to garner additional **HORIZONTAL and VERTICAL markets** with each new release. If *you* don't, your **competitors** will, in today's connected world.

ALL PRODUCTZATION LISTS should be NO LESS THAN 5 ENTRIES EACH! *The more bullet point entries the better!* The more FEATURES your offering has, the more likely you are creating, or have created, a substantive offering of value. The more BENEFITS and SOLUTIONS your offering provides, the more likely you'll find several MARKETS and USERS to sell it to. Identifying your COMPETITION helps you find or create DIFFERENTIATORS, unique value (UVP) to position (brand) your offering from competitors with similar offerings already on the market. The more HORIZONTAL and VERTICAL products you envision, the more target markets and users you'll have to sell to, and the easier it'll be to stay one step ahead of your competitors, by consistently producing *unique* upgrades, and new offerings.

Remember, the Productization process begins anew with each new product or service you imagine. And if you've already produced your offering, and created marketing that isn't getting the traction you'd like, perform the **Productization process** on your existing product or service—all 8 steps—*before* rebranding your offering. Getting your product, service, or message **Ready**, in the **RAF Marketing Method,** means getting *intimate* with your offering. Before you create advertising that brands and converts, you *first* must thoroughly understand *what* you have to sell, what it actually *does*, and *who* will likely benefit from the features of your offering.

PROJECT #2: The Elevator Pitch

2. Create an ELEVATOR PITCH for your offering and startup.

► **WRITE a first draft ELEVATOR PITCH for your offering**, a PITCH SCRIPT of your product or service in 1 – 3 engaging, cohesive, informative sentences. Be sure to **BE SPECIFIC** with your words. No puff stories. NO FLUFF WORDS! **TELL** (don't SELL) **with a quick story** of how you thought of your offering, and WHO will likely find benefits in the features of your product, service, or [nonprofit] message. Be sure to say what makes your offering unique, great, and *better* than your competitors.

'Name dropping' other companies in your PITCH is only applicable when your offering is a combination of two current, *popular* businesses. (You do not need to, and should *not* name your direct competitors. You can use phrases like: "Five times faster, and half the price of any *X-industry* provider available today.")

Always **close your PITCH with a direct** or **implied CTA**. Suggest a sneak peek, exclusive trial or other incentive, to solicit engagement beyond the conversation. Ask for a card, an email, a phone number to further the dialog. NETWORK. NETWORK. **NETWORK**.

MODULE 7: THE ELEVATOR PITCH REVIEW

- Your #1 job as CEO of your **productized** offering is to market/*sell it*.

- An **ELEVATOR PITCH** is a 5 – 30 second **engaging speech** to spark interest in your potential offering, and company.

- At networking events, parties, gatherings, freely **PITCH** to whoever will listen, as it will help you:
  —Create buzz about your upcoming product or service.
  —Give you input to make your initial idea into a better offering.
  —Define your idea better as you're pitching it.
  —Show you what FEATURES excite your audience as you **PITCH** your offering.

- **Stealth mode**, or, fear of revealing your idea before launching it because it may get stolen, is unwarranted paranoia. IDEAS are intrinsically valueless. Most everyone has ideas. Hardly anyone puts in the time and energy to actualize them into useful offerings.

- Your **ELEVATOR PITCH** should *not* give away the algorithms to your new SaaS offering, or the recipe for your great cupcakes. But, passionately talking about your offering, even in broad strokes, will attract USERS, partners, employees, and keep all stakeholders on the path to actualizing your startup's success.

PROJECT #3: PROFIT MODELS

3. Establish a PROFIT MODEL for the LAUNCH of your offering.

► **Define and document a roll-out (initial launch) profit model** for your offering and/or startup. Review the PROFIT MODEL module in this workbook, and pick one that will **benefit your projected target USERS**, serve *their* needs, without imposing any real or implied risk, to solicit the greatest engagement at the launch of your new offering.

► **Create a CHART of your projected costs vs. earnings** over Q1 through Q4 (one year) from the launch of your new venture. Include the **costs** of **development**, **redevelopment** (if you discover you must iterate your fully developed offering), as well as your **pre-launch** and **launch marketing** efforts. Be sure to include hires, consultants, equipment, manufacturing, workspace, and all other costs associated with creating your startup.

Project the number of users or customers you hope to garner in each quarter of the first year of operation. Assess the amount they will pay for the use or ownership of your offering, if any, as trial offers are great for launch! **Earnings** are NOT profits, but the amount of money you've made on your offering at launch and throughout the year. It is likely the first year (and often well beyond) your new venture will not realize a profit over the operation's cost of running your business.

▶ **Create additional CHARTS of your projected costs vs. earnings, three to five years down the line.** Make the charts clear, professional, and you'll be able to use them in your presentations to solicit financial support, such as venture capital (VC), or crowdfunding.

▶ **Project new or additional PROFIT MODELS for your established offering,** such as **Subscription, Premium,** and/or **Affiliate Marketing model,** for three to five years from launch, after your company has acquired an **established customer/user base**. Identifying financial milestones and goals early on, will keep all stakeholders on the path to creating and marketing an offering of value, for *profit*.

MODULE 11: TYPICAL & SAAS PROFIT MODELS REVIEW

- **BRICK & MORTAR** locations should have some type of online component—feature or service—to encourage in-store sales, even if it's only pre-order for pick-up.

- The acronym **VAR** means **Value Added Reseller**. **VARs** typically add features or functionality to the original offering. *Amazon* offers retailers a platform to sell their products, and also offers software companies servers on their **cloud** platform. **VARs** make a profit from an agreed price per transaction, or subscription for service, and/or commission fees.

- The typical **profit model** for **HUMAN SERVICES** is an agreed upon price, or fee for the service.

- A **NONPROFIT** organization shows no profit, and pays no taxes. Net earnings (including donations) are invested back into the company at the end of each fiscal year. Government entities, religious, charitable, or political organizations are **nonprofit**, tax-free businesses.

- Your **Profit model** should change over time as your business grows. A LAUNCH **profit model** should encourage user engagement with **incentives**, such as a **FREEMIUM** profit model.

- A **SUBSCRIPTION profit model** should be implemented *after* a company has an established, and loyal customer base.

- A software **LICENSE AGREEMENT** means the original developer permits the use of their software as a FUNCTION within another company's product or service, for a fee, as well as a royalty stream.

- Utilize new **profit models**, such as a **PREMIUM UPGRADE**, by adding HORIZONTAL and/or VERTICAL features to your first product release.

- Determining a **profit model** for LAUNCH during the **Productization process,** helps keep all stakeholders on the path to actualizing an offering of value, for *profit*.

MODULE 11: AFFILIATE MARKETING REVIEW

- To make money with **AFFILIATE MARKETING**, become a *popular* online internet property. Create a trending blog, vlog, website, podcast, or social media platform, that gets a *lot* of unique visitors, and sell advertising space *and* time on your site.

- **Affiliate ADVERTISERS** are the businesses that market their offering on the **affiliate MARKETER'S** website, or popular internet property.

- The acronym **CPC** stands for **Cost-Per-Click**. In **CPC** campaigns the **advertisers** pays an **affiliate PUBLISHER** or **affiliate NETWORK** every time a viewer clicks, or sometimes even passively 'views' their ad online.

- **Affiliate networks** [ostensibly] perform extensive analysis to place your ads on sites relevant to your target audience, for greater response to your marketing efforts. However, begin with caution, and don't spend money you don't have for '*impressions*' of your adverts. Post your **PPC** (pay-per-click) **display ads** as **click-campaigns** on your startup's profile pages, and other social media groups and forums, for free!

- **SPLIT (A/B) TEST** PPC campaigns to a limited number of affiliate sites to identify which keywords in your headlines garner greater response, *before* rolling out a full affiliate network campaign. Always post your click-campaigns on your startup's social feeds for free, to see if the campaign garners equal or better response than your paid **PPC Affiliate Marketing** plan.

- **Click-farms** are a form of **click fraud**. Large groups of low-income workers fraudulently click on your **PPC ads,** to pocket your advertising dollars that they are depleting with each click.

- *Effective* **PPC campaigns**, as with *all* marketing efforts, should be highly targeted for the greatest possible response. **Affiliate networks** can *not* target your campaigns near as well as *you* can! By initiating the **Productization process**, and populating the eight required **Productization lists**, you now possess an *intimate* knowledge of your upcoming product or service, as well as **target markets** and **users** who will find value in your offering.

Ongoing Productization for the Life of Your Offering

► **Continually add to, and refine all eight of your offering's PRODUCTIZATION LISTS** throughout the life-cycle of each of your offerings.

► Go back to your **Productization lists**, and get **very specific** about what your offering IS, what it DOES, and for WHO *before* you begin the branding process in **LSB Workbook 2**. *Bigger, faster, stronger, more powerful*, are all meaningless words. Take all fluff words out of your lists, and replace them with facts—the actual FEATURES of your product or service. Remove the fluff words from *all* your lists, including the BENEFITS list, in which you should have actual and perceived BENEFITS of the features of your offering.

► **Add additional bullet entries to your Productization lists** all the time, every time an additional FEATURE is implemented, or a new BENEFIT or SOLUTION is uncovered. And the **Productization process begins anew with every new offering developed**.

Don't forget, the **#1 place startups fail is neglecting to productize their idea**, or developed offering. If you already have a salable product or service, and have yet to **productize** it, well, better late than never. Do it *now!* Working with your offering's **Productization lists** will enable you create, or direct those you hire, to produce marketing campaigns for your new venture that get the greatest response, and conversion.

LSM Workbook 1
RAF Marketing Method REVIEW

Knowledge Gained in LSM Workbook 1

We actualized our idea by identifying its *space* in the marketplace, then defining some of its **FEATURES and BENEFITS**, in **Productization lists 1A and 1B**.

We identified **solutions**, and the value our product, service or message provides for broad **TARGET MARKETS**, and *specific* groups of people, our likely **TARGET USERS**, in **Lists 2A and 2B**.

We've written an **ELEVATOR PITCH**, encapsulating what makes our offering extraordinary in 3 – 5 sentences or less. And we are chatting up our PITCH to whoever will listen, to define it clearly for ourselves, and to get feedback on how to make our offering even better.

We've researched our **COMPETITION**, found some, and identified them in **List 3A**, then created a COMPETITIVE ANALYSIS CHART to discover **differentiators** that make our offering unique, and *better* our competitors. We've identified our offering's **UVPs** in **List 3B**, and if we've found we don't have enough uniquely valuable features, benefits and solutions after performing competitive analysis, we iterate our original offering and CREATE them.

We've populated **List 4A and 4B** with potential **HORIZONTAL and VERTICAL markets** to sell our offering, in addition to the **target markets and users** we've already identified. And if you are a wise entrepreneur, you've projected at least a few possible new features that can be added to iterate your initial product before launch, if need be, or released as upgrades down the line. **New offerings** should be projected as well, both **horizontal and vertical product ideas** that align with your original offering.

And, to keep all stakeholders on the path to producing an offering of monetary value, we've established an initial **PROFIT MODEL** for launch, as well as projected other revenue streams for three years, and five years down the line, after our offering has established a loyal base of customers/users.

LSM Workbook 1: PRODUCTIZATION gave you a step-by-step process to getting *intimate* with your projected (or even fully-developed) offering. This workbook provided doable steps to discovering the features, benefits and solution of what you plan to sell; a realistic assessment of the people that will find value in your product, service, or message; and some differentiators that make your offering unique, *better* than your competitors. By taking this first step and **Getting Ready**, performing the Productization process also provides you with relevant keywords and content to use in your branding and advertising campaigns, that you'll learn to produce in **LSB Workbook 2**.

The **RAF Marketing Method** is a *process*, a sequential series of steps, like a math equation. Even if you have no idea in mind to develop into a business right now, when an idea you'd like to actualize does come, follow the steps of the Productization process introduced in Workbook 1, *in order*, to turn most any idea into a marketable offering of value, for profit.

LSM Workbook 1 is available in a video series. *Actualize IDEAS into PROFITS with Lean Startup Marketing* is *not* a boring talking head, but a series of videos presented in movie trailer format to keep you engaged in learning. View the *Lean Startup Marketing* video series, Step 1: Get Ready and Productize, here:
https://www.udemy.com/lean-startup-marketing/

One More Thing...

Be sure you have a thorough understanding of the Productization process, before moving on to LSB Workbook 2! Once Productization is established—FEATURES, BENEFITS, TARGETS, COMPETITORS, and HORIZONTAL and VERTICAL MARKET lists are populated, an initial ELEVATOR PITCH is constructed, and PROFIT MODELS defined, it's time to **BRAND** your newly productized offering.

LSB Workbook 2—Step 2: BRANDING, in the Lean Startup series, delivers step-by-step instruction, that guides you through the process of creating a brand identity—giving a 'face,' and 'voice' to your new venture with **corporate and product logos, taglines/slogans**, and **brand standards,** that build brand awareness for your offering and startup across campaigns and various media.

We'll review effective **layout, graphic and responsive design,** so your online marketing campaigns will look as good on a cellphone as they do on a laptop screen. We drill down on **internet operations**, how **URLs** work, what **web-hosting** is, and why you need it for your online marketing. You'll learn to identify **images with impact**, and begin a low to no-cost professional-quality **image and video library**.

Next, you'll give your product, service, and/or startup a form—a body of **branding and advertising campaigns**, extolling the virtues, UVPs and differentiators of your new 'baby.' Chatting up your new pride and joy, and producing marketing efforts to reach others who may find interest in your new offering, are integral to creating and establishing a BRAND.

You'll learn to create stunning **websites**, attention-grabbing **digital and print**

advertising, newsletters, blogs, vlogs, social media marketing, PR and email campaigns, at little to no cost.

You'll utilize your Productization lists from LSM Workbook 1 as **SEO content** for your marketing campaigns, and discover trade secrets to writing **content marketing** that gets response, in **LSL Workbook 3**.

LSB Workbook 2—**Step 2: Take Aim**, in the **RAF Marketing Method,** teaches you how to BRAND *and* market, i.e. SELL your offering. After completing the BRANDING modules, you will have the knowledge *and* the branding and advertising campaigns to effectively pre-launch your projected product, service, or message. You will also engage in creating launch campaigns for your fully-developed and quality-tested offering, with tightly targeted marketing efforts that will build your startup's brand awareness and achieve the greatest possible response and conversion rates for your new venture.

Find LSB Workbook 2 on Amazon, in ebook or print today.

◆◆◆◆◆

-About the Author-

J. Cafesin is the founder of **IPP Entrepreneurial workshops**, helping entrepreneurs and innovators actualize their ideas into startups and sustainable companies.

A Stanford marketing educator, and MarCom specialist for over 20 years, she has helped facilitate the launch of many Silicon Valley startups, including Stac Electronics (sold to Altiris); Bay Networks (sold to Northern Telecom); MD2 (sold to Sybase); Tea Leaf (sold to IBM); The Learning Company (sold to Mattel); Southland Associates, and others. Her corporate clients have included Six-Flags; Bay Alarm Systems; Intuit; Change.org; Location Labs; CA Technologies; Genetech; CBS; NBC; Xerox FCU; 1st Nationwide Bank; and Hewlett Packard, among many others.

For updates on new blog posts, videos, upcoming live and online workshops in entrepreneurship, marketing startups, education, plus stories and insights into Silicon Valley life, find J. Cafesin on *Twitter, LinkedIn, Instagram*, and *Amazon.*

Have questions or comments about LSM Workbook 1, or the Lean Startup Series? Please email: connect@jcafesin.com.

www.ingramcontent.com/pod-product-compliance
Lightning Source LLC
Chambersburg PA
CBHW050452110426
42744CB00013B/1964
* 9 7 8 1 7 3 2 5 4 3 1 0 2 *